Defying the Nazis

Defying
the Nazis
THE SHARPS' WAR

—— ARTEMIS JOUKOWSKY ——

WITH A FOREWORD BY KEN BURNS

BEACON PRESS
BOSTON

BEACON PRESS
Boston, Massachusetts
www.beacon.org

Beacon Press books
are published under the auspices of
the Unitarian Universalist Association of Congregations.

19 18 17 16   8 7 6 5 4 3 2

This book is printed on acid-free paper that meets the uncoated paper
ANSI/NISO specifications for permanence as revised in 1992.

Text design and composition by Kim Arney

Library of Congress Cataloging-in-Publication Data
Names: Joukowsky, Artemis, author.
Title: Defying the Nazis : the Sharps' war / Artemis Joukowsky.
Description: Boston, Massachusetts : Beacon Press, [2016] | 2016 |
Includes bibliographical references and index.
Identifiers: LCCN 2016007704 (print) | LCCN 2016008561 (ebook) |
ISBN 9780807071823 (hardcover : alk. paper) | ISBN 9780807071830 (ebook)
Subjects: LCSH: Sharp, Waitstill, 1902–1984. | Sharp Cogan, Martha,
1905–1999. | Righteous Gentiles in the Holocaust—Massachusetts—Wellesley
Hills. | World War, 1939–1945—Jews—Rescue. | Holocaust, Jewish (1939–1945)
Classification: LCC D804.66.S48 J68 2016 (print) | LCC D804.66.S48 (ebook) |
DDC 940.53/180922—dc23
LC record available at http://lccn.loc.gov/2016007704

CONTENTS

───── FOREWORD ─────

Many people approach me to collaborate on films with them. Usually I must decline for the simple reason that I'm involved in too many full-time projects of my own. I expected to respond exactly this way when my friend Artemis Joukowsky sent me an early, very rough cut version of his documentary, which, like this book, recounts the amazing and largely unknown saga of his grandparents, Unitarian minister Waitstill Hastings Sharp and his social worker wife, Martha Sharp. On the eve of World War II, the Sharps ran toward not away from what Winston Churchill called the "gathering storm." They helped scores of people to escape, many of whom surely would have died in the war and the Holocaust.

I agreed to look at his film, fully expecting that a few minutes in I'd decide that the project wasn't for me. Yet what I saw turned out to be an extraordinary diamond in the rough. I'm interested only in stories that talk to us about *us. Who are we?* is the driving question in all the work I do. And here was a story that answered that basic question in a dramatic, compelling, and unexpected way.

I saw in the Sharps an exceptional couple. While their story is clearly heroic, it's also nuanced and complex, full of unexpected turns and dangerous "undertow." It took both personal courage and the strong moral calling of their Unitarian faith to face the dangers they did and to sacrifice so much of their emotional lives to serve desperate refugees. These two "ordinary" people—a minister and his wife, a father and a mother—left the quiet, snug, and secure world of Wellesley, Massachusetts, for prewar Prague and, later, Vichy France, where they mastered the dark arts of espionage in order to outwit the Nazis.

VII ·

They devised codes and found ways to detect and defeat surveillance, lose people tailing them, finesse Fascist bureaucrats, launder money (Waitstill's specialty), and smuggle to safety everyone from toddlers to so-called *Kulturträgers* —artists, intellectuals, and scientists on the top of Hitler's most-wanted list. This is not the stuff they teach in divinity school!

So I surprised myself—and possibly Artemis too—when I agreed to help. Soon I was drawn into the project not just as an advisor but as co-director and executive producer, fully invested in telling the Sharps' fascinating and truly American story.

We live in such a narcissistic age that it is difficult today to conceive how the Reverend and Mrs. Sharp—so deeply connected to their church and congregation, their community, and their family—would willingly give up their comfort and safety to lead double lives in order to save the lives of strangers amid the daily horrors and deprivations of wartime Europe.

Defying the Nazis hooks you, catches you up in the narrative, and pulls you along by all the elements of great storytelling. Will the secret police finally stop them? Will they be captured or killed? Whom can they trust? What risks are they willing to take? Ultimately, will they save these people?

It reads like a spy novel, but it's all true.

The reason I call *Defying the Nazis* an American story is that it explores that rare level of character—selfless sacrifice for the greater good—that we have always admired and celebrated in this country. Abraham Lincoln, in his first inaugural address, called it "the better angels of our nature."

The Sharps saw there was a job to be done and, quite simply, *did* it. Their objective was to rescue enemies and victims of the Nazis. Personal glory wasn't the point. It was just the right thing to do.

Their story also transforms and deepens our understanding of the Holocaust. The notion of six million dead horrifies us, yet the massive number numbs and insulates us from the full reality of individual suffering. Existing records show that the Sharps rescued somewhat over one hundred people. Much documentation is missing, so the number is likely higher. At first, any number might seem inconsequential compared to six million murdered Jews or the obscene total of nearly sixty million human beings killed in the course of the Second World War.

It is clear that nothing gets done except by individual acts of courage, individual initiative. When someone risks his or her own life to save a stranger's life, you get a sense of what real heroism is.

You also can begin to sincerely grieve for those people who did not get out alive, for those who could not be saved.

Through their existential commitments and actions, Waitstill and Martha help us understand our own fundamental obligation to one another. Martha once said that neither she nor Waitstill saw themselves as anything but ordinary, that anyone else in their circumstances would have acted in the same way. It's hard for me to believe that's true, but their remarkable story shows us why we should at least try.

—KEN BURNS

I remember the moment with absolute clarity.

It was 1976, and I was a freshman attending the Allen-Stevenson School in New York City. One afternoon I casually mentioned to my mother that John Pariseau, my history and social studies teacher, had assigned a class report on the subject of moral courage. He said our papers were to be built around a personal interview.

My mother just as casually suggested that I talk with her parents about their adventures in Europe during World War II. "They played an important role in rescuing Jews and other people from the Nazis," she said. "Their story would make an interesting paper."

What? I was momentarily speechless--rare for me. "Mummy Mummy and Grandpa Sharp?" I blurted. "You're kidding me!"

"Not at all," she answered. "Go talk to them. They'll tell you."

She might as well have said that my grandparents, Waitstill and Martha Sharp, had conquered polio, invented jazz, or built the Empire State Building. Waitstill—Waitstill Hastings Sharp, a retired Unitarian minister—had never so much as mentioned World War II to me, much less acknowledged that he'd played a role in it. Likewise for Martha, from whom he had been long divorced. It was difficult for me to picture the two of them together under any circumstance, let alone as a dauntless duo carrying out dangerous rescue missions in enemy territory. To think that these unassuming people were heroes of the Holocaust astonished me, and I eagerly looked forward to learning more.

It wasn't practical to interview both Martha and Waitstill for the paper, so I decided to focus on Mummy Mummy, as we grandchildren had always known her, who lived in an East Eightieth Street brownstone, near the Metropolitan Museum of Art, a short walk from our apartment. Just as my mother suggested, Mummy Mummy said she'd be very happy to talk with me. Days later, I showed up for our first interview. She was seventy-one at the time, slender and graceful, beautiful as she always had been, and one of the warmest people I have ever known. My grandmother had a knack for making you feel you were first in her affections no matter who else was in the room.

She greeted me at the door and showed me to a room where we would sit across a table from one another in a formal interview setting. I set up my audiocassette recorder, turned it on, looked up at her, and said something like, "Well, tell me what you and Grandpa did during the war."

She gave me one of her radiant smiles and began slowly with a description of the January night in 1939 when she and Grandpa Sharp learned, to their utter surprise, that they'd been invited to undertake the Unitarian Church's first-ever international relief project, a mission of mercy to the imperiled citizens of Czechoslovakia. Gradually she became more animated, regaling me with amazing tales from her six months together with Waitstill in Nazi-occupied Czechoslovakia. Later she would speak of Vichy France, North Africa, Israel, and the Middle East.

Martha told me about the frantic work of securing travel papers for Social Democrats, Jews, artists, philosophers, and the long list of others in Czechoslovakia who faced certain extermination if they couldn't escape. She described their desperate schemes to pluck these otherwise doomed souls from the Nazis' grasp: how exhilarating it was to succeed, how heartsick they were when they failed.

She taught me a little spy craft too: secrets of writing codes, watching for tails, dealing with tapped telephones, and gauging who could be trusted and who could not. From time to time it was necessary to remind myself that this was my tender-hearted grandmother talking, not some retired OSS operative.

I was amazed to hear what she and Waitstill had accomplished, and nearly as amazed to have known nothing of their exploits until that moment. I asked her why she had never spoken of it, nor had anyone else in the family. She shrugged it off, as if to say that risking your neck for strangers speaking strange tongues in a strange and hostile world thousands of miles from home didn't merit discussion, certainly not special recognition.

It was just something that needed to be done.

We spoke together several more times, and out of these conversations came an eight-page document, entitled "A Matter of Faith," for which Mr. Pariseau gave me the only A I ever received in high school.

I understood, of course, that Martha had confined herself to the highlights of her story. Exciting as it was, I instinctively realized that it was part of a much deeper and broader saga. And the more I reflected on it, the more I realized it would be up to me to tell this important story.

After high school, I entered Hampshire College in Amherst, Massachusetts, which is about twenty-five miles from the house where Waitstill then lived in Greenfield. The Reverend Sharp's life since retirement from the pulpit in 1972 was fairly circumscribed, partially as a consequence of age-related infirmities. He no longer was quite so square-shouldered, strong, and resolute as he always appeared in photos, although he did still wear his signature wire-rimmed spectacles.

Waitstill read the *New York Times* each morning, watched the news with Walter Cronkite, and read a lot of historical nonfiction and biography, with particular emphasis on World War II and its causes. He was especially interested in books about the rise of Hitler.

Raised on a farm, he also taught me how to compost.

We attended church together on Sundays, and we often discussed religion, faith, and its role in both his public and private life. Though retired, he continued to deliver guest sermons from time to time. I attended a few of them and each had a profound effect on me. Each was fully considered and powerful. If there was an overarching theme to them, it was the importance of finding the joy of serving others. Since it was exactly that search that then occupied much of my time, I listened closely as he spoke.

The past seemed to interest him only insofar as it illuminated the present. He did humor me when I asked about the relief missions to Europe. He filled in a few blanks in Martha's narrative, told me a tale or two of his own derring-do, and generally agreed that humans rebuffed my admiring suggestions that he and Martha had received insufficient recognition for their remarkable sacrifice.

Like Martha, he saw their deeds as just something that had needed to be done.

I saw the situation otherwise. Of course I was proud of them, proud to be their grandson and certain that their story needed to be told. My purpose, naturally, would be to learn from the example of Martha and Waitstill and their lives, but I also wanted to rescue their example as an object lesson for a new age.

As they both emphasized to me, if the civilized world learned anything from the Holocaust it was that to placate or ignore an evil such as Nazism is morally wrong and practically ensures there will be great suffering as a consequence. They had seen and deeply experienced it for themselves, firsthand.

Yet on the evidence of subsequent experience with the likes of Cambodia's Pol Pot, Slobodan Milosevic in the Balkans, or the slaughters in Rwanda, Congo, and Darfur, the world's people must relearn the hard lesson with every generation. What the Sharps demonstrated by example was their fundamental belief that this moral imperative—to confront evil wherever it appears—holds true for the individual as well as society. I can't think of a more important message for me to carry from their generation to mine and beyond.

Unfortunately Waitstill died before I could begin systematic interviews with him. Martha survived him by sixteen years, but her memory was irretrievably lost to senile dementia before I was able to capture and fully record her story.

There seemed to be no way forward until a short time following her death in 1999, when we discovered among her possessions a trove of documents, photos, and personal artifacts dating back to her school days. The vast and eclectic archive includes everything from personal letters, official reports, and photos to maps, handwritten notes, calendars, datebooks, hotel tabs, ticket stubs, playbills, and other souvenirs of Martha and Waitstill's travels. There are many deeply touching love notes between them in the collection as well.

In all, more than two hundred thousand of these and other documents discovered in my research are now digitally housed at the US Holocaust Memorial Museum, Brown University, Harvard University Divinity School library, and the Cohen Center at Keene State College in New Hampshire. Much of this book is drawn from those primary sources, as well as from Martha and Waitstill's oral histories recorded in 1978; Waitstill's unpublished autobiography; and several of Martha's unpublished manuscripts, plus taped and filmed interviews with those who knew them and those whom they rescued.

The Sharps as they emerged from the research were quintessentially American, in the best and truest sense. They were relentless optimists but also realists, fearless but not foolhardy, resourceful and quick-witted, brave, and, more importantly, determined and tireless. They persevered through terror and anger, joy, frustration, privation, tragedy, and innumerable heart-stopping moments when lives hung in the balance. Through it all, they were buoyed by a fullness of spirit that only intensified as the threat of death lurked ever nearer.

For them it all came down to simple truths. I remember a wonderful, provocative question that Martha often asked me through the years: "What are you going to do in your life that's important?"

I've learned to answer that question in many ways, but, as I will always be the Sharps' grandson, I have taken on a lifetime commitment to make sure that the memory of their work and the legacy of their lives are carried forth. The actions and achievements of Martha and Waitstill deserve to be honored, and their courage and principles deserve to be celebrated so we may build a more just and fair society. The story of the lives of Martha and Waitstill Sharp deserves to be told, and now I'm telling it.

To me, nothing could be more important.

—ARTEMIS JOUKOWSKY
August 2016

CHAPTER ONE

The Eighteenth Choice

On a frigid Sunday evening in the winter of 1939, the Reverend Waitstill Sharp had just wearily arranged himself in front of his fireplace when the parsonage telephone rang.

Sharp regarded the ringing phone for a moment.

His exhausting Sabbath had begun with his usual sermon—forceful, closely reasoned, articulate, and sometimes poetic—delivered to the Unitarian Society of Wellesley Hills, Massachusetts, west of Boston. Then he led a confirmation class before spending the balance of the winter day trudging through the snow on personal calls to mostly elderly, housebound parishioners. By nightfall Sharp was spent and loath to stir from the warmth and comfort of his hearth.

"Hello?" Waitstill finally answered what he would describe until the end of his life as "the most momentous call I've ever received."

"Hello, Waitstill!" boomed a voice that Reverend Sharp knew at once. It was Everett Baker, vice president of the American Unitarian Association (AUA) and a member of his congregation.

Reverend Baker got to the point at once.

"Say, Waitstill," he wondered, "has your day been too much that you and Martha can't come over to talk with me?"

The summons—Baker added nothing more—was puzzling. After AUA president Frederick May Eliot, Baker was the second most powerful figure in the national Unitarian Church. Waitstill Sharp was a rising star within the hierarchy, but at thirty-seven he was comparatively new to the ministry, leading just his second pastorate. *Why on a Sunday evening,* he wondered, *would the Bakers require Martha and me at their house on a moment's notice?*

Martha Sharp, thirty-three, Waitstill's wife of ten years, was equally clueless—and intrigued. She called a neighbor girl to come sit with their two children, seven-year-old Hastings and two-year-old Martha Content, then headed out with her husband into the winter evening, both turning over in their minds what this urgent business might be.

Ev Baker wouldn't disappoint them.

He sat Martha and Waitstill down in his living room and announced that they had been chosen by the "highest authorities of the church"—that is, President Eliot and the AUA board—to perform a unique and historic service. As soon as possible, Waitstill and Martha were to sail for Europe on an emergency relief mission to beleaguered Czechoslovakia, then menaced by Nazi Germany. Never in the AUA's 114-year history, Baker told them, had American Unitarians reached out in this way. The Sharps had been selected, as he described it, for "the first intervention against evil undertaken by the denomination."

Waitstill was savvy enough to recognize a sales pitch when he heard one. Still, as an ardent internationalist both by faith and personal inclination, he found the notion of a rescue assignment to Czechoslovakia compelling to contemplate. However, the obstacles seemed insuperable.

Foremost, there were their two young children and the congregation to consider. Moreover, neither of the Sharps knew anything of foreign relief work (especially in a potential war zone). Yet Sharp also bore the Nazis a deep personal enmity, and the sudden opportunity to act directly against the fascists, rather than just rail about them from the pulpit, was a powerful temptation.

He and Martha listened intently as Baker explained how the idea for the mission had been born the previous autumn. The Unitarian leaders were shocked and outraged in late September of 1938 over the Munich Pact, in which the British and French formally ceded the Sudeten region of Czechoslovakia to the Nazis.

The Munich Pact was yet another misguided gesture in British prime minister Neville Chamberlain's policy of appeasing, rather than confronting, Hitler's expansionism. Chamberlain (coincidentally a Unitarian) believed that appeasement would secure "peace in our time," as he put it. Subsequent events would prove him tragically wrong.

The betrayal at Munich struck a deeper chord among the internationally minded directors of the AUA and many of the sixty thousand US Unitarians than it did among most of their fellow citizens. Domestic revulsion at the savagery and enormous costs of World War I had fed a strong strain of isolationist sentiment, led by such prominent voices as that of Charles Lindbergh, head of the America First movement. Moreover, the majority of Americans were too distracted by the protracted rigors of the Great Depression to care much about remote events across the Atlantic.

Very few US voices were raised throughout the 1930s as Hitler consolidated absolute power in Germany, wove his violent anti-Semitism into the country's civil codes, then began methodically to spread the Nazi virus to his neighbors.

In 1935, it was little remarked in the United States that with enactment of the Nuremberg Laws, the Nazis effectively stripped German Jews of their rights *and* nationality. The next year there was minimal outcry when Hitler re-annexed the demilitarized Rhineland. Similarly, there was scant anger expressed in the United States over the *Anschluss* of March 1938, when Austria in effect disappeared into the Third Reich.

American Unitarians, however, took note and spoke out throughout the 1930s, regularly expressing themselves in the pages of the *Christian Register*, the Unitarian monthly journal. They condemned fascism in Spain, Italy, and Germany, as well as the anti-Semitic rants of Father Charles E. Coughlin, the popular radio priest whose broadcasts were heard by tens of millions of US listeners at the peak of his popularity.

In its December 1, 1938 issue, the *Register* published an essay by the Reverend Henry Wilder Foote, titled "The Deadly Infection of

Anti-Semitism." Foote rightly predicted that the Nazis would exile all Jews who could afford to emigrate, and exterminate those who couldn't. "Coming centuries," wrote Foote, "will record this anti-Semitic campaign as on one of the blackest and most discreditable pages of history."[1]

Unitarianism is part of the deep, wide stream of dissent and disagreement within Christian thought that for centuries has periodically cost its adherents dearly, most particularly their lives.

The faith emerged in the sixteenth century during the Reformation among theologians who dissented from the doctrine of the Trinity but still believed that Jesus was a divinely inspired moral teacher. Unlike most dissenters of the day, these Unitarians also insisted on religious freedom for all nonconformists, not merely for themselves.

The modern church promotes active, participatory democracy at all levels of political organization, as well as equality, defined as broadly as possible. Unitarians have been active in almost all American social reform movements, including abolition and universal suffrage, as well as the later civil rights, antiwar, and gay rights movements.

Unitarians also are generally united on one other point. They see humans, not God, as the source of most earthly ills, and they therefore believe that humans are responsible for healing these ills.

"Earth shall be fair," said the Reverend Howard Brooks, one of Waitstill's colleagues. "But only if we make it so."

The Munich Pact particularly distressed America's Unitarians for three major reasons. First, many in the AUA greatly admired the Czech government. Modern Czechoslovakia was founded in 1918 on the democratic models of France and the United States. It was led until 1935 by its founding president, Tomas Masaryk, whose American-born wife, the former Charlotte Garrigue, was a Unitarian from Brooklyn.

Second, Prague was home to Unitaria, a 3,500-member Unitarian church founded by Norbert F. Capek, a former Baptist minister who'd converted to Unitarianism in the United States following the First World War.

Unitaria, completed in 1932, was housed in a pair of buildings Capek purchased with considerable AUA financial help. He combined the structures—one ancient, one relatively new—into a sort of Unitarian spiritual and community center. Besides a chapel and meeting rooms, the complex featured living quarters for ministers-in-training and even a health-food restaurant in the basement. Unitaria was also going broke. Without financial intercession, Unitaria faced liquidation by May of 1939.

One of Capek's daughters, Bohdana, and her husband, Karel Haspl, who was involved in ministry at Unitaria, were graduates of the Pacific Unitarian School of Religion in Berkeley, California, and were well known in American Unitarian circles. Visits from American Unitarians to their coreligionists in Prague forged additional personal connections. Waitstill later recalled an almost frenetic anxiety among Unitarians following the Munich Treaty. *These are our friends!* he remembered thinking. *What are we going to do?*

The third American Unitarian concern regarding Munich was that the liberal National Czechoslovak Church, which maintained close ties with American Unitarians, had numerous congregants in the largely German-speaking Sudeten region, a major chunk of Czechoslovakia that the Nazis had long coveted. Even before Munich, members of the National Czechoslovak Church, many of them Social Democrats (both liberals and leftists), already were being harassed by a local Nazi organization, the Sudeten-German Party (SdP), led by "sharp-nosed, hard-lipped" Konrad Henlein, as *Time* magazine described him, the "Sudeten German Nazi No. 1."[2]

Canadian-born Robert Cloutman Dexter, director of the AUA Department of Social Relations, was fifteen years Waitstill's senior and one of his closest friends in the hierarchy. Dexter was in New York when he learned of Chamberlain's capitulation at Munich. He later wrote, "I spent every hour from the moment I heard about it in a sort of daze."

Dexter took the night boat to Boston but could not sleep. Out of his dark hours of agonized reflection, however, emerged a personal resolve. "I knew that there would be untold suffering in the Nazi-occupied territories," he wrote, "and I was equally convinced that something should be done about it by those of us who felt we had an obligation to aid our friends who had been so betrayed."[3]

Within a month, the AUA executive committee voted to send Dexter to Europe to assess the situation. He reported back in person on November 16, 1938, that the situation in Czechoslovakia was critical. With winter fast approaching, Dexter estimated a quarter-million refugees from Germany, Austria, and the Sudeten region already had poured into what was left of the country. According to Dexter, twenty-six thousand of these displaced people required immediate emigration assistance. That is, they were Jews, intellectuals, artists, labor leaders, political leaders, and others on the Gestapo's wanted lists who faced internment and death if they didn't somehow escape Czechoslovakia.

The Nazis delivered a foretaste of their agenda on the night of November 9, just five weeks after Munich, when Hitler dispatched waves of his goons to terrorize German Jews on what became known as *Kristallnacht*, the "crystal night," or "night of the broken glass." Wielding sledgehammers, storm troopers in Germany, Austria, and the newly acquired Sudetenland in Czechoslovakia smashed the windows of Jewish homes and businesses, ransacked and burned synagogues, and vandalized Jewish cemeteries. Two hundred sixty-seven synagogues were destroyed and seventy-five hundred Jewish businesses attacked and looted. An estimated ninety-one Jews were killed, and thirty thousand Jewish males were sent to concentration camps, where hundreds perished. The rest were released with the proviso that they start proceedings, which were to prove mostly futile, for emigrating from Germany and German-occupied lands.[4]

Waitstill and Martha had closely followed the unfolding crisis. In Wellesley Hills, they formed an international relations club that met regularly for in-depth discussion of world issues. In mid-November, the Sharps' own presentation to the group was entitled "The Rape of Czechoslovakia."

"The more we learned about Czechoslovakia," Martha later wrote in an unpublished memoir, "the more we admired this plucky little democracy. In our opinion, its progressive social welfare and economic programs had made it the leading and most financially sound country in Central Europe."

——— · ———

The Sharps, of course, had plenty of questions for Everett Baker.

"Now Ev, look out," said Waitstill in rapid-fire mode. "Who's going to take my confirmation class? Who's going to take all that a minister's supposed to do here for the church school? Who's going to take the preaching? Who's going to take the calling on the sick, the burying of the dead, the marrying of the connubially minded?"

"I am," Baker replied.

That seemed to satisfy Waitstill, who followed with a bit thornier query.

"How many men have you offered this to?" he asked.

Baker shifted in his chair.

The AUA leadership had deliberated at length over whom they should send to Czechoslovakia, before deciding that a married couple would be best. According to a document developed during their discussions, there were a number of other qualifications too. These included good health and the couple's willingness to leave almost at once and to remain in Czechoslovakia for four to six months. According to the paper, the commissioners should be "the type who would make a good impression on people there, government and otherwise," and "be well enough known to have their report accepted" among church members in the United States. They needed, as well, "some knowledge of Europe and preferably of Czechoslovakia," and they would "preferably" have "Anglo-Saxon names. Certainly not Czech or German or Hungarian names."

A remarkably high number of American Unitarian ministers and their wives met all of these requirements, giving the church a wide choice of potential commissioners from which to choose. Unfortunately, every one of those whom Baker had approached so far had refused the honor.

"Seventeen," he told Sharp.

There was a pause.

"Ev," Waitstill began again, "do I understand from you that I am the eighteenth choice?"

"Yes."

"Why did they turn you down?"

"For three reasons," Baker replied. "They didn't want to impair their professional advancement. They didn't want to break up their families. They think a war is definitely coming. They don't want to be in danger."

Waitstill, of course, would have to struggle with the same set of personal considerations, as well as the prospect of war in Europe at any time. And there was Martha. He couldn't go without her.

———— · ————

Some forty years later, Waitstill recollected that both he and Martha accepted the assignment almost immediately. "As we went home beneath the starry skies," he reminisced, "we went home with a promise to do it." Martha remembered the decision process differently, noting that Waitstill was eager to go, assuming, of course, that she would go with him. Missionaries, he reminded her, leave their children. It was a touching expression of his love, respect, and need for Martha. Yet he also was forcing her to choose between him and the children. She knew there would be consequences no matter how she decided.

Although Martha had serious doubts, she shared Waitstill's sense of responsibility, as she later wrote: "My husband and I felt that something should be done. Refugees in the Sudetenland had been murdered; people were being imprisoned and hurt." Her greatest concern, however, was for their seven-year-old son and two-year-old daughter: "I had never for one minute entertained the thought of leaving them." Knowing that Waitstill wouldn't go without her, she recalled being "torn between my love and duty to my children and to my husband."

Martha took the matter to an old friend and mentor, Edna Stebbins, whom she thought of as an aunt, and addressed her accordingly. Aunt Edna advised her to go. "If you prevent Waitstill from taking this assignment," Stebbins said, "he'll always regret the lost opportunity. He might subconsciously blame you for not helping him fight the Nazis. It would be a great experience for both of you. I think you ought to go."

Then Edna sealed the deal by offering to come with her husband, Livingston, to take care of Hastings and Martha Content while their parents were away.

The encouragement and offer to help persuaded Martha to give her consent. In later writings and in speaking about her public life, she often expressed ambivalence about having left the children. Those who knew her were aware of the guilt that followed her into old age at the choice of service over family that she repeatedly made.

———— · ————

The AUA booked the Sharps, and a secretary, Virginia Waistcoat, aboard the RMS *Aquitania,* departing New York City for Southampton on February 4, which left them just two weeks to prepare.

Besides the rounds of appointments, meetings, and errands, there was also the congregation to think about. Priscilla ("Puss") Sweet, Waitstill's part-time secretary and Martha's tennis partner, remembered that the Wellesley Hills congregation voted its approval of the mission unanimously, although not without individual misgivings. "We were concerned about their safety," she said, "because we didn't know what kinds of problems they'd get into. I know they were worried about leaving the children too."

Some members of the flock did question the advisability and appropriateness of the mission, particularly the role that the minister's wife played in it.

"A lot of people thought Martha was out of hand and irresponsible not to stay home and take care of her children," recalled Marnie Mette, a congregant who, like Martha, was a young mother in 1939. "There was a strong feeling at that time that a woman's place was in the home," she said. "Anybody who decided to have a career or wanted to do something for themselves as a woman was certainly wide open to criticism. It was not the thing to do."

Mette herself questioned Martha's decision to leave Hastings and Martha Content to go to Czechoslovakia, but she did not question

her friend's heart or instincts. "I think that Martha was very courageous," she said. "I like to see that in women."

By far the hardest part for Martha was saying good-bye to her
children. "I had been so driven by duties and details," she wrote, "that
it was not until the morning of our departure that I was suddenly hit
by the impact of the long absence from our children. We had talked
it over with our son, Hastings, and had tried to answer his questions
and set his heart at rest."

He had been very brave about it, even though he was quite upset.
The night before, he had wanted me to read to him for a long
time before he went to bed. I could see that Aunt Edna's arrival
before dinner had both given him security and alarmed him, for
it meant that our time for going was near. At seven years, he was
unusually sober and thoughtful. He went off to school that morning with hugs and kisses but with no tears.

It was a sleety day. Martha Content, my baby girl, was standing on the sofa in the library window watching Waitstill carry
our bags out to Ev Baker's waiting car. Ev would drive us to the
station to get the train to New York. Martha Content was jumping up and down, chanting, "Mommy and Daddy going bye-bye!
Mommy and Daddy going bye-bye!"

I gathered her up in my arms and hugged and kissed her, trying to explain that we would be gone for a while but that we would
come back. Fortunately, she didn't understand. She struggled to
get back to the sofa to see what Daddy was doing now. I suddenly
realized that it was better she did not know. Brushing away the
tears in my own eyes, which she had not seen, I kissed her again,
and with the sweetness of her neck in my nostrils, I bade Aunt
Edna and our loving maid, Alberta, good-bye and hurried out to
the car, waving as gaily as I could as we drove away.

─── CHAPTER TWO ───

Learning the Ropes

The Sharps' shared mission to Czechoslovakia was the continuation of a partnership formed in the earliest days of their marriage, when Martha sat in on Waitstill's classes at Harvard whenever his job with the American Unitarian Association took him out of town. Long attracted to the ministry, Waitstill had graduated from law school more to please his parents than himself. When he finally had to make a career choice, he rejected an offer from a leading Boston law firm to accept the job of director of religious education for the AUA.

During his first ministry, at the Unitarian Church in Meadville, Pennsylvania, and later in Wellesley, Martha was his "right hand." She led religious education classes, directed the Christmas pageant, held teas, helped with church visits, critiqued his sermons, and, perhaps most importantly, provided the social aspects of ministry that Waitstill, by his own admission, did not do naturally. She was far more effective then he at mediating disputes, stooping down to talk with a child, and making small talk after church with a perhaps too-loquacious parishioner. They saw themselves as helpmates, one indispensable to the other. Over the next six months, it was a connection that would deepen to an extent that even they could not have imagined.

Waitstill's last words from the pulpit before their departure for Czechoslovakia were a ringing denunciation of Hitler and the Nazis. Edna Stebbins was right: Waitstill's enmity toward Fascism ran deep, and this opportunity to confront evil was vitally important to him. To Waitstill, this was a transcendent mission. In a letter to the congregation, dated June 13, 1939, Waitstill put that sense of mission into words: "Our last night as we sailed down the Harbor is still very vivid in our minds, a great lighted statue—a monument to an ideal, towering into the night. We live and work very much in its memory."

By the time Martha and Waitstill were ready to leave, the Unitarians had raised more than twelve thousand dollars in donations (equivalent to about two hundred thousand dollars today), suggesting significant support among Unitarians for the mission. There was a second commission too, from the American Committee for Relief in Czechoslovakia (AmRelCzech), which was headed by Nicholas Murray Butler, then president of Columbia University. Butler had been a close friend of Tomas Masaryk. AmRelCzech came up with an initial twenty-nine thousand dollars to be used only for large-scale resettlement projects and only for the benefit of Sudeten refugees.

Most of these funds were wired ahead to banks in Prague. Waitstill would carry three thousand dollars in a money belt. Martha stashed a similar sum in a pouch against her leg. They also carried a letter of introduction signed by US secretary of state Cordell Hull, courtesy of Representative Robert Luce, a member of the Massachusetts congressional delegation. Seth Gano, a wealthy Unitarian financier who helped arrange the commission, also insisted they carry with them three ledger books to keep track of accounts. The ledgers would return to Boston unused. Auditors would affirm that the couple's accounting, largely from memory, was accurate within pennies.[1]

The Unitarian churches of the New York City area hosted a farewell reception for the Sharps on the afternoon before they sailed. It was a chance for them to meet the Czech ambassador to Great Britain, Jan Masaryk, the son of Tomas Masaryk. Masaryk made a deep impression on Martha, who remembered him as "an amazing personality, part philosopher, politician, lover of democracy, part worldly wise and cultivated diplomat with a gorgeous sense of humor. He made me feel that if he were representative of the Czechs, they must surely be wonderful people." The Sharps' friendship with Masaryk blossomed from that moment and would last until 1948 when, as foreign minister in the postwar Czech government, he jumped, or was pushed, to his death from a window.

Prague-born Karl Deutsch, a convert to Unitarianism who in the second half of the twentieth century would emerge as one of America's preeminent social thinkers, particularly on issues of war and peace, approached Waitstill soon before he and Martha sailed. Deutsch, twenty-six, had been an active antifascist in Czechoslovakia. He and his wife, Ruth Slonitz, were in the United States in September 1938 when the Munich Treaty was signed. At the strong urging of his parents, Martin Morris and Maria Deutsch, Karl and Ruth did not go back home.

Now a PhD candidate in the government studies program at Harvard, Deutsch was deeply concerned for the safety of his parents still living in Prague. His father, an optician who owned a factory and a couple of retail outlets in Prague, was a Jew. His mother was a leading leftist (she'd named her son for Karl Marx) and founding member of the Czech Parliament. Julius Deutsch, Karl's uncle, was a communist. Waitstill would recall tears in Deutsch's eyes. "Do what you can for my father and mother," he beseeched Sharp. "They are in terrible danger."

It's doubtful that Martha and Waitstill had more than the dimmest conception of how they would go about responding to Karl Deutsch's plea or to the needs of the desperate refugees who would come to them for help in Prague. But they were young and full of passion for life, partners in a courageous and daring enterprise that would mark both a beginning and an end in their lives.

In the iconic news photo of the Sharps waving from the *Aquitania*, Waitstill is every inch the carefully groomed Unitarian minister in his three-piece suit standing next to his smiling wife, who is bedecked in a stylish hat with ribbons, holding a bouquet of roses, and wearing an oversized corsage. Behind them appear the wings of a bomber aircraft secured to the *Aquitania*'s upper deck.

Seasickness kept Martha in her berth through much of the crossing. They docked briefly at Cherbourg, where, as Waitstill later wrote in a draft of their official report, they witnessed a foreboding scene: "Our welcome to Europe was the sight of a French warplane scudding out from the gray skies over Cherbourg and launching a torpedo at a target simulating a battle ship in the harbor; the steering gear of the torpedo went wrong and drove it in a wide circle to strike the side of our liner as we lay at anchor. The plane on the deck and the torpedo were a foretaste of the spring and summer of Europe's dying peace."

On February 10, six days out from New York, the *Aquitania* arrived in Southampton. A short train ride brought the Sharps to London where they had honeymooned ten years before. At that time they had visited all the tourist sites, inspected the churches, attended the theatre, and cruised along the Thames in the popular flat-bottomed, pole-propelled boat called a punt. This time they encountered a very different London, sober, purposeful, tense, and once again preparing for war.

Martha saw immediately that the British were not as blind as most Americans to the condition of the Czechs. "Average English citizens," she noted, "seemed to be more aware and more emotionally involved in Czechoslovakia's plight than their counterparts in America. Most of the people we met seemed to feel a sense of responsibility and shame for the steps Chamberlain had taken to appease Hitler."

That concern was reflected in a gift of 4 million pounds sterling from the British government for refugee relief and resettlement, as well as private donations to several relief agencies. One of these, the Lord Mayor's Fund, raised 318,000 pounds sterling in a very short time. Another, the Earl Baldwin Fund, raised 500,000 pounds sterling in six months. Soon after Munich, the British Committee for Refugees from Czechoslovakia (BCRC) was set up to provide relief and to help refugees arriving in England. Waitstill and Martha would work closely with members of the BCRC in the months to come.

For two weeks, the Sharps were put through an exhaustive series of interviews and debriefings in London and Paris with contacts among Unitarians, the British government, and international aid organizations. Their Unitarian contact was the Reverend E. Rosalind Lee, whom Waitstill affectionately described as someone who had just "stepped out of Mother Goose down to silver buckles and her towering Welsh hat." Eleanor Rathbone, MP, perhaps the most outspoken champion of refugee relief and emigration, who had spent time in Prague assessing the refugee situation, promised that she would raise in Parliament any issues the Sharps presented. Gertrude Baer, president of the Women's International League for Peace and Freedom (WILPF), gave Martha a lesson in elementary spy craft. "She noticed," Martha wrote,

> that I was writing in my little notebook the names and addresses of the women in danger whom she wanted me to find and help. "Do you know how to keep notes so that if found by hostile persons they cannot be understood?" she asked.
>
> "No," I replied, "I never heard of it!"
>
> "Would you like a few pointers?" she offered, and thereupon gave me a short course in some of the memo-taking techniques which cannot be easily deciphered and, if you can't make notes, how to memorize key words to remember important data. She also suggested various methods of destroying incriminating papers. She explained how to ascertain if you are being shadowed, and various ways to elude your follower.
>
> She warned me that we would probably be followed and spied upon the moment we reached Prague. This put a new complexion on things. I destroyed the old notes and adopted her new systems, wondering if I, who had been so used to openness and honesty, could ever get used to living with secrets and suspicion.

Martha fought another bout with motion sickness on the night boat-train to Paris, but recovered on the brief morning ride from Calais to the Gare St. Lazare. In Paris, their meetings with Malcolm W. Davis of the Carnegie Endowment for International Peace, whose refugee experience dated back to Russia in the days of the Bolshevik Revolution, provided them with an invaluable background briefing on Czechoslovakia, as well as a comprehensive list of in-country contacts.

Davis wrote the names of these key people, individually, on the backs of dozens of his business cards, then gave them to the Sharps to use as calling cards. Because he was plugged into the Carnegie Endowment's extensive international executive networks, Davis would also be a welcome and vital source of accurate, behind-the-scenes information about developments from Berlin to Moscow, Paris, London, and Washington, DC. Waitstill described him as the "most helpful single person" among all their contacts.

Davis made available to Martha and Waitstill the visiting lecturers' suite at the Endowment's exquisite *palais* on the Boulevard St. Germain and lined up a weeklong series of informational meetings as well. The Sharps met everyone from the Czech ambassador to France to labor unionists, members of PEN—Poets, Playwrights, Essayists, and Novelists—and various friends of the endangered Czechoslovakia, among them Donald A. and Helen Lowrie, who were then at the University of Paris. Donald Lowrie was an essayist and journalist and, like Davis, an old Russia hand. He had known Grigori Rasputin, and in August of 1916, in Moscow, had conducted an interview with Patriarch Tikhon, leader of the Russian Orthodox Church. He had been a YMCA executive at various European postings, as had Helen. Lowrie also had written a Tomas Masaryk biography.

These connections in London and Paris provided the Sharps with two legs of a supportive tripod. The third leg would be in Geneva, where they would soon work with Marie Ginzburg, secretary of the Committee for the Placement of Intellectual Refugees (Comité International pour le Placement des Intellectuels Réfugiés). Formed in 1936, the committee worked to match refugee journalists, professors, doctors, and other professionals with jobs in what were then safe countries. In the course of the next six months, Martha and Waitstill would make a total of ten trips out of Prague to one or another of those cities with piles of documentation from people desperate to get out of Czechoslovakia. They would return to Prague with the names of more people to find and, if possible, help. Waitstill would also transmit messages between the Czech resistance and Jan Masaryk in London.

The Sharps took the Orient Express from Paris to Prague, arriving at Wilson Station—Wilsonovo Nádrazí—at just after seven on the sub-freezing Friday evening of February 24, 1939.

The station, originally named for the Hapsburg Emperor Franz Josef, had been renamed in 1919 for the US president who had championed the creation of the Czech nation. Now Masaryk's bold experiment in democracy was teetering toward oblivion.

"The air," Waitstill later wrote, "was full of sorrow, disillusion and foreboding." From his compartment on the "majestic train" as he called it, he was puzzled and astonished to see another train headed out of the station filled with nothing but men.

Norbert Capek, founder of Unitaria, led a grave-faced greeting committee on the platform. Martha remembered that all were dressed in black coats and black hats. Five or six relief organizations had sent representatives, each eager to meet as soon as possible with the Sharps.

Martha was presented with a bouquet of red, white, and blue flowers.

Also on hand was Karel Haspl, Capek's son-in-law. Martha and Waitstill knew Haspl personally from his student days in the United States. He would help Waitstill sort out and record everyone's name, address, and telephone number in order to make appointments.

Dr. Capek stepped forward, extended a hand, and greeted them with what Waitstill described as "affectionate but restrained and sober joy."

"Brother Sharp, Mrs. Sharp," Capek said, "we are very glad and relieved to see you here. You've come to a nation in crisis."

Formalities over, Waitstill asked Capek, "What is the meaning of that very unusual train two platforms over? Who were those men?"

"They were Social Democrats, fleeing the Sudetenland."

"Where are they going?"

"London, if they can get through."

Capek noted Waitstill's confusion. "Here," he said, "we see the reverse of the law of the sea. It's not women and children first, but men first."

"These women," he continued, gesturing with his arm, "may never see their husbands again, nor the children their fathers. These men have to get out. And somebody is taking it upon himself to convey them."

Capek himself chose to stay in Prague rather than flee, knowing full well that the decision was tantamount to writing his own death warrant. Two years later, the Gestapo arrested him for high treason and the capital offense of listening to foreign radio broadcasts. About the same time, his daughter, Zora, was arrested for disseminating summaries of the broadcasts. A German court, sitting in Dresden, acquitted the elderly minister of treason and recommended a reduced sentence on the second charge. The Gestapo nevertheless used poison gas to execute the father of Czech Unitarianism at Hartheim Castle, near Linz, Austria, in October, 1942.

It is commonly assumed that Capek was killed as part of the Nazis' retaliation for the May 1942 assassination by Czech partisans of Reinhard Heydrich, "Reich Protector" in Bohemia and Moravia and a leading architect of the Holocaust. Zora Capek, sentenced to eighteen months in a Saxony prison, survived the war.[2]

———— · ————

AmRelCzech had reserved a room for Waitstill and Martha at the four-story Hotel Atlantic at No. 9 Na Porici, conveniently situated near the center of town. The place was odd and unappealing—"potty," Waitstill called it—fitted out with heavy, veneered pieces upholstered in bright rayon. It was a vivid contrast to the soft colors and antique furniture of their house in Wellesley Hills.

There was no bureau or closet, just a few open shelves and a hybrid secretary-armoire. The Sharps wondered what the Czechs did with their clothes. They were also confused by the room's upholstered beds. Neither was fitted with a mattress. Instead they were provided with large down puffs inserted into linen cases, like oversized pillows. Martha found them strange and uncomfortable.

The rent was eighty-eight korunas a week, or about two dollars and twenty cents. Food was cheap. Breakfast—coffee with a boiled egg on toast for the both of them—would be fifty cents or so. Dinner at the hotel, again for two, was less than a dollar.

They went out for their first meal, a substantial dinner of soup, bread, dumplings (*knedlicky*), meat and gravy, and a chocolate dessert. Martha was surprised by the Czechs' liberal use of caraway seeds in almost every dish. Then they tried to digest the meal on a brief, late evening walk around Prague.

Both were tired, hopeful, and apprehensive, eager to get started. Back in the room, as they started to unpack that night, Martha suffered a sudden attack of homesickness. She missed Martha Content and Hastings terribly. "I tried to figure out the time differential and picture what the children were doing," she wrote. "Hastings was probably home from school and either playing outdoors with one of his pals or up in his room taking something apart to see what made it tick. Aunt Edna might be reading or sitting before the fire in my upstairs study, or keeping an eye on Martha Content, who would be across the hall in her pink and turquoise nursery."

Waitstill caught her expression and put his arms around her.

"Tired? Homesick?" he asked quietly. "It will all be over before you know it."

Martha began to cry. "I miss the children so much!" she said.

Waitstill was not good at such moments.

"That's natural," he said. "But we can't dwell on it. Come, let's go to bed. We have to be up early."

—— CHAPTER THREE ——

Witnesses to History

"Waitstill," Martha later wrote of their first Monday in Prague, "looked so handsome dressed for our first formal courtesy calls. He wore a new black suit with his Phi Beta Kappa key dangling as usual from the gold chain across his vest, anchored on one side by 'the turnip,' a heavy gold pocket watch inherited from his Revolutionary War ancestor."

Prague, city of a thousand spires, was an architectural mélange of Gothic, Renaissance, Baroque, Art Nouveau, and more modern building styles. In 1939, its ethnically diverse population was about eight hundred thousand, mostly Slavs but also a significant German-speaking minority and a relatively large Jewish community of about fifty thousand. Like Vienna, Prague's days on the center stage of world affairs were long past. But prior to the mutilation of Czechoslovakia after the Munich Pact, it was the comparatively prosperous heart of a "plucky little democracy," as Martha called it, a showcase of economic development (in the midst of a global economic depression) as well as political and religious freedom.

But the flow of refugees into Prague—first a small stream of leftists, Jews, artists, and intellectuals fleeing the Nazis in Germany, then a river of terrified émigrés in the aftermath of the *Anschluss* in Austria, and finally a tsunami of the displaced and desperate following cession of Sudetenland—threatened to drown the Czech capital in sheer human misery and fear.

The Sharps' first stop that Monday was the office of Dr. Antonin Sum, head of the Czech government's Emergency Committee for Refugees, and a former consul in the Czech embassy in Washington, who provided them with an overview of the mounting catastrophe. As Martha recalled,

> Dr. Sum described the chaos as frightened, hysterical men, women and children, clutching whatever they could put their hands on as they fled, arrived at the new border by the thousands in every conceivable kind of vehicle, as well as on foot.
>
> Some did not even have sufficient clothing. Most were without money or any preparation for the journey. Families, jobs, everything was forgotten in their fear of torture and imprisonment by the Nazis. Shelter, food and medical care were their immediate needs.
>
> The Emergency Committee had filled the dormitories at Prague University with the first arrivals. Women and children volunteered to collect food and prepare it for the refugees. But thousands more poured in every day. The heads of the private welfare agencies offered their services. The government provided eight korunas (about twenty cents) per refugee per day for food. The Salvation Army opened vast soup kitchens. The Red Cross undertook medical care. Child welfare agencies assisted homeless and orphaned children. Youth groups in churches, together with the YMCA and YWCA, opened their summer camps, and made volunteer staff available. Social organizations such as the Sokols helped displaced persons find jobs, shelter, [and] provided essential furniture and bedding. The newspapers printed want ads for free.

When the government ran out of rooms for the refugees, giant sewer pipes were used as temporary housing.

The Sharps asked Dr. Sum, who had prepared a long, itemized list for the meeting, where best for them to begin. The Commission for Service in Czechoslovakia discovered that its modest financial resources were in urgent demand, many times over.

For their initial few weeks in Prague, Waitstill and Martha would work out of No. 55, Vysehradska 16, a large, two-room office suite provided at government expense on the third floor of the former Ministry of Health, in the southern section of the city, near the Vltava River. The immense building had been re-designated the Central Institute for Refugees, and it housed all foreign aid groups, including the British Committee for Refugees from Czechoslovakia. The Sharps forged a close alliance with members of that group, especially with Quakers Elizabeth ("Tessa") Rowntree and Beatrice Wellington, a Canadian working for the British.

They bought a few cheap desks and tacked up a US flag brought from Wellesley Hills for that purpose. They also displayed a Czech flag, the white lion rampant on the quartered arms of Bohemia, Moravia, Slovakia, and Ruthenia. Finally the Sharps pasted a Unitarian-Quaker letterhead on the door and opened for business. Since their commission was the de facto umbrella organization for practically all nongovernmental aid from the United States, they soon became known simply as "American Relief."

Business hours would be eight to six, with the office closed for lunch from one to two, roughly the norm for most governmental offices in Prague. Martha and Waitstill typically rose each day at six, listened to the ever-more-distressing international news on the BBC, breakfasted downstairs at the Hotel Atlantic, then took a trolley car across the city to work. They ate supper at about eight each night and turned in early unless they had a date for the philharmonic or opera.

At first they were frequently out of town, reconnoitering the countryside for suitable projects to support under their mandate from AmRelCzech. Their very first expedition, a trip thirty miles outside Prague to the village of Lysa nad Labem, would demonstrate to Waitstill and Martha the enormous amount of good they could accomplish, even with the relatively limited means then at their disposal. But the trip would also come to show them the futility of optimism.

They were escorted by Madame Ruzena Palantova, social service chief in the Lord Mayor's office, to an exceptionally beautiful, sixteenth-century Bohemian castle. The Czech baron who owned the enormous and superbly maintained residence no longer could afford to live in it and was willing to sell. The Institute for Refugees, Madame Palantova explained, wanted to buy the castle and convert it into housing for two hundred refugee families. According to the larger plan, the Czech army would later take it over as a military hospital. In the interim, there were local manufacturers eager to hire the refugees, including a dressmaker willing to employ sewing-machine operators to work on the grounds of the castle.

A little back-of-the-envelope math told Martha and Waitstill that the conversion could be undertaken for about twenty-five thousand dollars. They were excited. "The wonderful inventiveness of this social engineering filled me with admiration," Martha wrote. "I realized how important it was to be able to harness experience and imagination with money."

On another expedition, to a refugee receiving camp south of Prague, their host and guide was Alice Masaryk, Jan's sister, a founder and head of the Czech Red Cross. On the way to the camp in her chauffeured limousine, Dr. Alice, as she was called, guided the Sharps through Ceske Budejovice, home of the original Budweiser beer.

Unlike the rest of her family, Dr. Alice was not a Unitarian but a Presbyterian, a member of the Church of the Czech Brethren, another liberal denomination with old ties to the Unitarian Church. She had trained to be a social worker and had spent time as a volunteer in Chicago settlement houses in the early part of the century. Dr. Alice and Martha hit it off immediately.

"Her single-minded devotion to the Czech people and sense of humor were like her brother Jan's," Martha wrote. "But there the resemblance ended. She was a self-effacing, pious, kind and devoted daughter."

Dr. Alice had been enmeshed in the tumultuous and bloody events of central Europe and the Balkans following the 1914 assassination of the Archduke Franz Ferdinand in Sarajevo, the flash point for World War I. In 1916, the Austrians pronounced a death sentence for treason on Alice and her father, Tomas Masaryk, whom they accused of plotting with Czech nationalists. Because he was beyond the

Austrians' grasp in London, Tomas Masaryk was sentenced to death in absentia. His daughter spent nine debilitating months in prison until vehement and repeated protests from the United States persuaded the Austrians to free her. The experience permanently compromised Alice Masaryk's health.

Now her life again was in peril. Her late father was deeply revered among the Czechs, and Dr. Alice was widely admired in her own right. When the Nazis finally pounced, they would not let her remain as a symbol and possible rallying point for the nation. She'd have to be eliminated. Already the Germans had launched a propaganda campaign against her, alleging that Masaryk pocketed private funds sent in her care to aid Czech refugee relief efforts. These included substantial amounts from AmRelCzech.

———— · ————

Gustave A. Prochazka, patriarch of the Czechoslovak Hussite Church, which had separated from the Catholic Church, greeted the Sharps with a briefcase that bulged with church mortgages, for which he was guarantor at local banks. The patriarch, who spoke no English, was disappointed to learn that the Unitarians would not be relieving him of this financial burden, although the Sharps did offer to personally present the case for American assistance in Boston upon their return. What became of that effort is unknown.

The pious old fellow (once the local Roman Catholic archbishop) escorted Waitstill and Martha on a thirteen-parish foray that took them far and wide into the countryside. Crowded together in the snug rear seat of his official car, flying both the flags of the National Czechoslovak Church and the Czech Republic, they whizzed around the outskirts of Prague to the front steps of thirteen newly built churches, where they were greeted each time by a minister and board of directors.

Both Sharps immediately were in high demand as public speakers at parties and meetings, especially Martha. Invitations poured in for her to address suggested topics, such as "Feeding the American Baby," "The Two-Party System of American Democracy," and "American Women's Organizations." These innocuous public appearances, and day trips such as the serial church tour with Patriarch Prochazka, helped maintain the Sharps' cover as a visiting minister and his wife, at least for the time being.

"We accepted as many as we could," Martha said. "I began to wish that I really had more recent figures and wider knowledge about American medical, social and other sciences, and had brought reference material and photographs with me. But my audiences were enthusiastic, in spite of my slender facts, and the laborious translations necessary after nearly every sentence."[1]

———— · ————

By the start of their second week in Prague, Martha was seriously chafing over accommodations at Hotel Atlantic. Ugly and incongruous furniture was by no means the only problem. There was nowhere to comfortably read or write at night and no proper light by which to do so. They also needed a separate room for private discussions that occurred with increasing frequency and at all hours.

Their main concern, however, was security.

"As the city filled up with Gestapo," she remembered, "we found them taking extra special interest in us. For example, they lingered in the lobby to note the names of those who called in search of us. To make matters worse, whenever we came in sight the concierge would shout our most confidential messages at us, no matter who was there to share the news. We politely asked him to be a bit more discreet, but whether out of pride at his smattering of English, or naïve confidence that he was behaving responsibly, he also managed to forget our admonitions."

The deal breaker came one day when the Sharps returned to their room to find all the furniture and their possessions in the hallway. According to hotel staff, their room required a coat of paint. Afterward, they found that certain important papers and belongings had vanished.

Fortunately, friends connected the Sharps to a Czech businessman named Hans Wertheimer who was willing to rent them his two-room apartment within Prague's seventeenth-century Waldenstein Palace for a thousand korunas a month. The extra room would allow space for private discussions with their Czech contacts. The move-in date was March 10.

Shortly before they were scheduled to move, Wertheimer's sister, Lydia Busch, a well-known Czech actress, called the Sharps to ask if they could delay moving a few days and explained that the current tenant, a Russian diplomat, refused to leave any sooner. Since the Sharps now had the weekend open, Lydia invited them to visit her and her family at their villa at Roztoky, about thirty miles from the city.

Peter Busch, Lydia's husband, until recently had run Czechoslovakia's largest glass-manufacturing plant, in Sudetenland. Following cession, he had refused to work for the Nazis, and he and Lydia had relocated to Roztoky, where he owned another plant. Many of his senior personnel had followed him as well.

Hans Wertheimer picked up the Sharps in his Skoda at the Roztoky train station, and on their way to the Busch villa he explained how the Nazis had tried every inducement to get Busch to reopen his Sudeten plant. They needed his glass for windshields for their military vehicles, but Peter Busch was immovable.

Lydia, forty, made an immediate impression on Martha. "She was scintillating," Martha wrote, "striking in appearance, and grace itself as she moved about the house, or sat at the piano playing our favorite music. She had a lovely voice, and as she played and sang, her auburn, page boy hair swinging back and forth caught the light from the fire."

Dinner on Saturday night started out as a grand and convivial affair, served on antique Meissen china by candlelight. Both Sharps noticed, however, that Peter Busch said little and excused himself frequently during the meal to listen to his radio in the den. Evidently the news was not good, and as the evening wore on, their host looked increasingly gloomy.

Hitler originally demanded cession of the Sudeten region under the pretext that the Czechs there were mistreating the ethnic Germans. His actual aim, soon to be clear, was conquest of all Czechoslovakia. He intended to appropriate its extensive industrial infrastructure—including Peter Busch's glass factory—in advance of Germany's invasion of Poland, planned for September 1939.

Edvard Benes, Tomas Masaryk's successor as president of Czechoslovakia, resigned on October 5, 1938, and moved with his family to London, where Benes eventually set up a government in exile. The following month he was replaced as president over what remained of his country—Bohemia and Moravia, Slovakia and Carpatho-Ukraine—by Emil Hacha, sixty-six, a distinguished lawyer with few political enemies and almost no political experience. Hacha, who was in poor health and of widely questioned mental acuity, would be the first and only president of the Second Czechoslovak Republic.

Hitler secretly set March 15—the Ides of March—as the date for invading Czechoslovakia. Once again in need of a pretext, Hitler stirred up secessionist fever in Slovakia, where, with Nazi connivance, a virulently anti-Semitic priest, Jozef Tiso, seized power.

President Hacha had no choice but to respond.

"Why so grim?" Lydia Busch finally inquired of her distracted husband at dinner.

"President Hacha has put Slovakia under martial law," he answered angrily, "and put Monsignor Tiso under arrest." Busch went on to say that the confrontation between the Hacha government and the Slovak nationalists was just the sort of crisis the Third Reich needed as an excuse to intervene. He was plainly pessimistic.

"I feel we must make our own plans for the family," he said at last, signaling the end of the dinner party. Busch and his brother-in-law, Hans, immediately fell into a discussion of whether Hans, too, should consider leaving the country, and how the glass plant might continue operating in their absence.

The Sharps made their thank-you's and good-nights and withdrew. In their bedroom they spoke together until dawn, wondering and worrying about their mission. Deep foreboding gripped them both.

— CHAPTER FOUR —

The Dying Republic

On Tuesday, March 14, 1939, Slovakia declared itself independent under Tiso. When Czech troops mobilized to put down the insurrection, Hitler summoned Emil Hacha to Berlin, where he was given an ultimatum: order your soldiers back into their barracks or the Luftwaffe will level Prague. Hacha reportedly fainted on the spot. After regaining consciousness he reluctantly signed the document.

That same day, Martha headed for the Prague airport to deliver a package of outgoing mail, most of it sensitive, to Trevor Chadwick, an English schoolmaster who was escorting a group of Czech refugee children to London that morning. Among the documents Chadwick would carry for the Sharps was Waitstill's first report from Prague to Robert Dexter in Boston.

"The situation is serious here," Waitstill wrote,

> both for the Jews and the life of the state. I am writing you just after the Austrian putsch anniversary and the recent near-secession of Slovakia about which you probably have been reading. Five divisions of the German army are waiting at Bratislava. People here seem to think that the German intention now is to split Slovakia off on the pretext of rescuing the "abused" German minority there or the pretext of preserving order after an appeal for that purpose has been made by the anti-Czech government of Slovakia.

The Nuremberg laws are being steadily put into effect by this helpless government and by the various college faculties in the city. Medical students are being told . . . that if they are Jews they have no hope of being graduated. Dr. [Albin] Goldschmeid was dismissed from the German University because an ancestor was a Jew. He and others are coming to us, begging for help in escaping to America. They will starve or commit suicide if some large-scale plan of emigration is not worked out.

The situation was not quite as Waitstill portrayed it in his letter, perhaps because he had much to discover about Czechoslovakia and its "helpless" government. Not all refugees were treated with the same care as he saw from humanitarians such as Dr. Sum and Alice Masaryk. Trains carrying refugees were often turned back at the border by Czech authorities. The refugee camps outside Prague were deplorable. Food was inadequate and people suffered from the cold because of broken windows and the scarcity of blankets.

Czechoslovakia, in short, was not immune to the virus of anti-Semitism that infected most of Europe as well as the United States. A series of polls taken between 1938 and 1942 revealed widespread negative impressions of Jews among Americans and support by about one-third of the respondents for anti-Jewish policies.[1]

In Czechoslovakia, the Munich agreement had stipulated that Sudeten Jews, most of whom were now refugees in Bohemia and Moravia, were entitled to apply for Czech citizenship. But based on an analysis of British government reports, historian Louise London notes, "the pattern of bureaucratic discrimination against Jews from the Sudetenland emerged, and they were systematically denied access to funds they had brought out." According to London, all three hundred thousand Jews in Czechoslovakia were under threat from the national authorities. "The Czech government made it clear," she writes, "that Jews of Czech nationality were not wanted and put various forms of pressure on them to emigrate."[2]

——— · ———

Trevor Chadwick's departure with the refugee children from the Prague airport that March 14 was a landmark moment in the increasingly frantic effort to rescue high-risk refugees from Czechoslovakia before it was too late. It was also a particularly poignant for Martha.

The flight was to be the first of eight transports—the others went mostly by train—that ultimately brought 669 Czech children to England.

The operation had been initiated by stockbroker Nicholas Winton, a Jew by birth, whose German parents had him baptized an Anglican and changed the family name from Wertheim.

Winton's program was modeled on, and later integrated into, the famed *Kindertransport* rescue missions. Between December 1, 1938, and September 1, 1939, Kindertransport brought to England between nine thousand and ten thousand children (seventy-five hundred of whom were Jews) from Germany, Austria, Poland, Holland, and Czechoslovakia. Kindertransport itself was a response to the Kristallnacht carnage of early November 1938.

Following the savage attacks against Jews, British aid organizations, among them the Jewish Refugee Committee and the Society of Friends (Quakers), pushed the British government to relax immigration restrictions. Public opinion supported their efforts, and the government agreed to give temporary refuge to an indeterminate number of children under the age of seventeen. Each child's care and maintenance was to be guaranteed by individuals or by organizations. It was assumed at the time that the youngsters would eventually return to their families.

In December 1938, Nicholas Winton visited Czechoslovakia at the invitation of his friend Martin Blake, who was working for the BCRC, Tessa Rowntree and Beatrice Wellington's organization, with offices near the Sharps at the Central Institute for Refugees in Prague. Without any direct authority from the BCRC, Winton set up a subsidiary "Children's Section" and began accepting applications from people eager to get their children out of the country to safety.

As he later wrote: "Everybody in Prague said, 'Look, there is no organization in Prague to deal with refugee children, nobody will let the children go on their own, but if you want to have a go, have a go.'"[3]

The British Home Office agreed to issue visas to Czech youngsters under eighteen as long as Winton could find them homes, as well as deposit fifty pounds for each child to guarantee his or her eventual return fare home. Then Winton furiously set about raising money and recruiting families who were willing to take in the refugee children. The first twenty were lined up by early March, visas were issued, and Trevor Chadwick was ready to whisk his young charges—one was an infant who would fly in Chadwick's lap—away to freedom.

———— · ————

Martha ached at the unspoken certainty among all the families gathered to say good-bye to their boys and girls that they were probably saying good-bye forever.

"Each little family was a small island of emotion," she went on. "The parents had bought sweets or other small gifts using their precious funds to the limit. While saying the mundane things—'Don't forget to write. Do what Mr. Chadwick tells you. We'll be over to join you before you know it.'—the parents seemed to caress the children with their eyes, as if to engrave on their memories how they looked, spoke and walked in this last hour."

She could not help but think of her own two children far away, and she inwardly shuddered at the idea of standing there like these other parents, saying a final farewell to Hastings or Martha Content in order to save her darlings' lives.

Martha also found it easy, though painful, to intuit the departing children's thoughts, and she was acutely sensitive to their inner turmoil. They may have accepted their parents' decision to send them away, but few were old enough to fully understand it. All they knew at that moment was excitement mixed with fear and confusion.

"Some parents showed their love openly and tenderly and the children responded without embarrassment," she recalled. "They carefully unpinned wrapped treasures—a photograph, a ring, a watch—and made last-minute presentations. I offered to take their pictures, and they were very pleased, eagerly giving their names and addresses to me to send them copies." Then, the plane was announced, and "the boys and girls each were given a last hug, [presented with] kisses on both cheeks, and loaded with small parcels" before joining Chadwick in line for departure.

Among the group was eleven-year-old Gerda Stein from Carlsbad in the Sudeten. After Chamberlain's capitulation at Munich, Gerda's parents, Arnold and Erna Stein, had fled with her and her older half-sister, Johanna, to Prague where, for nearly six months, the elder Steins trudged from embassy to embassy, searching unsuccessfully for any avenue of escape.[4] Some Jews in Czechoslovakia, throughout central Europe, and around the world still refused to believe the Nazis' violent rhetoric. Not the Steins. They signed Gerda up for the Kindertransport. They would eventually turn to the Sharps in search of help, sending a desperate, typewritten note in broken English that survives in Martha's files.

"Dear Sir," it begins. "As I brought you the pictures of the children's and my little Gerdi's departures, you have had the amiability of allowing me to apply to you. I never should taken the liberty to write you, if I were not helpless. I have heard that a new action is established from America for the Jewish refugees. I don't know whether it is true, but having not other acquaintance I beg you politely to inform me about this matter. With many thanks beforehand, I remain yours faithfully, Arnold Stein."

Erna Stein appended her own scribbled postscript. "I should be very glad," she wrote, "if you and madam would allow to me to go to see you in your office. But I don't like to trouble you." In a separate box in the lower left-hand corner of the page, Frau Stein added: "Today is a great danger for us. Please tell us the time when we may come to see you. Please help us!"

The Steins' application reveals a couple in their thirties, parents of two daughters, Gerda and Johanna. Arnold Stein ran a knitting shop. Erna was a knitter. They were ordinary people with no connections, and their fight to save themselves and their older daughter—who, at eighteen, was too old for Kindertransport—failed.

Their daughter Gerda, now Gerda Stein Mayer, remembers fragments of that day at the Prague airport. "Trevor Chadwick was there, amusing a three-year-old with a glove puppet," she says. "My father took photographs, while my mother walked rather pensively, arm in arm, up and down with my sister. My mother also spoke with another mother, who had a girl of my age, a quiet, well-behaved child who, I knew instinctively, was going to be an 'example' to me. I loathed her on sight."

Martha gathered with the Steins and the other families at the enclosure where they could wave a last good-bye to their children.

"As each boy and girl stepped out of the exit they waved at their parents, ran across the snow-covered field, waved again and climbed aboard the plane," she wrote.

Their parents' self-control was marvelous. Smiling brightly, eyes brimming with tears, they waved back. Chadwick was the last to board.

Then the door of the plane was slammed shut with a finality that rocked the little group. Suddenly we were all one large and bereft family. A few muffled sobs escaped as the engines warmed up. The children could see us from the windows. The plane was moving. The pilot brought it as close to the enclosure as possible so that all the children on one side could get one last look, and wave; then he turned, wheeled, so that children on the other side had a chance to say goodbye.

Then the engines raced and the plane took off, disappearing at once into the low clouds. I returned to Prague on the airport bus with the parents. We disembarked, exchanged handshakes and bows, and then each of us withdrew into [our] private misery.

Gerda Stein Mayer's very last memory of the departure was her father running after the airplane with his camera, trying to take one more photo. She would never see him, or her mother, again. They were both interned at Terezin, a concentration camp outside Prague, and later transported to Auschwitz, where they died.[5]

Gerda and the rest of Trevor Chadwick's charges—most of whom got airsick—made a refueling stop that day in Holland. When refreshments appeared, she recalls, "We were given the choice of lemonade or milk. We all asked proudly for lemonade, like cowboys calling for whiskey. Only one boy without shame asked for the babyish drink, milk. I looked at him with amazement, awe, contempt. Clearly an individualist."

The transport landed safely at Croydon that evening.

———— · ————

Vera Gissing, one of the 669 who owed their lives to Nicholas Winton, later wrote a book about him: *Nicholas Winton and the Rescued Generation*. In it, she describes the tragic attempt to bring out one last group, the eighth train. "The next transport, the largest," Gissing writes, "was due to leave Prague on 1 September 1939. Hitler had invaded Poland that very day and the borders were closed; 250 children were already at the station, but the train was not allowed to depart. The despair of the parents on hearing this fateful decision is unimaginable. As far as it is known, all these children were later deported to concentration camps where they perished, my two young cousins among them."[6]

Nicholas Winton died in July of 2015 at age 106.

———— · ————

The evening of March 14, 1939, the Sharps sat in the Prague National Theatre's presidential box, ordinarily occupied by Alice Masaryk. With the Gestapo determined to silence her, Masaryk had decided against attending the performance and instead gave her tickets to the Sharps. Both loved opera and were grateful for any respite from the oppressive tension everywhere around them.

Yet the National Theatre would be no refuge that night. Whispered rumors and endless speculation over President Hacha's mission to Berlin and Adolf Hitler's intentions flew through the nervous and distracted audience in the ornate old opera house all evening.

The performance that night, as recalled by both Sharps, was a Dvorak opera. The scene that followed the final curtain was very emotional. The audience rose and in tears sang the national anthem, "Kde domov muj?," "Where is my country?"[7]

Einmarsch—The Invasion of Czechoslovakia

After the opera performance, on what usually was a ten-minute walk back to the Hotel Atlantic from the National Theatre, the Sharps encountered Nazi thugs roaming the Czech capital, carrying out Berlin's directive to provoke as much chaos as possible, thereby underscoring the urgent need for authority—the Reich's ostensibly beneficent, pacifying hand.

They saw one young man under a street lamp wound himself superficially with a pocketknife. As the blood ran, he smeared some on his face, then hurried over to a Czech policeman, complaining in German that he was "a poor German student" who'd been attacked by a young Czech, whom he pointed out in the crowd.

The policeman grabbed the suspect, who protested that he had never touched the German youth. Waitstill jumped into action, charging across the street to inform the cop of what had actually occurred. The potentially violent confrontation quickly cooled into a routine incident, with the policeman instructing everyone to move along, and the young Czech thanking Waitstill in broken English for intervening.

As they approached their favorite *kavarna*, or coffee house, intent on a quiet nightcap, the Sharps encountered a riot, as Martha put it. "Chairs, dishes and all sort of movable objects were flying out the door."

The police arrived to restore order. The Sharps asked the owner what had touched off the melee. He told them a group of German students had arrived early that evening and had tried to provoke fights with every Czech student who came in. "Our boys refused to take them up," he said, "but finally the Nazis went too far. It was a point of honor for the Czechs to defend their country."

Waitstill and Martha took a taxi the rest of the way to the hotel, each lost in private, sober musings.

"There's a heaviness in the air," she said at last. "Do you feel it?"

"Are you afraid?" he replied. "Do you want to go home to Wellesley and let the Czechs fight their own battles?"

Martha didn't answer at once. But as their cab wound carefully through the increasingly crowded streets—very unusual at that hour in Prague, a city that habitually got its sleep—Martha reflected on their original reasons for coming to Prague and on the Czechs' clear need for their help.

"I'd like to stay if you want to," she said in the dark.

"Good!" he answered. "I want to stay too."

——— · ———

Although it was well past twelve when they finally reached their room, Martha telephoned Alice Masaryk.

Dr. Alice told them that a mob of Nazis had gathered below her apartment windows, shouting threats and insults. At one point the crowd had tried to rush the building's front door. The Czech police finally broke up the demonstration.

"We'd be happy to come over and stay with you," Martha offered.

"No," Masaryk answered, "I think I must undergo this myself. Why should I involve you with my personal problems?"

Before Martha could answer that she and Waitstill were already deeply involved with Dr. Alice's personal problems—that's why they were in Prague—Masaryk changed the subject.

"I have heard that some of the embassies are offering asylum," she said. "If the United States should invite me, I might consider it. I must think about it. Please keep in touch."

As Martha rang off with Masaryk, there was a knock at the hotel room door.

"Who under the sun is calling at this hour?" Waitstill wondered. He opened the door to discover Jiri Vranek, a Czech diplomat and member of former president Benes's staff in London. The Sharps had met Vranek in Paris.

"Come in! What a surprise!" said Waitstill. "When did you get in?"

Martha watched as Waitstill practically yanked the Czech into the room.

"Just a couple of hours ago," Vranek replied. He had brought along some of their mail, and a note from Malcolm Davis, but that was not his reason for calling at such a late hour.

"Have you heard the latest?" he asked.

"What is it?"

The story spilled from Vranek in a torrent.

"Hacha just telephoned from Berlin," he said. "Hitler has ordered the Nazi army to march into Czechoslovakia at six this morning. They entered one of our frontier barracks at midnight. Our men were outnumbered. Every one of them was killed. Hitler has threatened to wipe out the whole Czech army and to bomb Prague unless all resistance is called off."

In all, two hundred thousand Wehrmacht infantrymen would pour over the Czech border in the coming hours.

"Hacha told the cabinet that he already has signed an agreement that the Czechs will offer no resistance. He asked for their confirmation. Poor weak Hacha! To save Czech lives he signs their death warrants."

Vranek slumped in a chair, overwhelmed for a moment. Then he continued: "Dishonor is worse than death. This is the end of the republic. It was too successful. Everyone wanted to grab us."

Martha stepped forward.

"We are going to stay and keep on working as long as we can, whatever happens," she told him.

"Thank God!" he said, looking up with a smile. "Some of our friends have guts."

He advised the Sharps to destroy any incriminating documents and warned that the Nazis were certain to search their files, openly or in secret.

"We set to work to review letters of introduction, commissions to be discharged, and lists of people to be found and helped," Martha recalled. "Fortunately, many of the projects discussed in these documents were already underway and could be continued without the original paperwork. They made a rather large pile, however."

"Too many to flush down the toilet?" Vranek asked. "How about burning them? I know the way to the hotel furnace."

It was by now nearly 4 a.m.

Martha described the somber scene:

Deep under the Hotel Atlantic we came upon a queue of people, all waiting their turn to approach the furnace. It was a silent line. Evidently all of us there understood that from this night on, no one was to be trusted. I watched as they threw their papers in the fire. For a few brilliant moments, the flames illuminated each face, betraying each person's fear, dejection, pensiveness and hopelessness. As each turned and was swallowed in the darkness, their shoulders seemed to give away something lost in the ashes. Memory? Hope? Honor? Freedom?

The Sharps said good night and good-bye to Jiri Vranek, and returned to their room. From the window, they could see that a snowstorm had driven the crowds indoors. But there was no sleep in Prague. Lights burned in all the buildings along the street, in banks, offices, and apartments, throwing yellow patches on the newly fallen snow.

"Waitstill," Martha remembered, "was going through his futile nightly ritual of trying to anchor the four-by-six down puff on his bed by tucking a steamer robe around it. He muttered. 'This barbarous custom! No sheets! No blankets! Arms and legs exposed! You either swelter or freeze! How the Czechs have survived—'"

Martha interrupted her husband's tirade to help him secure his bedclothes.

"Then I fixed the one on my bed, and snapped off the light," she said. "But it was not so easy to turn off my mind."

———— · ————

Two hours later, at 6 a.m. on March 15, 1939, German troops crossed the border into Czechoslovakia, reaching Prague a little more than three hours later. The *Einmarsch* (invasion) had begun. Waitstill recalled that "every trace of Czechoslovak democracy vanished as the grey troops poured in through the falling snow."

International condemnation quickly followed. Neville Chamberlain, admitting to the failure of appeasement, said, "World opinion has received a sharper shock than has ever been administered to it."[1] In Washington, the acting US secretary of state, Sumner Welles, condemned the invasion. "It is manifest that acts of wanton lawlessness and of arbitrary force are threatening world peace and the very structure of modern civilization," he said.[2] The Soviets called Hitler's actions "arbitrary, violent, and aggressive."

Treaty obligations notwithstanding, no government intervened.

The Einmarsch was front-page news everywhere and proof, in case anyone had held lingering doubts, that the Nazis would not be stopped at the negotiating table. On March 17, the British *Guardian* headline read, "German Rule in Prague, Rounding Up the 'Harmful' 10,000 Arrests?" The unsigned article reported:

> Prague, a sorrowing Prague, yesterday had its first day of German rule—a day in which the Czechs learned of the details of their subjection to Germany, and in which the Germans began their measures against the Jews and against those people who have "opened their mouths too wide." Prague's streets were jammed with silent pedestrians wandering about, looking out of the corners of their

eyes at German soldiers carrying guns, at armoured cars, and at other military precautions. . . . Suicides have begun. The fears of the Jews grow. The funds of the Jewish community have been seized, stopping Jewish relief work. The Prague Bar Council has ordered all its "non-Aryan" members to stop practising at once. The organisation for Jewish emigration has been closed. Hundreds of people stood outside the British Consulate shouting: "We want to get away!" This is only the beginning. According to an official spokesman of the German Foreign Office in Berlin last night, the Gestapo (secret police) will have rounded up hundreds of "harmful characters" within the next few days. So far about fifty to a hundred men have been put in local jails. "There are certain centres of resistance which need to be cleaned up," said the spokesman. "Also some people open their mouths too wide. Some of them neglected to get out in time. They may total several thousand before we are through. Remember that Prague was a breeding-place for opposition to National Socialism." The head of the Gestapo in Prague is reported to have been more definite: "We have 10,000 arrests to carry out." Already, says a Reuters correspondent, everyone seems to have an acquaintance who has disappeared.

——— · ———

The enormity of the Czechs' national disaster was evident everywhere, from the crowd's hollow stares to the huge bright-red, white, and black swastika flags snapping arrogantly in the cold wind. However, the true nature of the calamity was at first unclear to Martha and Waitstill, and it would take time for them to grasp the full extent of Nazi evil.

——— · ———

At 7 a.m. on March 15, the Sharps arrived as usual at the refugee institute, only to discover an enormous crowd standing outside in the snow. They approached one of the Czech police officers helping to hold back the throng.

"What office do you wish to visit?" the officer asked.

"American Relief for Czechoslovakia."

"You must wait your turn. All of these people are waiting in front of you."

"But that is our office!" Waitstill said.

"Who are you?"

"Sharp."

A policeman led them through the crowd toward the door, patiently asking each person to stand aside—"*Prosim,* please move, please move"—and then up the staircase toward their office. With each step the mass of humanity shifted and quivered, as if ready to explode. The sheer pressure of so many desperate people jostling and shoving one another frightened Martha.

"These people have been gathering all night," one of the volunteer staffers said as they finally made it into the office. "They think this is American territory and if they can just get inside the office, they'll be safe."

"Didn't you tell them we are not on US property?" Martha asked.

"Of course, but they don't believe me!"

Waitstill went out into the hall, raised his arm for quiet, then addressed the crowd in English and some German.

"American Relief for Czechoslovakia is here to give medical and material help to Czechoslovak refugees," he said. "We are not a visa agency. We are not an emigration agency. We are not an official branch of the US government. You are endangering yourselves and your families by being here, for the Gestapo may be among you and they think that if you are here you must need to escape. For your own protection, and that of your families, please go home."

The speech had negligible impact. Some people left, but others kept trying to elbow their way forward. Meanwhile, inside the office, Martha was confronted by a hysterically frightened husband and father waving a handgun. "I came here for help, to save my family!" he cried. "Here are my wife and two sons. I am hunted by the Gestapo! I am only one step ahead of them! I have no place to go. If you force me out of here I shall shoot my family, and then myself! There is no other choice!"

Martha took him into her private office alone, offered him a cigarette, and gradually calmed the man. He told her he was an attorney, from the Sudeten, where he had come to the Gestapo's unwelcome attention by winning cases against a number of their leaders in the Reichenberg area.

He had learned just in time that he was marked for elimination, and he had escaped to Prague with his family. Now that the occupation was a fait accompli, he knew that he and his family were doomed unless they could escape again. He had no money, no connections, and, without help, no hope.

Martha offered to do what she could, if he would leave his gun with her. The lawyer finally agreed and said he thought perhaps he could hide out for a bit longer. They agreed to meet again the next morning.

"Thank you," he said as he gathered his wife and sons to leave. "Thank God for you."

———— · ————

Since the crowd outside their office would not disperse in spite of Waitstill's entreaties, the ad hoc solution to the crisis was to take everyone's name, note their place in line, and then promise to take up their cases, one at a time, beginning the next morning.

The Sharps conferred by telephone with Dr. Alice, who now asked that they request that she be given asylum at the US embassy, and with Lydia Busch, who reported that her husband, Peter, was safe within the French embassy, but that her brother, Hans, was being hunted by the Gestapo, who intended, if they could, to use him as a bargaining chip as they continued to pursue Peter. She asked Waitstill and Martha not to move into the Waldenstein Palace apartment just yet. Hans was hiding out there.

The Sharps assured her not to worry. Moving was their last concern at the moment.

Martha later noted in her datebook that Hans Wertheimer was arrested by the Germans. Nowhere does she write that he was released, and it's likely that their new friend was one of the 263,000 Czech Jews who died in the Holocaust.[3]

Peter Busch escaped to France inside a large box labeled "Furniture" that was included with a French diplomatic shipment. Even more artful was the way Karl Deutsch's mother took her leave of Prague.

The former Leopoldina Scharf, named for a Holy Roman emperor and nicknamed "Poldy" by her friends but known generally as Maria, had suddenly been stricken with appendicitis. She was recovering from emergency surgery in a Prague hospital as the Germans marched into the city. When the Gestapo checked patient rosters, as surely they would eventually, Frau Deutsch without question would be arrested. Although largely incapacitated by major abdominal surgery, she had to be moved as soon as possible to save her life.

According to Waitstill, Maria Deutsch's salvation was a clever trick conceived and executed by the hospital nursing staff. They wrapped her as a corpse in an undertaker's basket and sent her to the train station in a hearse. Her destination was the German Baltic port of Sassnitz, from which it was a short ferry ride to southern Sweden and her destination, the city of Malmo.

It is unclear for how much of the journey Frau Deutsch needed to pretend she was dead. According to her granddaughter, Margaret Carroll, who is today a professor of art history at Wellesley College, the train passed through Deutsch's old Parliament district as it neared the German border. Luckily, the local train inspector recognized her and did not betray her to the Nazis. We know she did make it safely to Malmo, and ultimately to New York City. She died in 1969.

— · —

The Sharps held a brief and unsuccessful meeting on Dr. Alice's behalf with US ambassador Wilbur Carr, who said that he could not help. "United States State Department regulations which, by the way, I helped draft myself," Carr explained, "allow us to take into the embassy only our own nationals in time of crisis."

Although Martha and Waitstill never were publicly critical of the sixty-eight-year-old ambassador, Carr had for his entire State Department career supported the restrictionist immigration policies he had helped promulgate in the 1920s. Anti-Semitic, not unusual for the State Department at the time, he also was a stickler for regulations, never inclined to relax the quota rules for anyone.

Evidence suggests that Carr in 1930 advised officials in several European consulates to restrict immigration visas to just 10 percent of their allotments. Fortunately for the Sharps, he was succeeded a month later by Irving Linnell, who proved to be a far more compassionate and helpful official.

Martha and Waitstill conveyed Carr's unwelcome news to Masaryk, and promised to carry their appeal to the British embassy. They ate a brief lunch they hardly could taste on St. Wenceslaus Square, then walked back out to the street. It was shortly past noon.

"The snow still was falling and now was about ten inches deep," Martha remembered.

In spite of the piercing cold, and the difficult footing, the whole Nazi Army, blue with cold, seemed to be marching down the main square of Prague. Goose-stepping to martial music, with their primitive battalion symbols and flying animal tails encrusted with snow, they came proudly along in endless ranks, it seemed.

Every building flew the Czech tricolor as far as the eye could see. Unless one knew that a policeman had visited every house and ordered that it fly the Czech flag before noon, or its owner would be arrested, one would think that the Czechs were welcoming the Germans!

Loudspeakers had been placed at all main intersections, and between the military music we heard, "*Achtung! Achtung!* Congratulations, Czechs! You are now citizens of the Third Reich and will be protected by the Führer, who will come to speak to you, himself! Stay off the streets tonight, for your own safety. After eight p.m., Prague is under martial law. Anyone who disobeys this order will be shot on sight."

As we stood in a scattering of people, looking at the parade, I made a snide remark to Waitstill in German about the broadcast. Most of Czech adults had turned their backs to the parade, and were seemingly absorbed in the show windows. A man nearby, who heard me speak German, turned to me with a raised hand, and livid face.

"You are a Nazi, Fräulein?" he snarled.

"No, I am an American," I answered.

"Then why are you speaking their filthy tongue?" His arm still was raised, as if he was going to strike me.

"I'm sorry," I said in English. "I don't speak Czech, and I just came out of a shop where I was speaking German—"

"Then, by God, speak American!" he interrupted angrily. "It may be the last time you have a chance!"

I nudged Waitstill along, and we spoke quietly in English from then on.

As we moved along in the gathering dark, a number of Czechs drifted into earshot, whispering, "Go to the Old Town Square. Go to Starometske Namesti." Soon, these voices were everywhere, so we turned and as if drawn by a vast human tide we joined the crowd departing the spectacle of triumphant Nazism for the genuine expression of Czech pride and unity at the traditional gathering place, the Old Square and fourteenth-century Prague Town Hall, where enshrined was the casket of their Unknown Soldier from World War One. Starometske Namesti was the hallowed heart of the ancient city.

As we entered on foot we saw thousands of people standing or kneeling in the snow before the Town Hall chapel, bareheaded, praying, indifferent to the frigid snow and their own tears. Before them on the pavement were thousands of tiny bouquets of snow drops or violets arranged in instinctive designs, frequently the heart shape of Bohemia.

There was no sound, only the heavy silence of a tomb, broken by sobs quickly smothered. Impotent hands clenched and unclenched. The Czech Republic was dead. Their naked despair was terrible to see and share. We placed our offering among the others and slipped away.

Waitstill's later summary in his report to the Unitarian constituency was brief and grim: "Civilization as it is understood in administrative practice, in banking practice, in government by principles and common law, had ended at noon on March 15."

———— · ————

At about 4:30 p.m., Martha and Waitstill met with several other workers from foreign aid agencies at the British embassy. Likely among them were representatives of the American-Jewish Joint Distribution Committee, the Jewish emigration agency HICEM, the Quakers, the BCRC, and the YMCA and YWCA. At the embassy they learned that in advance of the Einmarsch the Gestapo had raided the Social Democrats' Prague headquarters, where they seized the passports of three hundred workers ticketed for escape to Great Britain the next day. All three hundred were immediately picked up and jailed.

In contrast to Ambassador Carr's by-the-book refusal to help shelter the hunted, the British had put a priority on emigration assistance to political refugees, especially German Social Democrats from Sudetenland and the "Old Reich" refugees—those who had fled to Prague from Germany and Austria.

At the British embassy that afternoon, the Sharps and the rest of the gathered relief workers learned that the British were offering asylum to eight endangered individuals, among them Wenzel Jaksch and Siegfried Taub, leaders of the Sudeten Social Democratic Party, a communist named Katz, and Werner T. ("Bill") Barazetti, a Swiss-born BCRC volunteer who worked closely with Nicholas Winton.[4] Several aid workers, Waitstill and Martha among them, were dispatched to bring in those people.

Martha's job was to escort a man she always and only referred to as Mr. X. For some reason, she would never disclose his identity, if indeed she knew it. For a young minister's wife, Sunday school teacher, and mother of two from Wellesley Hills, Massachusetts, it would be a defining Mata Hari moment on the freezing, snowy streets of occupied Prague.

"I found a taxi in the darkness," Martha wrote, "and noting that the driver had a companion with him in the front seat, gave an address which was near my destination, but not the exact address."

She had listened well to Gertrude Baer in London.

"The 'extra cargo'"—clearly a Gestapo agent—"tried to engage me in conversation, but I parried his questions. Arriving at the place, I hastily paid the driver and hurried around the corner to hide in the first doorway to watch and see whether I was being followed."

The Nazi operative soon rounded the same corner on foot, looked up and down the street, as well as into several alleys, and walked on, very alert. The cab driver honked.

"My heart skipped a beat," Martha wrote. "I flattened myself against the entrance. In the darkness, he walked right by me! Once he heard the taxi horn, however, he evidently decided I wasn't worth following."

The bitter cold and a rising wind might have affected the Gestapo man's inclinations, as well. "He returned to the cab," Martha reported, "and soon after they drove away."

She slipped from her hiding place, turned the corner, and found Mr. X's address, a five-story walk-up. The vestibule was dark. Martha fumbled along the wall for a light switch, then pressed it to illuminate the first floor long enough for her to climb the stairs to the second floor, where she repeated the process until she achieved the topmost story—Mr. X's floor.

Martha rang the bell. A woman answered. "No," she said. "There wasn't anyone by that name here. Never heard of him."

Martha wrote: "I begged. I told her there was little time. I produced my American passport. When she saw it, she said in Czech, 'a moment,' then snatched my passport from me and shut the door in my face."

Martha's first foray into clandestine operations looked at that juncture to be a bust. *What will I do,* she asked herself in the unlit hallway, *if she never opens the door again?* To her immense relief, the door did open. A man stood before her.

"I asked him if he was Mr. X. He replied in English that X could be given a message. I explained it had been arranged for X to proceed to the British Embassy for safety until he could be convoyed out of the country."

The man asked Martha to wait a moment and shut the door once more. Moments later he emerged in his overcoat and handed back her passport. "I am X," he said quietly, as if his identity were a secret even from his neighbors, and they headed down the stairs together.

Back on the street, they noticed that nearly every cab now carried a minder. "We better walk to the embassy," X said, and he led the way at a brisk pace through the icy wind. Within twenty minutes they reached the ancient Charles Bridge over the Vltava River. There, a young German soldier stepped out of the shadows to challenge them. He was shivering from the cold in his thin uniform; icicles hung from his cap.

"Identity cards!" the guard demanded in German.

"Americans," Martha responded in English, adding, "en route to the US embassy." She pulled out her passport to show him.

"Passport?" she said. "I don't speak German."

Martha later surmised the guard figured it was too cold to argue. "*Gehen,*" he said—"Go"—and they did, straight across the cobblestone bridge.

The same ploy worked just as well on the opposite side of the Vltava, leaving Martha and Mr. X about a half-mile uphill walk to go. Then came the hard part. As they approached the British embassy, they encountered a Gestapo detachment stationed at the courtyard gate.

"My heart thumped again. Were we to fail with the doorstep to safety in view?"

Luckily another strategy popped into her head. As Martha and X neared the gate, she began complaining loudly and angrily about the cold and the wind and the lack of taxis on the street. "We never should have accepted this appointment with the secretary!" she snapped angrily at Mr. X, who stood silently at her side. "If I had known we'd have to *walk* here!"

Martha accosted one of the German agents, and asked the bewildered man if he knew whether Mr. Swanson was still in his office. "We are so-o-o-o delayed!" she added dramatically.

"Uh, I do not know," the German replied in broken English.

Martha produced her passport once more, handed it to him, and regally inquired, "Will you please tell Mr. Swanson that Mr. and Mrs. Sharp are here?"

"I am *not* the British embassy guard," he answered testily, handing Martha back her passport as he spoke. "He is there," he said, gesturing to a British soldier in the distance. "Go ask him."

———— · ————

Once inside the embassy, Martha warmed up with a cup of tea and bade farewell to a grateful Mr. X. She learned that her husband had gone to Alice Masaryk's apartment and was waiting for her there.

While Mr. X's identity probably never will be known for a certainty, records show that all eight of the people brought in that night eventually got out of Czechoslovakia. British embassy officials were able to obtain permission from the Gestapo for all but Jaksch to immigrate to Britain. The seven left by April 1, and Jaksch, disguised as a workman, left secretly and escaped to London by way of Poland.

Martha caught up with Waitstill before the crackling hearth in Dr. Alice's drawing room. He struck Martha as being tense but calm. Dr. Alice's worn expression and nervous manner told the story of her previous twenty-four hours. She would be gone from Prague in early April, ultimately spending the war years in the United States.[5]

But for the time being, Masaryk explained, she realized her place was not under the protection of a foreign embassy, but here inside her own home in Prague. Duty and the Masaryk name demanded it.

If Dr. Alice was as frightened as she'd recently seemed, she did not show it.

———— · ————

As the Germans' eight o'clock curfew drew near, Martha and Waitstill reluctantly departed Dr. Alice's company, found a free taxi, and headed across the city for their hotel. This time the Nazi minder in the front passenger seat actually served a useful purpose. The bridge crossings were a snap; all the Gestapo man had to do was flash his credentials.

"We entered the hotel just as the clock was striking the hour," Martha recalled, "and loudspeakers proclaimed, '*Achtung! Achtung!* Anyone on the street will be shot on sight.'"

The lobby and dining room teemed with officers of the Wehrmacht. No tables were immediately available, so the Sharps retreated to their room to freshen up and kill a little time. When they returned to the dining room, there still was no table free. A monocled German officer rose and with a courteous gesture offered to share his table with them.

"Waitstill thanked him," wrote Martha, "and said that he was sure the officer would understand that 'we wished to be alone.' He bowed to me, clicked his heels and with a knowing wink at Waitstill murmured that he did not wish to interfere with a 'tête-a-tête,' and sat down once more." As for the "tête-a-tête": "When a table was finally free, we had no appetite, and anything we could think to say was so innocuous that we felt perfectly safe in saying it. The weather was vile. The cook looked to be in a temper. We were preoccupied by the problems of the day."

They retired to their room. There a huge roar from outside drew them to the casements. "Below us," Martha wrote, "were lines of German military trucks, evidently the ones that had brought the army to Prague that morning.

"I immediately understood the need for the curfew. Tons of food, sugar, wool, machinery, and raw materials were taken away that night in the trucks, and every night thereafter. When they returned to re-load, the Czech word for robber frequently was found scrawled on both sides of the vehicles."

"The looting went on every night for months," Waitstill recalled, "carrying the goods westward to the Third Reich."

The looting of Prague soon extended beyond the obvious and easily portable. Iron benches disappeared from parks and other public spaces, as did fences. The Germans even appropriated the brass chains from water closets, replacing them with ropes.

From their morning confrontations with the fear-maddened lawyer and other refugees, to the heartbreaking scene at Starometske Namesti, to their clandestine human rescue work that night, and now this, the vast plundering of Prague, the Sharps were overwhelmed.

"It was not possible for us to understand all at once, either intellectually or emotionally, what was happening," Martha remembered. They passed a sleepless night discussing the astonishing events of the day, trying to figure out their next move.

─── CHAPTER SIX ───

Under the Swastika

Next morning, Martha and Waitstill tuned in to the BBC as usual, only to hear a harsh buzz. The Nazis already were jamming the radio waves. At breakfast there was no morning newspaper, no mail. They learned that no trains or planes were entering or leaving the country. The only officially sanctioned news was of Hitler's address, scheduled for eleven that morning, March 16.

The Führer arrived in Prague at about dusk the previous day, after a train ride from Berlin to the Czech border, and then a motorcade to the capital, where he was driven up to ancient Hradschin Castle and escorted to the suite of rooms that Tomas Masaryk had once occupied. It was exactly one year plus a day from the moment Hitler had entered Vienna after the *Anschluss*. In a further imperial affront to the Czech people and their government, his personal, gold-edged swastika was hoisted overhead, visible for miles around.

According to a story that went around the capital that morning, Tomas Masaryk's ghost visited Hitler in Masaryk's old bedroom in the night, and harassed him till dawn.

"So," Martha remembered, "at eleven a.m. we stood in Hradcany Square and saw Hitler standing in the window from which pronouncements of importance always had been made to the people throughout the centuries. I thought, *He sounds even wilder than the broadcasts we've heard on the radio. But he looks just as he does in all those pictures.* He was jubilant."

"I now proclaim this state the Protectorate of Bohemia and Moravia!" Hitler shouted. He touched on a favorite theme, *lebensraum*—literally, living space—the lands surrounding the Fatherland that according to Nazi doctrine shared primordial kinship with the German people and thus were intrinsic parts of the German Reich. Bohemia and Moravia had been part of that greater Germanic family for a thousand years, he said.

Hitler returned to the canard of civil unrest and persecution of ethnic Germans as the cause for the invasion. The German Reich, no longer able to tolerate disturbances on its borders, would restore order and discipline to central Europe.

Hitler announced the men he had selected as leaders of the new protectorate: Konstantin von Neurath, protector; Karl Hermann Frank, secretary of state; and Konrad Henlein, leader of the Sudeten German Party, *gauleiter,* or Nazi party chief, in Sudeten. Von Neurath was an aging member of the upper Nazi hierarchy who had served in the foreign ministry. Though ruthless even by Hitler's standards, the sixty-six-year-old von Neurath would have trouble suppressing the Czech underground, and he was removed in 1941. His successor, Reinhard Heydrich, would be assassinated by the resistance the following year.

Frank and Henlein were typical Nazi thugs who'd worked together in the Sudeten to foment the troubles Hitler used as his pretext for annexing the region. Frank, a protégé of the SS and Gestapo head Heinrich Himmler, was characterized by Irving Linnell as "the perfect image of the German *Halbgebildeter* [half-educated individual] whom National Socialism has raised to power."[1]

Frank was most famously hated among Czechs for carrying out Hitler's order to avenge Heydrich's death. Besides the execution of Norbert Capek, an estimated thirteen hundred men, women, and children died either directly or in concentration camps. Among the slaughtered were all the men and many of the women and children in the village of Lidice, northwest of Prague. A few of the surviving children were given to German families, but the rest, along with the surviving women, died in concentration camps. Lidice was reduced

to ashes. The Nazis triumphantly proclaimed that the village was forever erased from human memory.

After the war, Lidice would become a national memorial. Homes
were built nearby in the early 1950s and a rose garden planted with
twenty-nine thousand roses donated by thirty-two countries.[2]

———— · ————

Martha felt a chill up her spine at the prospect of Konstantin von
Neurath, aided by gangsters such as Frank and Henlein, assuming
dictatorial control of all Czech governmental and security affairs.
Waitstill squeezed her hand and whispered "Courage!" in the square
as the crowd began to break up.

March 16, the day after the Einmarsch, was a busy one. The
Sharps had appointments with at least ten people that day, most of
whom were identified in Martha's datebook only by their initials.
Among them was Ambassador Carr. Neither Martha nor Waitstill recorded the substance of that meeting, but certainly they asserted that
the Einmarsch had not shaken their determination to carry on their
work in Czechoslovakia, a decision that Waitstill later downplayed in
his official report to the denomination as one that "any other American in our position" would choose.

Martha had a lunch appointment with Ruzena Palantova. After
the two women found every restaurant overflowing with German
military, they retreated to Palantova's office in the city department of
social welfare and ordered in their meal.

"I was glad," Martha remembered, "because we never would have
had a chance to talk about the events of the day so freely if we were
in a public place. She showed me the directives her division had received that morning from the Nazis. They were printed in Czech and
German. She was ordered to post them on all bulletin boards. Palantova also was personally summoned to a meeting with her new German overseer, where the new order was spelled out in more detail.

He instructed her that for the time being all direct financial support to non-Jewish indigents would continue, except that each welfare check henceforth would bear the legend "Gift of the German

Reich." He said that the source of the funds, of course, would remain the same, the national treasury, newly renamed the Treasury of the Protectorate. Soon, she was told, subvention policy toward the "unproductive" aged would be amended to give the unemployed elderly a chance to support themselves through unspecified, "useful work." Palantova asked what the Reich intended to do about the Jews. "Our police are rounding up all the Jews on refugee rolls," he said, "and will send them back to their countries of origin. After the problem of the German, Austrian, and Sudeten Jews is disposed of, we shall attack the problem of the resident Czech Jews."

———— · ————

Over the coming days, the Sharps would look on in horror and grim amazement as the Nazi python first crushed Czechoslovakia and then methodically proceeded to swallow it. "The Protectorate of Bohemia and Moravia," Martha wrote, "was sealed off from the outside world. Each day our lives grew more restricted, and nobody had any idea how long this period would continue."

CHAPTER SEVEN

Changing the Rules

The Nazis' continued hold on Czechoslovakia was firm.

"All radio broadcasts were jammed, except for propaganda messages," Martha later wrote. The free press vanished at once, leaving a shaken nation at the mercy of the rumor mill's fantastic distortions. "I remember," Martha wrote, "it was confidently believed that the Chamberlain government in Great Britain had fallen, and that Sir Anthony Eden was now Prime Minister. Wishful thought!"

The Sharps tried to restrict their daily conversations to the few key people whose information generally was reliable. "It was time-consuming but necessary, not only in order to keep up with the refugee picture, but to stay current with the whole life of the Protectorate," Martha explained.

Unfortunately, the Nazis soon caught on. They dispatched special patrols that quickly separated any two people they discovered in earnest conversation, then questioned them separately. If the two individuals' versions of the discussion topic did not match, both were taken off to prison as "dangerous conspirators."

Therefore, we began each such meeting with, "What shall we discuss?" We then quickly got down to cases. Also, we noticed that the patrols tended to follow the same route each day, like beat cops in big US cities. So we adjusted for that, as well. The time and place of the next day's conversation was always the last thing we discussed.

I found myself so disturbed by the pressures and the potentially-serious consequences of making the slightest mistake that I changed from a rather naïve, friendly and outgoing person who trusted everyone into a self-contained, reserved and increasingly wary individual. I weighed every word and watched where it was spoken, how and to whom. I recall that the safest place to talk in those days was inside a private car as you drove along a back country road. Since that was rarely practical, most of our conversations were held in a hotel or office room in the city.

There were immediate shortages of food and many consumer goods, a consequence of the systematic looting and the appetites of the German occupation troops coming off months on short rations. Since by decree the "liberators" were to be served first in all cafés and restaurants, there was less remaining for other customers. Martha and Waitstill grew accustomed to soup and dumplings for dinner every night.

The eight o'clock curfew put an end to trips to the opera and symphony. A prohibition against all public gatherings of a dozen or more people effectively did away with most other sources of entertainment or relaxation. Churches became the only places people could come together in numbers; attendance skyrocketed accordingly. The many Czech clergy who were fiercely defiant of the occupation delivered coded sermons from their pulpits, exhorting their parishioners via allegory and other devices to resist the Nazis and to assist one another.

The spirit of Good Soldier Svejk was abroad as well. Svejk, the inspired comic creation of Czech novelist Jaroslav Hasek, was a hapless fool who bumbled his way across four volumes of one of the most acclaimed satires ever written. But despite his manifest shortcomings— Svejk was not only stupid but also a fat, bald, middle-aged cipher—he survived, even thrived in the face of constant misadventure by dint of a very carefully camouflaged shrewdness. Although the novel was banned by the Czech army in 1925, Svejk was widely known and admired in the country. With the advent of occupation, he became a role model too.

"Svejk," Martha wrote, "was not created in vain."

> Czech civil servants, without previous collusion or direction, stopped working. Everyone found some valid reason why he could not understand, and had to have the new regulations explained to him, again and again. From the very first day the Czechs exhibited a patience, resourcefulness and originality behind a bland mask of incompetence that continued to vex their German masters despite all threats, persecution or blandishments.

> One of the intended results was to seriously undermine German plans for Czech industrial and agricultural production, a key component of their overall war strategy. Since it was impossible for the Nazis to detect whether Czech workers could, or could not, understand a directive, their frustrated German masters could only rewrite and rewrite, and explain and explain. Meanwhile, the famously organized and highly efficient administration of the rich little republic slowly fell to pieces, as if struck by some mysterious internal dry rot.

———— · ————

The effects of fear and deprivation, compounded by a claustrophobic sense of absolute isolation during the occupation's first few days, formed the backdrop of dread against which Martha coped with her deepest anxiety of all—the Nazis' plans for the Jews. Before coming to Czechoslovakia, she was well aware of National Socialism's anti-Semitic agenda. But from the remoteness of Wellesley Hills, the disease was more of an abstraction, like some dire tropical malady that posed no peril in suburban Massachusetts. In Prague, however, the fate of the Jews was very much a local matter, one in which Martha would take a personal stake. The Sharps had hired a group of eight young Jews from the Sudeten as office staff. They were all bright and hardworking, spoke German and Czech among other languages, and skillfully bridged the inevitable cultural divide between central European refugees and a pair of earnest American relief workers.

Among these office helpers was a young woman named Lisl. "Lisl was the lovely blond wife of a former industrialist from the Sudeten, whose chemical plants had been seized by the Nazis," Martha remembered. "She had maturity and charm as well as linguistic ability and had become a real asset. She told me, 'I am so happy to be working here. I get so absorbed in other people's troubles, I forget my own! I usually find that most people are worse off than I am!' The small amount we could pay her allowed Lisl and her otherwise destitute family to escape the unheated loft where they, and hundreds of other Sudeten refugees, had been housed."

On the morning of March 17, Lisl showed up for work with her arm in a sling, her face marred by a burn that left her practically unrecognizable. She explained to Martha that just before curfew the night before, she, her husband, David, and her brother, Friedl, had been enjoying an after-dinner coffee at the Kavarna Artia, a café popular with Jews from the Sudeten. Suddenly a live hand grenade flew through the window and landed at Lisl's feet. Her brother grabbed it to toss it back into the street, but it had exploded in his hand, killing him instantly.

"I was burned by some of the fragments," she said. "David grabbed my arm before I could bend over Friedl. 'Come, we get out of here,' he said. 'Friedl is beyond our help.'" David tried the front door, but it was barred shut. Through the *kavarna* window, they could see German soldiers with their weapons trained on the door, ready to shoot anyone who came through it. So her husband pulled Lisl with him to the back entrance, up a staircase and over the roof to the building next door, where they descended a second staircase and escaped through a back door into the alley. Besides her brother, two other customers had been killed by the grenade, and several more were badly burned.

Lisl's experience and the persecution of Czechoslovakia's Jewish population brought a dimension of concern that would stay with Martha forever. "Nazi discrimination against a whole people because of their religion challenged every crusading corpuscle in my being," she wrote. "I had read reports of the persecution of the Jews in Germany. But the printed pages of *The New York Times* never got under my skin the way that seeing indignities heaped upon innocent people did." She labeled anti-Semitism "Christianity's greatest sin." Within four years, she would be deeply involved in Jewish-Christian interfaith relations and, later, in the resettlement of Jewish survivors of the Holocaust in Palestine.

CHAPTER EIGHT

Helping the Kulturträgers

The few days that the Sharps had spent in Czechoslovakia prior to the Einmarsch had mainly been devoted to reconnaissance and consultation. According to their commission, their role was to scout out worthy projects—particularly government-sponsored refugee relocation programs for Nicholas Butler's group, AmRelCzech—and, as representatives of the Unitarian Association, "to assist the people of Czechoslovakia in making adjustments to the new order in their land, and in all ways to render constructive friendly service."

March 15 changed all that. "Refugee relocation" was now a euphemism for shipment to Nazi death camps. As far as Martha and Waitstill were concerned, the best "constructive friendly service" they now could, and should, provide was immediate escape from the protectorate.

The opportunities for moving many of the hunted at one time—such as the London-bound trainload of Social Democrats that Waitstill noted on their arrival at Wilson Station—quickly grew scarce. Instead, the Sharps would run a small-scale operation, glad for any small triumph in a deadly cat-and-mouse game with the Gestapo.

The wild crush of terrified refugees that greeted them at their office on the morning of March 15 convinced Waitstill and Martha that in order to help the maximum number of "clients," as they called them, they needed a system to quickly and efficiently capture each person's vital information, so they and their staff of eight could then customize assistance according to the individual's situation. Martha's answer was to create a written questionnaire covering germane information that any refugee could complete without assistance.

Three hundred of those files survive today at the US Holocaust Memorial Museum in Washington, DC.

For the balance of their time in occupied Czechoslovakia, Martha's energies mainly would be devoted to steering clients through, or around, endless bureaucratic labyrinths in Prague and across Europe, the United States and Latin America. "We had lists of thousands of names," Martha wrote, "all of them requesting exit visas. But it wasn't as easy as simply requesting a visa from a foreign country. Through our contacts in Boston, New York, London, and other cities, we had to arrange for jobs, places to live. We had to match refugees in Prague with opportunities to live and work abroad."

They had to master the intricacies of immigration law in dozens of countries, lobby contacts for money, arrange for escorts, coordinate with other aid organizations, and manage endless details while trying to avoid trouble with the Gestapo.[1]

The Sharps' contacts in London, Paris, and Geneva (the YMCA and YWCA, Women's International League for Peace and Freedom, the British Committee for Refugees from Czechoslovakia, and the Committee for the Placement of Intellectual Refugees) would try to match those clients with jobs or invitations of some kind anywhere in still-free Europe or in North and South America. At home, a Unitarian Case Work Committee, led by their friend Marion Niles of the Wellesley church, worked feverishly to find sponsors who would sign affidavits guaranteeing the financial solvency of refugees and to pry US visas from the State Department's tight fists. The Sharps were losing hope that the US government would respond compassionately to the refugee situation.

"For a fleeting moment," Martha recalled, "when we first arrived in Prague, we had the vain hope that the urgent needs of the Czech people might move the US Congress to open the country's doors. But our requests for special consideration were being ignored in Washington. The old US quota for Czechoslovakia allowed 2,800 Czechs to enter the US yearly on immigration visas. At that pace, most refugees realized that they might wait several decades to get an American visa."

———— • ————

Waitstill soon was specializing in even chancier business, one that put his prodigious memory and compulsive command of detail to full use. As the Nazis tightened their financial clamp on the Czechs, making it impossible for him to legally receive and distribute US dollars, he became a black-market currency broker and bagman. Not only did Waitstill risk expulsion, at minimum, and possible imprisonment and death if caught, he also enlisted the vital assistance of the US consul general in Prague, who acted as his banker.

Sharp's career in financial crime began two days before the Einmarsch when a messenger accosted him at the Hotel Atlantic. The man saluted Waitstill, then said, "Mr. Sharp, will you prove that you are Mr. Sharp?"

"Goodness!" Waitstill replied. "Pardon me?"

"This is very important," the messenger said at length, then drew Sharp aside to quietly explain that he'd been sent by Dr. Alice. Before he said anything more, however, Masaryk's emissary required identification.

Waitstill produced his passport for inspection, which satisfied the man.

"We must separate now," he said. "Dr. Masaryk presents her compliments and asks you to take a taxi to her apartment as quickly as you can. Do not mention her name to anybody, particularly to the taxi driver."

Sharp proceeded as instructed to Dr. Alice's apartment door. "I was scrutinized through a peephole," he remembered, "I suppose by Dr. Alice herself. She let me in. Her usual aplomb was somewhat ruffled. There were no sweet introductions or anything."

Masaryk had with her two five-thousand-dollar checks, each made out in her name, from Nicholas Butler at AmRelCzech. She showed Waitstill the envelopes in which the checks had been mailed. Each had been opened. It appeared that the checks had been removed and replaced and the envelopes resealed. The only explanation, she said, was that the Gestapo was opening her mail. If she attempted to cash either of the checks, the Nazis would immediately revive their old allegations that Masaryk was diverting humanitarian aid to her own uses. At this sensitive moment, she could not risk another round of such accusations.

"What am I going to do with this money?" she asked. "The Nazi Party here knows I have it. I cannot go to any bank. Surely, you see the situation clearly?"

"Well, yes," Waitstill replied. "But what shall I do with these?"

"That is your problem," she answered.

Left to ponder the matter on his own, Waitstill headed by taxi back to the hotel in the gloom of a late winter afternoon. By the next day, March 14, an idea had formed. In the collection of calling cards that Malcolm Davis had provided Waitstill in Paris, there was one for Dr. Vladimir Pospisil, governor of the National Bank Czechoslovakia. Waitstill slipped the card into his pocket and headed out the door at once, hoping to catch Pospisil before the bank closed its doors for the day.

He made it just in time, and presented the Davis card, along with one of his own, to a bank employee. Minutes later, he was seated opposite Dr. Pospisil at his big desk in the bank governor's private office, where Waitstill explained the business with the two checks.

It was Pospisil's best advice that the American clergyman deposit the checks with the National Bank, unaware that by morning the bank would be under Nazi control. Sharp was willing, but by now it was too late, so he returned the checks to his wallet. Had he deposited the checks as Pospisil suggested, the ten thousand dollars would have been lost forever.

The occupation introduced a whole new set of challenges when it came to financing foreign relief work. Henceforth it would be pointless to transfer hard currency into the protectorate. If the money came via normal, legal channels, the Nazis would grab it. If it arrived in some clandestine fashion, one risked imprisonment or worse. Moreover, the flow of donations, particularly from the United States, slowed precipitously with the fall of free Czechoslovakia. American donors weren't about to risk seeing their dollars stolen to support the German war effort.

Thus it was clear to Waitstill that the only way to make practical use of the ten thousand dollars—and keep the money out of the Germans' hands—would be to take the two checks somewhere outside the protectorate. While he waited for the travel restrictions on foreigners to be eased, he considered his options, finally hitting on a variation of an old stratagem that perfectly suited his purposes. Like Martha, Waitstill would discover he had a talent for subterfuge.

He headed by train for Geneva on March 22 with the two AmRelCzech checks tucked away in his money belt, hoping that the deference the Nazis had so far paid US citizens meant that he would not be subjected to the exhaustive personal searches that all other travelers were forced to endure. The gamble paid off. Waitstill's US passport and a Gestapo *Ausreise,* or travel permit, were all that he needed to show.

In Geneva he selected one of the larger banks, walked in and asked to speak to a bank officer, to whom Waitstill revealed his letter from Cordell Hull, which assured him of the banker's close attention. Then he laid out his proposal.

Sharp explained that he wished to open an account with the two checks, and to make a special arrangement for withdrawals. He said that on this account the only withdrawal form the bank was to honor was a torn calling card such as the one Waitstill produced to show the man. The amount of the withdrawal would be printed in pencil on the back of a torn calling card. Any person presenting such a card was to receive the amount indicated, no further questions asked.

"The conditions in the Third Reich, where I am now living, preclude any documentation at all," he said. "If you require documentation from me, anybody attempting to leave the Third Reich would go to the gibbet or the gas chamber after a Gestapo investigation. So we must have an agreement that this will be the way that these two sums, aggregating ten thousand dollars, will be drawn down. Do we agree on that?"

One can imagine the bank officer's wonderment at such a strange proposal coming from this bespectacled American with his gilt-edged bona fides from the US secretary of state. He gave Sharp a dubious look and said that this was a "highly irregular matter" that would require the attention of the bank's legal department. Nevertheless, in just half a day the bank produced a contract that covered the necessary issues, and Waitstill shook hands on the deal.

Next stop: Paris.

There he confided the stratagem to Malcolm Davis, who endorsed more checks from the United States to Sharp. Waitstill then took the money and a copy of his Swiss bank contract—executed in English and French—to two Parisian banks, where he made identical arrangements. "I said, 'This is a highly risky venture. Any recipient of one half of these cards could alter it. That person and I must gain as much confidence in one another as possible, and I must assume they will not alter that figure.' Hatred of Germany being endemic, they agreed that this was the only way in which we could outwit the monster."

In the course of a second excursion, Sharp set up one of his special accounts with a Belgian bank, then moved on to London, where he left the balance of his funds with the British Unitarians, who would also dispense the money according to Waitstill's plan. As it turned out, the London connection would be by far the busiest, followed by an account subsequently set up in New York.

Finally Sharp returned to Prague to put in motion the second part of his operation. As he did so, Martha set out on an expedition of her own.

On Friday, March 24, she met in her office with Tessa Rowntree of the BCRC. "She had a plan to lead about one hundred refugees, ostensibly household workers, to England," Martha recalled. "All of them had British visas and Gestapo *Ausreise* and were ready to go. She would take half the group out on the first train to leave the Protectorate, scheduled to depart at 4 p.m. that afternoon, and asked me if I would take the next fifty on the next train at 4:30. I responded that I didn't have an *Ausreise* and besides, Waitstill hadn't yet returned. I couldn't just go off without telling him."

"Nobody can do it as well as you, Martha," Rowntree replied, "a clergyman's wife and an American. Perhaps your consulate can get you the exit permission. If you'll try, I'll have your transport ready to join you at the station."

Martha knew full well that the transport entailed significant personal risk, Rowntree's reassurances notwithstanding. The "household workers" included some of the most ardent and well-known political enemies of the Reich. Her US passport would not be much good if she was caught assisting these enemies of the state in escaping.

On the other hand, she remembered thinking that saving these people seemed worth the personal risk. She went back to her office to pick up some papers and to leave a note for Waitstill when Lydia Busch appeared.[2] When she learned that Martha was headed for London, Busch asked her to take along a bag of jewelry that was needed to help pay for a cancer operation for Lydia's mother. Martha agreed to do so, and managed to get back to the hotel, pack a suitcase, pick up the jewels, and get to the train station by 4:15. Tessa Rowntree had already departed without incident at the head of the first group of refugees. A Miss Bull, who worked with Rowntree, was on hand to assist Martha with the second group.

"Miss Bull had a typed list of my transport members ready for me," Martha recalled.

But not everyone had yet assembled. "Some will come out of hiding just in time to board the moving train," she explained, and as she spoke new ones arrived, which she added to her list, using a pen she borrowed from a doctor standing near her. I noticed the pen wrote in green ink.

She then gave me a ticket for each of my charges, apologizing as she did so that we were going to travel fourth class. This would mean wooden benches all the way across Germany and the Netherlands to the North Sea. As I discovered once we entrained, it would mean a single, non-flushing toilet for us, too.

In all, thirty-three refugees showed up at the station for the trip.

They were about to depart when two more men jumped on. Miss Bull cried, "They're yours!" then disappeared altogether as the shriek of those piercing whistles and the swirling smoke from the locomotive enveloped us.

As the train rolled west out of Prague into the Czech countryside, Martha glanced over her list of "household workers." Some names were familiar to her: a doctor, an actor, an agricultural scientist relocating to a university in Canada; a brother and sister, twelve and fourteen, whose parents had committed suicide the previous week. There were a pair of European news reporters, one from United Press and the other from the Associated Press. Most of the rest of the members of the transport were average citizens who had family or other connections in England or elsewhere who had vouched for them. Martha introduced herself to each of them, trying her best to soothe their anxiety and put them at ease.

At the German border the guards unhitched their car from the train and moved it onto a siding. Martha asked the border station personnel why they were being made to wait, but could get no answers. With no choice but to wait and see what happened next, they bought food from local vendors, washed up as best they could from a single available water spigot, and stayed close to the car through the night.

To everyone's immense relief, another train picked them up at dawn, and they headed west toward the Netherlands once again. Before they arrived at the Dutch border, however, they were twice more shunted to a siding and made to wait without an explanation. Finally, they were attached to a long express train headed for Vlissingen, in the Netherlands, where with luck they might catch a night boat to England.

But first there was another inspection to negotiate at Rheine, in Westphalia.

Before disembarking, Martha put on Lydia's diamond bracelets, necklaces, and earrings and carried her luggage from the car for customs inspection. Her bags were casually opened and OK'd without a search. The refugees' luggage received considerably different treatment. Every possession of value, from silver to jewelry to cash, was confiscated. The Nazi officials even removed wedding rings from refugees' fingers and forced the women to hand over the small gold rings in their pierced ears.

Martha remained on the platform while the group re-boarded to make sure that no one in the transport was detained. As she stood there, she heard her name being shouted from the rear of the customs shed. She ran back and through the door before the guards could stop her and found the two reporters, their bags torn apart on a table in front of them. They had, for some reason, raised the guards' suspicion. One of them was trying to show a letter with the US seal to the guards.

Martha's semester of graduate-school German and the lessons she and Waitstill were taking from Professor Albin Goldschmeid, one of their clients, became very useful.

"Have you orders to arrest these men?" she asked.

"No," one of the Nazis answered. "But we must get special permission from headquarters before they can leave."

Martha then took a calculated risk. Based on her brief experience with the Nazis, she believed their police would act only on a direct order. If an unusual circumstance arose, they did not dare use their own judgment. Like Waitstill, she also counted on their reluctance to provoke an American. She took the letter from the journalist. It was written by Ambassador Carr, vouching for the men as reliable friends of the United States. Waving the letter in front of the guards, she translated, noting that the men were under her protection as an American citizen. She announced emphatically that she would not leave without them.

At that moment, the engineer signaled with his whistle that the train was about to depart. Martha swallowed back her fear that it would leave without her and the two reporters. "I will call my government if you insist on holding these men," she said to the German officer.

The Germans conferred among themselves in low voices. Martha folded her arms and waited silently.

"They may go," the officer said at last. Martha swallowed hard once more. She'd gambled and won.

She helped the wire-service reporters stuff their belongings back into their bags and sprinted with them to the train. They reached the border without further problems, but the ordeal was not quite ended. They now had to deal with Dutch customs inspectors. The station was filled with refugees, whole families with children and little babies who'd been able to get out of Germany but now were being refused permission to enter Holland on their way to England, where they had jobs or relatives. There they sat at the German-Dutch frontier, afraid to go back, unable to go forward. Martha took down their names and passport information and promised to get in touch with their families when she got to England.

The Dutch officials came aboard and again their visas and passports were examined. They asked Martha for the names of those in her party, and she gave them her list to check against their documents. Suddenly, Martha heard someone call her name.

The two newspapermen were in trouble once more. The Dutch officials had ordered them off the train and were going to send them back to Germany because their names did not appear on Martha's list. Trembling with fear, they were standing on the platform with their luggage. Martha had to think quickly. She recalled,

I asked the passport officer for my list and realized instantly that we'd neglected to add their names to it back in Prague. There was one chance of rescuing them. I found the doctor with the green-ink pen and used it to add their names on the reverse side. Just as the train was about to depart, I found the passport officer.

"These two men are in my party," I told him. "You should have turned over the list." He was dubious. "I am sure the names were not there before," he said. I assured him that they were—it was just an oversight—and that the two men were part of my transport. Shaking his head, the official OK'd their passports and we all climbed aboard the train once again. This second near-miss drained me emotionally. Such a thin line between life and death!

The farther west they proceeded from the German border the more relaxed they became. Their luck even improved. In the dining car, where Martha went to get a cup of coffee, a charming couple, both Czechs traveling on British passports, asked her about the transport. When she explained who they were, and how they were essentially penniless, they casually pressed fifty pounds sterling in Martha's hand, saying that she could pay them back in London if she liked. Feeling suddenly rich, Martha went back to the fourth-class car and brought all thirty-five of her charges to the diner for their first real meal in more than a day.

Night fell. At about ten o'clock, the train pulled onto the dock at Vlissingen. The night boat was waiting. The refugees wearily gathered their things and lined up on the dock, waiting to be checked aboard the vessel. An official emerged from his office in the distance. In the dark, he called out in English, "Is Mrs. Sharp here? Does anybody know whether she and her party got through?"

"Here I am!" Martha called.

"How many did you get out with you?" he asked as he approached her.

"All of them."

"Thank God!" he said, and led her back to his office. She handed the official her stack of fourth-class tickets.

"Wait just a moment," he said, then disappeared out the door. Moments later he returned, grinning broadly. "I can put you all in berths—with a little doubling up! And this will be at the company's expense!"

Martha was near tears. After all that she and all the refugees had been through, to hear, in English, a message of kindness and consideration for her tired and emotionally exhausted group nearly overwhelmed her.

She and the official assigned everyone rooms aboard the boat. Then she took the excited children on deck. They had never been on such a large vessel or even seen the sea. As the ship pulled away into the North Sea, Martha turned their attention to the night sky and pointed out the major stars and constellations.

The next morning they were met at the dock by Margaret Stevenson, president of the British Unitarian Women and a representative of the British Committee for Refugees from Czechoslovakia.

To an anxious group waiting for people who were not on the boat from Holland, Martha showed the list of refugees she had encountered at the frontier and the telephone number of the train station. A couple on the dock saw the names of relatives on the list and hurried to the telephone. They somehow got through and were soon speaking to their family members.

The British Committee took the group to the hotel for a bath and breakfast. As they walked along, Margaret Stevenson could not resist a bit of teasing. "My dear," she said to Martha, "your face looks as if you have been in a coal bin. But your diamonds are glorious!" Martha had completely forgotten that she still was wearing Lydia Busch's jewels.

Martha treated the members of the transport to a bus tour of London that morning before dropping them off at the British Committee offices to begin their new lives. As she finally said good-bye to them all, the doctor stepped forward to present her with a thank-you note from the group, written in green ink. "Dear Mrs. Sharp," it read. "We shall never forget what you have done for us and wish to thank you from the depths of our hearts. Yours and gratefully." Twenty members of the transport signed the note, found, carefully preserved, among Martha's papers more than sixty years later. One of those who signed is Heinz Oestreicher, who escaped to England with his family and then reentered the RAF as Henry Walsh to fight the Nazis.

———— · ————

Martha wrote reports to New York and Boston, and wired Aunt Edna in Wellesley Hills to assure the Stebbinses, as well as Martha Content and Hastings, that she and Waitstill were safe and well. She met with Jan Masaryk, who debriefed Martha and then entrusted her with several messages to be delivered upon her return to Prague. Some of them were concealed in toothpaste tubes.

Then Martha moved on to Paris to confer with Malcolm Davis of the Carnegie Endowment and others on how best to assist the many artists and intellectuals—the so-called Kulturträgers, or bearers of the culture, as the imperiled intellectuals and artists sometimes were known—still trapped in the protectorate. An emergency committee of French thinkers and artists and diplomats arranged for French visas to automatically be issued for these individuals on Martha's authority. Don and Helen Lowrie agreed to head a committee focused on finding teaching positions and other employment for the émigrés as they came out of the protectorate. Dr. Clayton Williams, minister of the American Church in Paris, where the Sharps attended services, offered office space for the Lowries' committee.

Martha allowed herself a single indulgence during her brief stay in Paris, a new hat. Then on Wednesday, April 5, she boarded the Orient Express at 3:40 p.m. and was bound once more for Prague.

The train carried only a few passengers out of Paris, and for the first several hours Martha's journey was uneventful. Toward dinner time, still in France, a military transport was added to the train, as was a dining car. Unfortunately for Martha, her walk to and from dinner that night took her through a long string of coaches filled with rowdy French soldiers.

She knew that the German frontier was just ahead, and that she'd have to show her papers at the border. But the long days of work and worry and short nights of sleep finally caught up with her. After dinner, Martha lay down in her dressing gown and shut her eyes.

Her next conscious impression was the sound of a key turning the lock on her compartment door, which then loudly slammed open to the limit of the chain bolt. At first, Martha assumed it was the steward. Then she looked up to see a crowd of drunken French soldiers pushing against the door, trying to get at her. One of them was able to grab the coverlet and pull it off her.

Confused and terrified, she rang for the steward. No answer. The laughing, shouting soldiers yanked again and again at the door as Martha pressed against it from the inside, hoping that the four small screws holding the bolt anchor to the door jamb wouldn't break, as they appeared likely to at any moment. The door handle already had fallen clattering to the floor.

"Then," she recalled, "the cursing, laughing men stopped. There was a short silence. I heard the conductor and the steward coming through the car, checking tickets as we slowed for the German border. When I told the steward what had just occurred, he expressed his regrets and said the French military transports would not cross the frontier."

Still thoroughly frightened, Martha nevertheless composed herself in time to deal with the Nazi border agents. They gave her US passport a respectful look and searched her suitcase. A young officer commented on what a lot of papers she was carrying but did not attempt to examine them. He made no mention of her several tubes of toothpaste.

The great Orient Express picked up steam once again and rolled eastward into the night. Martha slept in her clothes. The next morning, with the French troopers long since gone, the walk to the dining car was peaceful and brief. She made no mention of her previous night's ordeal at the breakfast table that she shared with three businessmen, but was not surprised to hear one of them mention that the steward was under arrest.

The charge, however, was a surprise. The negligence that nearly had gotten her gang-raped, or worse, had nothing to do with why the steward was taken from the train. His crime, according to the businessmen, had been currency smuggling.

—— · ——

Waitstill greeted Martha at the Wilson Station that Thursday night, April 6, with news that the Germans had requisitioned the entire Hotel Atlantic, so he had moved them to the Hotel Pariz, about half a mile away by foot. The Pariz turned out to be a very welcome upgrade. The hotel was (and remains today) an Art Nouveau citadel, a lovely structure of beautiful interiors. The room rate was ninety korunas a night, at which Waitstill must have winced.

In the cab on the way to the hotel, he motioned for Martha not to speak aloud and pointed at the driver's back by way of explanation.

After the short respite in London and Paris, where such precautions were as yet unknown and unnecessary, Martha felt herself quickly slip back into the habits of silence, fear, and distrust. The hopefulness of sunny April days in Paris immediately gave way to the wintry reality of Prague.

When they entered their new room at the Pariz, Waitstill silently looked under the beds, in the closets and bathroom, and every place large enough for a recording machine. Finally he took off his jacket and draped it over the telephone.

"Last week, I found my bed wired for sound," he explained. "There was a machine hidden underneath. I disconnected it." The next day, as Waitstill had been conversing with a Czech engineering professor in the room, a man identifying himself as a telephone repairman had arrived to adjust the room handset, he said. After he left, the engineer had examined the telephone and explained to Sharp that it was now a microphone, capable of picking up and transmitting conversations in the room. He showed Waitstill how to foil the device by covering it with a thick piece of cloth, such as a jacket.

Henceforth, Waitstill warned Martha, they had to assume that every telephone in Prague also had been "adjusted" in the same way. Similarly, he said, if they attempted to access a forbidden radio station, it was imperative to spin the dial afterward so there'd be no trace.

Then he produced a sheaf of much-delayed letters from Aunt Edna, the first news of their children since they'd arrived six weeks before. "She wrote as from another world," Martha recalled,

> long newsy accounts of the children. Hastings had required a vaccination and booster, which he took "like a stoic," as Aunt Edna put it, and later made "scornful comments on those who cried." He was bringing home good grades from school.
>
> Martha Content was growing. She now weighed 25 pounds and her slips were beginning to look like "longish shirts" and her dresses just barely covered her panties. Aunt Edna felt that Hastings might be experiencing resentment over the attention given to his younger sister, so she became especially mindful of giving

our son "equal time," and calling him "dear" or "darling" as often as she did little Martha. I was strengthened in the sense that the children were in good and loving hands.

———— · ————

Within a few days Martha and Waitstill had assembled a thick file on Czech Kulturträgers who required immediate rescue. Waitstill left for Paris with the dossiers on Saturday, April 15. Martha had intended to accompany him but decided at the last minute that she had too much pressing business in Prague. Ever since the Einmarsch both Sharps had realized that their mission was now a moment-to-moment endeavor, conducted under the Nazis' increasingly intense and hostile scrutiny. Time was drawing short; even the loss of a moment's work could cost lives.

On Monday morning, April 17, Martha arrived at Vysehradska 16 to discover that the Germans had forcefully evicted American Relief from their third-floor offices. All their furniture lay in a pile on the sidewalk in the snow. With the help of the volunteers, she found new operating space at Studensky Domov, a cramped student bungalow not far away.

Waitstill wrote her from Paris on April 19, after learning of the incident:

> You are not only beautiful, but a brick. That rare combination spells out the PERFECT WOMAN, the answer to the quest of the ages. I really mean this—Venus and Minerva cast in one blended statue of loveliness and wisdom. THAT'S YOU. Ever, my beloved madam, your most fortunate servant, Waitstill.

On April 23, Martha left Prague to join Waitstill in Paris, where visas were being prepared for the Czech artists, intellectuals, and "politicals" on their endangered list. Don and Helen Lowrie and their committee were busy finding jobs for them. The Sharps returned on April 30 to Prague, where their first priority was to contact those Kulturträgers for whom visas or employment had been secured.

High on Martha's list was Jan Blahoslav ("J.B.") Kozak, a prominent Protestant thinker and professor of philosophy at Charles University. Kozak had aroused the Nazis' attention as head of the local Thomas Mann Society, a strongly antifascist group of intellectuals then active across Europe in helping their colleagues and one another escape persecution.

As Martha approached the professor's residence, she could hear a deeply sad violin solo from within. After she knocked several times the music stopped and a maid timidly peeped out the front door. Martha quickly tried to explain who she was and why she had come. Kozak himself then appeared, violin in hand.

"Don't you realize you've endangered yourself by coming to my home?" he asked sternly.

"I have a very important matter to discuss with you," Martha replied. "Why are you so apprehensive?"

The professor had no end of reasons for apprehension, all stemming from the Nazis' adamant refusal to let him leave the protectorate. "I am suspect," he told Martha, "and everyone who sees me is suspect."

The older of Kozak's two sons had escaped to join the French air force, and the professor interpreted his problems with the German authorities as reprisal. He told Martha that he might have escaped along with the older boy, but his wife was seriously ill with cancer, and they had the much younger second son to worry about.

"I have tried every means to leave this country," he said. "The last excuse the Nazis gave for denying me exit permission is that they accuse me of being non-Aryan. I brought them my family tree to prove we've been gentiles for ten generations on both sides."

Martha handed the professor a letter inviting him to join the faculty at Oberlin College in Ohio. In most cases, such a letter would trigger issue of the necessary travel documents, and the lucky invitee would be as good as gone from Prague. But Kozak was a special case.

"It's no use," he told her. "I know they won't give me an *Ausreise*. It would take a miracle." He added that he would not leave without his family.

Martha asked him if he would at least apply for a passport.

Kozak said he would, just because she had made such an effort on his behalf. But he held no hope of securing the vital exit visa. "It will be for no good!" he said.

"Let me worry about that," Martha said as she prepared to leave. On the way out the door, she noticed a man standing in the window of a house across the street. When he saw Martha, he raised a camera and took a picture of her.

——— · ———

Consul General Irving Linnell, who with Ambassador Carr's recent departure had become the senior US diplomat in the protectorate, was a veteran and battle-tested foreign-service professional. His last posting had been Canton, China, which Linnell had fled the previous autumn, just ahead of the advancing Japanese columns.

The Sharps and the consul general had come to know one another better as Martha and Waitstill had appeared repeatedly at the embassy in support of Czech academics and intellectuals seeking US visas.

Linnell warmly received Martha in his office. After she explained the situation, he was more than willing to intervene on the Kozaks' behalf. "This is probably a tough one, Martha," he said. But Linnell also had a potential solution. "Suppose I call up the Gestapo," he said, "and ask whether they'll give him and his family an *Ausreise* as a personal favor to me?"

"That would be wonderful," said Martha. "I hope with all my heart that you succeed."

Against all reasonable expectations, Linnell succeeded in getting exit visas for the Kozak family. "They said okay!" he reported with delight to Martha by telephone the next day. "Send your professor around as soon as possible." In less than two weeks, an incredulous J.B. Kozak, together with his wife and youngest son, were safely bound by steamer for the United States, where they rode out the war years at Oberlin.

—— CHAPTER NINE ——

Money Talks

The second stage of Waitstill's covert refugee finance program—
which he would later describe as "the most risky and perhaps the
most dramatic aspect of the operation in Czechoslovakia"—began
with tentative outreach to the wealthier individuals, Jews and gentiles, still hoping to slip out of the protectorate before it was too late.
Besides their prominence and their peril, many of these individuals
shared a problem—no access to the hard currency necessary to finance their escape.

Within occupied Czechoslovakia they could not liquidate their
property—land, buildings, inventory, personal effects—for dollars,
pounds, or any other hard currency lest the ever-vigilant Reich instantly seize the proceeds. Their Czech korunas, nominally worth
about twenty to the dollar, were spendable only inside the protectorate; they were valueless elsewhere.

This was the financial gap that Sharp would bridge. Carefully, he
let it be known through intermediaries that a mechanism was now
in place for those holding korunas to trade their currency inside the
protectorate for dollars or pounds or francs held in accounts outside
the protectorate, and therefore safe from the Nazis' greedy fingers.

"People approached me in increasing numbers," he remembered,
"complicating my safety problem. They'd open a briefcase or a small
trunk or go into large pouches under their suit coats and pull out
bales of Czech money. I soon stipulated that I did not want to see

notes in denominations of less than a thousand korunas. I agreed to exchange their Czech money with US currency from what was left of our operating funds. There was a sliding scale: the most needy getting the best rate of exchange. They couldn't cross the border with foreign currency so I went in and out of Prague seven times and placed the dollars in banks strategically in Geneva, London, and Paris, so that if they could escape their money would be waiting for them."

Waitstill would meet these "clients" in the safest possible surroundings, often in open fields, removed from the Nazis' ubiquitous listening devices, and sometimes at Unitaria when time was a problem.

The first phase was to agree upon an exchange rate for the transaction. As Waitstill recalled,

> My business was to negotiate, even mercilessly, as high a rate as I could. I knew it was illegal, but I did it because I had no other choice. I was beyond the pale of civilization. I owed no ethics to anybody. I owed no honesty to anybody at all if I could save imperiled human lives.
>
> Everything had to be carried out in my head and as a word of honor. I had never been a good bargainer, but there was an excess of adrenaline [born] of my hatred of the Nazis, and my intention, which may qualify as a Christian intention, to do as much as I could for the welfare of both the refugees and the indigenous populations. I drove the hardest bargains with big farmers and landowners. I felt that I could soak them, did not have to respect their economic needs as much as I might some tailor or schoolmaster or college professor.

When he later told Martha of the operation, she gently chided him. "And you a minister and a graduate of the Harvard law school!"

"Yes!" Waitstill rejoined. "And I am proud to refuse to obey those who have taken this country illegally and have no morality!"

Although Sharp was careful not to retain incriminating evidence of his illicit dealings, a couple of his account sheets, doubtless created outside the protectorate from memory, have survived. One page, styled "CONSOLIDATED ACCOUNT, Receipts in Crowns," includes a column headed, "Remarks—Clients Classification." It reveals that a Joseph Krebes qualified for the "social worker rate" of thirty-seven korunas to the dollar. Otto Munz received the "industrialist/lawyer" rate of seventy-five korunas to the dollar. Waitstill negotiated with an individual named Ruzicha for his highest, "merchant" rate of one hundred fifty korunas to the dollar.

Among familiar names on the sheet, Lydia Busch paid 75 korunas per dollar. Karl Deutsch's father did a little better at 60. According to Waitstill, the absolutely highest rate he ever charged was 160 korunas per dollar.

In a June letter to Robert Dexter from London, Waitstill reported that he so far had pledged twenty-one thousand dollars' worth of calling-card chits in return for nearly two million korunas in cash. Thus the average rate of exchange to that point was about ninety korunas to the dollar.

Once the dickering was done, Waitstill would stuff the proffered korunas into his handy black bag. Then he would tear a business card in half. As he had told bank officials in several countries to expect, he wrote the agreed-upon dollar sum in pencil on one piece of the card and pocketed the other as his only record. The consolidated sheet indicates that Mr. Krebes cashed his card stub in New York. Ruzicha picked up his money in pounds sterling, in London, as did Otto Munz. Lydia Busch took her card to the Paris branch of a London bank.

Business was brisk, which created a new problem for Sharp. He was collecting so much Czech currency that its sheer bulk was proving difficult and dangerous to manage. Their room at the Hotel Pariz, which had been searched three times, offered no safe hiding places. "Thus," he recalled, "I was driven to a desperate act."

That was a visit to Irving Linnell to enlist the consul general in his clandestine currency operation. With few words of explanation, Sharp opened his black bag and pulled out approximately two million korunas in thousand-koruna notes, two hefty stacks of illegal cash.

"He looked at them, almost like a man in shock," Waitstill remembered, "and said, 'To put it very mildly, Mr. Sharp, you are in plenty of

trouble. I have here on my desk somewhere the legal code of the German occupation, printed in several languages. Do you realize what
you have been doing?'"

"Yes," Waitstill answered, "I very much realize it, and I am aware
that indeed I am in trouble, and the trouble is as near as this black
bag." Reverend Sharp reminded Linnell of all the causes and needs
of the Czech people that the little mountain of korunas resting on his
desk could help support if only he might deliver the goods.

The consul general took careful note. "Well, what are you asking of me?"

Waitstill said he had a simple but pressing dilemma: where could
he find a secure hiding place for his stash as he went about his work of
gathering more Czech currency and then distributing it? The answer
floated in the air between the two men. Waitstill later remembered
that Linnell looked steadily at him for a while. "Mr. Sharp," he said,
"I have made some tough decisions before but nothing approaching
what I am about to do; that is, set aside a Foreign Service regulation."

"I am going to open my own personal safe here in my office," the
consul general continued, "so that you can put that money in it and
walk out of here until you get the next lot of this illegal stuff. There
will be one other person privy to this arrangement, because there are
times when I have to leave the office or am tied up with somebody in
the Czech government, what's left of it."

Linnell hit a buzzer to summon his secretary. "Take a good look at
Mr. Sharp," he instructed her, then pointed to the korunas stacked on
his desk. "I want you to honor whatever requests Mr. Sharp makes of
you for whatever increments of this money."

As Waitstill recollected the moment, "Her eyes opened up as big
as harvest moons. She was flabbergasted."

"Do you understand?" Linnell asked her.

"Yes, sir," she replied.

"Give Mr. Sharp what he asks for, and just keep a ledger here in
the safe."

Waitstill departed Irving Linnell's office in high spirits. "Now I
was free," he explained, "to begin the program of financial assistance."

His very first stop was the Salvation Army's soup kitchen at their Prague headquarters. For the several months preceding the Einmarsch, Mrs. C. M. D. Benjamin, a Briton, had operated a refugee feeding operation at Prague's Labor Temple. After the Nazis shut down that service, the Salvation Army stepped in, trying to fill the relief gap.

Thousands of Social Democrats still were trapped in Prague, subject to immediate arrest and imprisonment by the Gestapo. Most lived on the streets because they couldn't risk staying at the same address for more than one or two nights. Others continued to inhabit the giant sewer pipes they'd first colonized in the months before the occupation. They could not take advantage of public relief, such as it was, including medical care. For many, their only hot meals, or food of any sort, were provided by the Salvation Army, which was perilously close to shutting down its daily service for lack of resources.

Waitstill rescued the soup kitchen with a gift of 129,000 korunas—around $3,500—which provided two hot meals a day to 350 homeless refugees through the spring and summer of 1939. "It was a moving experience," Waitstill wrote in his official report, "to stand in the dark dining room and to watch these fugitives eating, unaware of the origin of their food." The whole operation, including the source of the Salvation Army's funding, had to be kept strictly secret. There was one close call, as Waitstill related: "One day the Gestapo came to our office, lined the refugee men facing the wall, and an officer beat the refugees' heads with a revolver until they fell senseless in their own blood. The Gestapo was looking for refugees reported to have eaten at the Salvation Army." Waitstill was happy to note in his official report that 294 of the 350 managed to escape the protectorate by late August.

Children were always a priority with the Sharps, and Waitstill peeled off another twenty-five of the thousand-koruna notes for the Salvation Army to expand and upgrade a summer country rest house for the poor children of Prague. Located in a pear orchard on the banks of a little stream in the village of Uvaly, the concrete structure could house twenty-five children, who were brought from the city for three-week stays. Waitstill's donation paid for construction of a so-called American Wing. The three-story addition consisted of a storeroom and lavatory on the ground floor, a sleeping porch and sunroom on the second, and a waterproof attic as well as a sun-bathing deck on top. The added space made it possible to increase the number of children to fifty or sixty for each three-week session.

In such grim times, the sudden advent of this free-spending American left staff members at the Uvaly rest house dumbfounded. As Waitstill handed over the money, one of the women who worked there inquired about its source.

"Don't ask, madam," Sharp admonished her. "You don't catechize Santa Claus."

He gave seventy-five thousand korunas to the YMCA and another fifty thousand to the YWCA to expand their summer camp programs. The money also helped underwrite national programs designed to monitor the incidence of deficiency diseases such as rickets among children (which would become more common as the occupation wore on), as well as the health effects of poor diet and restricted exposure to sunlight.

Waitstill later noted, "Here at the heart of beleaguered Czech culture, the welfare of the children, the health and nervous stability of the inheriting generation, came first. It was a life-long lesson in the devotion of which a wise generation may be capable."

Still another initiative he funded, especially remarkable under the circumstances, was reconstruction of the Karel Farsky Refugee Children's Home, a project of the Czechoslovak National Church that British Unitarians were helping to rebuild. Waitstill donated seventy-five of his thousand-koruna notes to support what he called "a really shining example of institutional reconstruction. Here, forty little refugee orphans were to live the year round—children whose parents had been shot, imprisoned, or lost or who had committed suicide."[1]

Since the children already in residence each owned, at best, one change of clothes and for modesty's sake were sent to bed on laundry day, Sharp spent another three thousand korunas on clothing for them, and threw in a few extra korunas to raise the house's matron's monthly wage.

One group of beneficiaries was Prague's small colony of mostly elderly Russians. Waitstill paid about fifteen dollars so an elderly Russian philosopher could have a glaucoma operation to restore his eyesight. Another scholar received a set of false teeth. "We cooperated with the Red Cross," Sharp remembered, "to pay the boat fare for an aged Russian woman to South America to join her family. We paid the boat fare to England for a Crimean nurse with a fine record and a good future who, because a foreigner, had no other possible source of funds to turn to for a way out of the country. We assigned 2,400 korunas to Dr. Ivan Georgievsky to support needy children of the Russian colony at summer camps in preparation for the winter of privation which we could see ahead for all children whose families could not emigrate from Prague."

Waitstill did not neglect the Czechs' spiritual need. He donated nineteen thousand korunas to the Czechoslovak National Church to start a publishing program with the proviso that there would be an English-language version of whatever they produced. Unitaria was very near his heart. Waitstill contributed seventy-five thousand korunas to the church's social service committee to help them lay in some increasingly scarce food staples (possibly purchased outside the protectorate) for the coming winter—sugar, flour, powdered milk, chocolate, dried fruit, and the like—as well as bulk wool fabric and some medical supplies. Waitstill helped them hide it all under the church floor: "We lifted up the floor by night. We lifted some of the great tiles by light of lanterns with all the lights turned out and the windows and doors concealed. And we dropped into the open area beneath certain valuable medicaments for the disbursal by ministers of the church during what then seemed certain to be the paralysis of everything by an oncoming European war."

The greater gift to Unitaria, however, would be its continued existence, for which Sharp deserved fundamental credit. Unitaria, which faced chronic money problems from the time Norbert Capek founded the church in 1932, needed approximately $1.2 million korunas, and soon, to avoid a forced sale and liquidation.

Then came two unlikely interventions. The first occurred on March 15 when Otto Schonberger, a Jewish glove manufacturer in Prague, loaned the church about 780,000 korunas in the form of bonds, shares, and currency he left with the Unitarians as he fled to London. In return, Unitaria pledged Schonberger $180 monthly until the loan was retired.

The second crucial intervention came in the person of Otto Schleim, a blind industrialist. Schleim supplied the several hundred thousand additional korunas that Unitaria required in a clandestine currency swap with Waitstill. The deal was supposed to finance Schleim's escape from Prague.

On May 3, 1939, Schleim traded Waitstill 1.25 million korunas at 125 to the dollar (merchant rate) and received his torn business card with the figure "$10,000" scribbled on the back. There is no record of the glove maker's fate, but it appears that he did not make it. According to Waitstill's records, in the late autumn of 1939 the ten thousand dollars still awaited Otto Schleim's claim at Lloyd's Bank, in London.

In a letter from London to Parker Marean, the Unitarians' accountant in Boston, dated June 13, 1939, Waitstill explained the deal, in part, and closed with a stern warning. "Absolutely no word of this arrangement should ever come into the Protectorate," he wrote. "It certainly would mean my surrender to the Gestapo and in all likelihood my imprisonment, as well as that of Dr. Capek and his son-in-law, Mr. Haspl. Mr. Haspl and I have to handle Dr. Capek's affairs in this way, as the officers of the Association understand he is not fully dependable in money matters. All the foregoing, with all the irregularities which it introduces into your ordinary procedure, may be some indication of the extraordinary circumstances under which all business has to be conducted in Czecho-Slovakia."

In case his missive was not clear, Waitstill appended a postscript: "All of the foregoing is of life and death significance to the persons named herein. If you want to see us back in America please keep this letter in your confidential files, and make no reply to me."

—— CHAPTER TEN ——

Last Days in
the Protectorate

Occupied Czechoslovakia was a world of predators and prey where among the hunted the paradoxical consequence of surviving today was a reduced likelihood of making it past tomorrow. The strain of coping with such tension and fear took a physical and emotional toll on both Martha and Waitstill.

Martha in particular was afflicted by depression and anxiety. She had trouble sleeping, and suffered through a succession of chest and head colds.

Waitstill kept his sights resolutely fixed over the horizon. On June 1 in Geneva, he took time from his work with Marie Ginzburg of the Committee for the Placement of Intellectual Refugees to share some thoughts in a letter to Martha. He blended his optimism over "the coming victory of democracy" with lyrical asides on the Swiss capital's physical beauty and the suggestion that she quit Prague's grimness for a few days to join him where "the weather is like wine."

In one of her several later attempts to set down her life story, she reproduced this letter from her husband at length, including a passage in which Waitstill compared her to the famous Emily Balch, professor, pacifist, and moving force in the Women's International League for Peace and Freedom. In 1946 Balch would share in the Nobel Peace Prize.

"You will be returning from this experience abroad with, I believe, a good deal of prestige," he wrote, "and some rather steady glances fixed your way. . . . I see no reason why it is not a laudable ambition to qualify for as influential a post as Emily Balch occupies, or even one higher, in the liberal forces of our country's life." He closed the letter, "Ever yours and most gratefully, Waitstill."

Martha didn't require much coaxing to leave Prague's oppressive atmosphere behind, if only for a brief while.

Martha and Waitstill's stay together in Geneva was a working vacation. They met with various contacts in Switzerland, among them John Winant of the International Labour Organization (ILO) and Marie Ginzburg. Ginzburg had with her curricula vitae for 5,700 intellectuals desperate for employment outside the Reich. When Waitstill asked how many of the applicants had secured their lifelines to freedom, the answer was 299—about 5 percent of them. Martha had brought with her files on hundreds more Kulturträgers, all also in need of jobs.

Martha returned to Czechoslovakia by way of Paris, where she met with the Lowries and Malcolm Davis, who passed along some teaching invitations from US colleges. Waitstill traveled from Geneva to London to meet with colleagues and carry back any of the precious documents that might save a young student, a professor, or an artist.

In the pile of letters awaiting them at the Hotel Pariz, there was one from Aunt Edna, who reassured them that life was proceeding smoothly at home in Wellesley Hills.

"Hastings brought home his report card today," Aunt Edna wrote. "Satisfactory in everything except penmanship, unsatisfactory. The report said he can do better in arithmetic and spelling. When I asked why he was not trying to do his best, he replied, 'But Aunt Edna, yesterday and the day before I was brilliant in both.'"

Aunt Edna reported that on Mother's Day she and Martha Content took tea with Marion Niles, the Sharps' close friend from Wellesley as well as a trustee of Waitstill's church. Dr. Frederick Eliot and Mrs. Eliot also attended.

"Martha had a beautiful time," she wrote. "We christened her new spring coat and bonnet, periwinkle blue. It was a real bargain at $3.97. When we tried it on at Jordan's, Martha climbed up before the mirror and liked so much what she saw that she wept loudly and copiously when we took the coat off. But she behaved beautifully and enjoyed herself at the party, winding about among the people and smiling at all who greeted her."

———— · ————

By June, the Anglo-American colony in Prague had shrunk to no more than a couple dozen diplomats and aid workers. Although the circle clearly was closing, the upside was that with fewer nationals to watch over, consular officers such as Irving Linnell could act on their behalf more quickly.

The day after their return, Martha realized that she had acquired a permanent Gestapo minder, installed in the room next door. "One morning when I went to the office door," she remembered, "I saw him outside posing as a relief worker, questioning the people as to why they were there. They told him everything, thinking they were safe."

After weeks of practice, Martha was adept at losing a tail. But this particular minder soon was inhabiting her head as well. "His evil face and burning eyes began to appear in my dreams," she said. "His ruthless look made me shiver." Henceforth, she would rarely be alone.

In mid-July, she received a surprise visit from the vice president of the Czech National Women's Council, who explained that the council needed her help. Frantiska Plaminkova, founder and president of the council, as well as a former senator, Czech representative to the League of Nations, and a prominent feminist, was returning to the protectorate after some meetings and a lecture tour abroad. The council leadership feared that the outspokenly antifascist Plaminkova—known familiarly as "Pani" or sometimes "Plam"—faced almost certain arrest and imprisonment.

"We must prevent her from returning," the woman said. "She has turned aside every effort which we have made personally, in letters, to dissuade her from coming back. We feel she does not understand how difficult and changed life is here now, and that she can be of more help to us on the outside."

"Why do you tell me all of this?" Martha asked.

"Because we feel you understand what is happening," she answered, "and because we feel she will listen to you."

Martha was doubtful but agreed to help if possible.

Plam was expected in two days at Lovosice, known in German as Lobositz, which coincidentally was the site in 1756 of the first battle of the Seven Years' War. "Since we heard you have been able to go in and out of the country," she continued, "we hoped you might be willing to meet her at the border and explain to her why she must turn back. If she still insists on coming in, you will journey back with her and be a witness if the Nazis try to abduct Plam and take her to prison. She has been saying some strong things about them!"

Martha considered the question overnight, weighing the risk to herself and to the mission against the importance of trying to protect such a leading figure in Czech political life. She decided to give it a try. On the morning of Tuesday, July 18, Martha took a five o'clock train out of Prague for the German border, where she showed her papers, carefully counted and registered the korunas in her possession, and then set out on a short walking tour as she awaited Plaminkova's train to arrive from Switzerland.

She had brought along her camera, and was clicking away when suddenly she heard a voice behind her. It was a German officer on a bicycle. "Do you like to take pictures?" he asked casually.

"Very much," she replied.

"Would you like to see some of the picturesque spots?" he wondered.

"Yes," she said cautiously. "But I must be here to meet the train from Switzerland."

"We shall be back in time," he said. "I must be here for that too."

"Why?"

"Because I must check the passports. Don't you remember me? I checked your American passport when you came off the train. I couldn't imagine why an American lady was getting off here. But now I see that you are a photographer."

Worried lest the officer suspect her of spying, Martha explained that she had not come to take pictures but to meet an older woman, whom she'd help with the balance of her trip.

"What is her name?" he inquired.

She hesitated, uncertain if Plaminkova might be on a border watch list. "Oh, she has a funny Czech name you'll never remember."

"I will show you!" he said genially. "Tell me and I will introduce you to the commandant who will let you through the wicket before the others, as soon as her train stops, so you can join her at once."

There was no way out. Martha could not very well say she didn't know the woman. At least it would give her more time to talk with Plaminkova while they checked the rest of the train.

"Pani Plaminkova," she said.

The German officer laughed. "No wonder you thought I wouldn't remember," he said. "It *is* a funny name."

They walked on to the edge of town where Martha noticed that a whole section of houses had been gutted by fire. The officer pointed at the ruined structures. "See these?" he said. "They are the houses Jews lived in."

"What happened to them?" she asked.

"We blew them up!" he said, pride in his voice.

Martha instinctively wanted to document what he said. "Let me take your picture," she asked. "Won't you pose in front of the houses?"

"No," he answered. "I don't like the composition."

Martha got her pictures anyway.

When the train from Switzerland pulled into the station, she was led as promised to the front of the line to board first. Her escort, a young passport officer, pointed out Frantiska Plaminkova, then moved on to check the other passengers, saving Martha a potentially sticky moment. Plaminkova was mystified and wary of her.

"I quickly explained my mission," Martha recalled. "I begged her with all the strength at my command not to go into the Protectorate."

Plaminkova was immovable on the subject.

"Shall I stay in comfort on the outside, while my women are suffering?" she asked. "Shall I have to go about with my lips sealed, so as not to endanger them while I do nothing to help? No! I must go back and fight. But I am most grateful to you for being willing to accompany me to see that I arrive safely in Prague."

Martha recognized the same implacable resolve she had seen in Norbert Capek. Logic dictated that if they stayed in the protectorate both no doubt would pay with their lives. In neither case, however, was logic a principal consideration.

The train bumped to life. The passport officer called *auf Wiedersehen* as they passed by. "Thank you very much!" Martha shouted back.

She was apprehensive about the Gestapo guards at the frontier, but Plaminkova reassured her that her visa was good. "I went all the way to Berlin," she explained, "to get permission to enter the jaws of the wolf!"

But to what end? she thought to herself.

The next morning Martha overslept, and in the rush to catch the streetcar had forgotten a paper she needed for a meeting that day. She hurried back to the room to find people in it. A maid was running her hand over the new bed mattress. A man sat at the desk, reading papers from the drawers. They were equally surprised to see Martha, who realized that she should leave her hotel room as nonchalantly as possible. "Oh, excuse me," she said, "I will just be in your way." Closing the door behind her, she was serene. Gertrude Baer's lessons in London had come in handy once again. Anything of potential interest to the Germans already had been turned to ashes and flushed down the toilet. All she'd preserved were the letters from home.

The increased surveillance was no surprise to Martha. The Germans had been clamping down on foreign refugee groups for some time. In mid-April, American Relief (and probably all other foreign relief agencies) had been evicted from their headquarters at the former Ministry of Public Health. At about the same time, the Gestapo took in Beatrice Wellington of the British Committee for Refugees from Czechoslovakia for grueling interrogation, during which time she was made to stand for six hours. All British Committee staff, except for the indomitable Wellington, returned home by May 9. Wellington would finally leave on August 3, shortly before Martha did.[1]

———— · ————

At lunch that day with other aid workers the topic was Frantiska Plaminkova and her continuing defiance of the Nazis, who had ordered Czech women to donate their furs to line German soldiers' winter coats. The Wehrmacht had tried to enlist Plam in the campaign, but she adamantly refused. "My women will assist the poor," she said, "as well as the sick and homeless. They will work for peace. But they will not move to enable you to carry on a war."

After the invasion of Poland, Plam was briefly arrested. She was rearrested in 1942 and taken to Terezin, where, according to what Martha learned, she was tortured. On June 30 of that year, Plam was executed in another Nazi reprisal for the ambush assassination of Reinhard Heydrich.[2]

———— · ————

The Germans finally shut down all refugee aid programs on July 25. The volunteers at American Relief by then had interviewed and enrolled 3,500 would-be émigrés. Security dictated that no master list ever be prepared.

Over the several weeks leading up to July 25, Waitstill repurposed a few bales of korunas to help young people—mostly students— make their own escapes from the protectorate. A favorite route took them northeast of Prague into the rich coal region on the border with Poland.

As Waitstill described it, the student refugees donned mining gear and headed down into the mines, crossed under the border into Poland, and then reemerged on the other side. There, members of the Polish resistance took over, conveying some of the émigrés north to the Baltic port of Gdynia, where British submarines picked them up by night. Many ended up in the Allied armed forces.

Waitstill was very proud of his role as financier of this underground railroad. His standard donation was ten thousand korunas per student. An unknown number of these otherwise doomed young men and women were rescued as a result.

But these final weeks also brought him his most bitter and painful failure. Despite Martha and Waitstill's considerable efforts, all eight of the young Sudeten Jews who ran their refugee office—four couples— eventually died in concentration camps. In the case of one couple, a simple typographical error—an "O" instead of a "D" for a middle initial on the British visa application—led some bureaucrat somewhere to deny the application and thus consign the two to the gas chambers.

On August 7, his penultimate day in Prague, Waitstill met with Karl Deutsch's father, Martin, who had finally perfected his own escape plans for Sweden. If nothing went awry, Martin soon would be reunited with his wife, Maria.

But suddenly a glitch had occurred.

"Mr. Sharp," he said, "I am in a very serious emergency. If we cannot solve it, it may cost me my life. I have everything arranged but have just been told that the Swedes accept only hard currency for the ferry ride from Sassnitz to Malmo. I cannot raise the three dollars and twenty-eight cents American that I need. What can I do?"

By this time Waitstill was not at all surprised to hear that a human life hinged on $3.28.

"In my pocketbook," he later said, "I happened to have a hoard of five one-dollar bills, which I kept against such an emergency as this. I gave Martin Deutsch four dollars. He said, 'This is my ticket to life.' It was the last I saw of him."

Martin Deutsch successfully escaped to Sweden, where he rejoined his wife. The Deutsches subsequently made their way to New York City, where they lived out their years in peace in an apartment on the corner of Seventy-Fifth and Broadway.

Karl Deutsch's in-laws were not so fortunate. According to their granddaughter, Margaret Carroll, Hugo and Hermione Slonitz "were convinced that what happened couldn't happen. They didn't try to leave until it was too late. They first were transported to Terezin and then to Auschwitz, where they perished, as did one of my mother's sisters."[3]

——— · ———

Waitstill left Prague for the last time on August 8 to address a meeting in Arcegno, Switzerland, of young people sponsored by the International Association of Religious Freedom. When he tried to return to Czechoslovakia, his *Ausreise* was confiscated and he was not allowed back in. He nervously waited for Martha in Paris.

Martha hoped to remain in the protectorate until as near as possible to their sailing date, August 30. However, on August 14, a Monday, Jaroslav Kosé, former Czech representative to the ILO in Geneva, warned her that the Gestapo intended to arrest her in two days. So Martha left for Paris aboard the first available train on August 15. Thirteen friends gathered to see her off at the station, laden with flowers and presents.

Martha also was carrying pearls, gold bracelets and diamond rings for the wife of Pavel Eisner, a noted Czech literary scholar and translator. Her assignment was to deliver the jewelry into the safekeeping of novelist H. G. Wells in London.

In Paris she rejoined her relieved husband for whom the five-day wait and the knowledge that she was in danger would have been almost unbearable. Uncertainty is hard for anyone, but for a man of Waitstill's energy, and with his tendency to be proactive rather than passive, enjoying the safety of Paris while his beloved wife was still operating under the Nazis' watch would have had him climbing walls.

They met once more with Malcolm Davis, the Lowries, and other members of refugee aid organizations there. Martha took ill but continued to work from her bed, classifying the refugee cases in preparation for a final trip to London on August 23 (the day Josef Stalin and Joachim von Ribbentrop would conclude the Nazi-Soviet nonaggression pact).

The Sharps spent just two full days in London, where Wells duly accepted Frau Eisner's jewelry and even signed a receipt, which Martha preserved.

They then returned to Paris on August 26 and filled their remaining days there with more refugee work and long strolls together through the city they both cherished.

Martha would write of walking down the Champs-Élysées and after a dinner one night watching Notre Dame "fade into darkness." They browsed through a flea market where Waitstill bought Martha a silver buckle. They hoped for a day trip to Chartres, but the trains were running late and there wasn't time.

On September 1, the day after the Sharps boarded the *Queen Mary* at Le Havre for New York, the Germans invaded Poland. Two days later, England and France declared war on Nazi Germany. "I was standing over the propellers when the British radio cracked out the news," Waitstill recalled.

We were summoned to the grand saloon where we heard the voice of Neville Chamberlain: "Calling all radio stations in the British Commonwealth of Nations, the Parliament of England declares a state of war obtains now between the United Kingdom of England, Ireland and Scotland and the Imperial German government."

We were no longer aboard a civilian ocean liner. We had become a war target. The course of our ship was changed to run north, for German submarines had been reported due west, waiting to sink this pride of the British fleet. Portholes were fastened and painted black to prevent light from showing, and nobody was allowed to smoke on deck at night.

The order had been sent down from the captain's bridge. "Give her the max!" The ship came alive, and we went up to very cold waters. She hit the great waves of the North Atlantic with such violence that the sea came right over the ship.

The great ship steamed on past Newfoundland and then southwest for New York, where she safely berthed on September 4 with no further alarms. On September 3, while the Sharps were still at sea, the SS *Athenia,* a British passenger ship, became the first casualty in the Battle of the Atlantic. It was sunk by a German U-boat west of the Hebrides. One hundred and eighteen lives were lost.

The Sharps felt the tension drain as they disembarked and headed for Grand Central Terminal to board the New York–New Haven train for Boston and home.

"We were back in another world," Martha later wrote. "Love, children's arms, plentiful food, and the only thing that concerned Americans that September seemed to be which team would win the World Series."

CHAPTER ELEVEN

The First Choice

Martha and Waitstill returned as heroes to Wellesley Hills and the American Unitarian Association. That autumn the AUA laid on a heavy schedule of press interviews and public appearances—particularly for Martha—to capitalize on their new celebrity and to raise money as well.

Accolades notwithstanding (as Waitstill put it, "[They] filled our cup"), the Sharps were slow to recover from their months of nervous stress, long hours, chronic illness, poor food, and emotional turmoil. Waitstill had been so wound up during the last hectic days in Prague that he found two days in Lucerne on the way to Paris after the Arcegno conference "nerve-wracking" instead of a respite.

More troublesome from a parental perspective, despite the fine surrogate work done by the Stebbinses, Hastings and his little sister Martha Content had suffered from their father and mother's long absence. It "had made them fearful that whenever we left the house we might not come back," Martha remembered. "Fortunately, they were too young to understand the risks and the difficulties of living in the front seat of a tragedy during war conditions, which had been our daily lives. They did know that they needed us and they missed our love. And I knew that I missed them terribly. Every suffering refugee child had made me think of home and wonder how *my* children were. Since we sometimes were cut off from news for two or three weeks, the not knowing was even worse."

The Sharps might reasonably have collected their honors and resumed their old lives and responsibilities, assured that they had done more than their share. But they didn't. Coordinating with the AUA Case Work Committee, which had been set up to support the Sharps' work in Czechoslovakia, Martha and Waitstill continued to press the State Department for visas. During speech-making events, Martha tried to find people who might give affidavits of support, indicating that potential immigrants would not become public charges. Without these affidavits no visas would be issued.

One of their few successes in Washington was to obtain visas for Dr. and Mrs. Albin Goldschmeid, who arrived in New York in mid-November of 1939. Dr. Goldschmeid had been their German tutor in Prague, hired perhaps as much to provide him with a small income as to learn the enemy's language. The Goldschmeids stayed at the parsonage until they could find a place of their own.

Martha switched back and forth among several personas: mother, wife and social and political activist. Her schedule for November and December 1939 was a blur of conferences, sewing circle meetings, teas, dinners prepared at home for visiting clergy, speeches, school pageants, press appearances, and shopping trips. Among the few unscheduled days were Thanksgiving and Christmas. The only two dates that apparently were canceled were dances. Martha loved to dance.

Just before Thanksgiving, she traveled with Robert Dexter to Washington to lobby Ernest Gruening, governor of the Alaska territory (and later a US senator), on behalf of Interior Secretary Harold L. Ickes's proposal to relocate as many as ten thousand non-quota refugees to the sprawling, remote, and underpopulated land. A proposal, the King-Havenner Bill, reached Congress the following year, but was voted down.

— · —

Meantime, AUA leaders, including Waitstill, met to create a permanent organization that would carry the Unitarian message and continue humanitarian efforts in Europe during the war and in the world to come after the fighting stopped.[1] The model would be the American Friends Service Committee (AFSC), founded in 1917 for the relief of civilian victims of World War I.

In early January 1940, Waitstill wrote to Dexter, suggesting that the new organization be called the Unitarian Service Committee (USC). "Prepare now," he advised, "for a standing service record like that of the Quakers." Nearly a quarter century later, the USC merged with the Universalist Service Committee to form the Unitarian Universalist Service Committee (UUSC), a respected international social-change organization.

——— · ———

Although Great Britain and France had declared war on Nazi Germany immediately after Hitler's invasion of Poland, not much else of military significance happened right away. The so-called Phony War, or *sitzkrieg,* had set in, seven months in which the principal declared belligerents—Germany, Great Britain, and France—made no important moves against one another. Great Britain and France were focused on rearmament and mobilization, looking west across the Atlantic to the Roosevelt administration for much-needed money and materiel. The Germans were interested in consolidating their gains in Poland, and preparing for the next stage in the Führer's grand design.

In January of 1940, the AUA dispatched Dexter and his wife, Elisabeth, on another survey trip to Europe, this time to assess the Czech refugee situation outside the protectorate and then to return with recommendations for possible further action. The Dexters traveled through western Europe and Britain, meeting with contacts Martha and Waitstill had made the previous year. They discovered that the Sharp name, as Dexter put it in a letter, was "an open sesame here."

They reported back that Czech exiles in France, mostly intellectuals and civic leaders, were in great need of services, and they proposed opening a Unitarian center in Paris, funded at twenty thousand dollars a year, to aid Czech refugees and to act as liaison with their separated families wherever in unoccupied Europe they might be.[2]

The obvious choices to head the new office were Martha and Waitstill, although they saw it otherwise. Dr. Eliot urged them to accept the challenge, writing to Waitstill,

> I most earnestly hope that the first act of the [Unitarian Service] Committee—after making Robert Dexter the Executive Director—will be to invite you and Martha to go to France as our ambassadors extraordinary. Then you will have to face a momentous decision. My personal hope is that you will decide to go. There just aren't words to express my feeling of admiration and deep respect for what you two people have done and for what you are. My dream for the USC centers on you, and it is a very big dream.[3]

The Sharps declined to be considered for the post. The leadership of the Wellesley Church, care of their children, and heavy speech-making on behalf of the AUA was time-consuming enough. They felt that they had done, and were doing, their share. Martha, especially, didn't want to leave Hastings and Martha Content yet again for another extended assignment to Europe.

——— • ———

Before the Dexters returned, the Phony War turned real. In April of 1940, the Wehrmacht marched on Denmark and Norway. On May 10, German forces began to smash their way into Holland, Belgium, and Luxembourg. Using tanks, Stuka dive-bombers, and ruthless aerial bombings, they took Holland in five days and Luxembourg, which had no army, in one. Belgium surrendered on May 28.[4] That's when the mass evacuation of Allied soldiers at Dunkirk began. This heroic water-borne rescue of close to 340,000 mostly British troops, as well as some French, Dutch, and Belgians, was the single bright moment in a catastrophic spring for the Allies.[5]

On May 23, as the grim developments in Europe dominated the front page, Eliot summoned Waitstill to his third-floor office at 25 Beacon Street. The soft sell hadn't worked, so he employed stronger tactics, offering the assignment again but not as an option.

Waitstill was thunderstruck.

"Dr. Eliot," he said, "my family has been broken up since early February of last year. I have two young children who need steady parenting. We've been eagerly counting upon a vacation at our lakeside cottage on Lake Sunapee."

At this Eliot exploded.

"Vacation!" he shouted. "Europe is falling to pieces and you talk about vacation! I won't hear the word! Let me tell you something. It is your moral obligation to go overseas and resume what you have proved you can do so ably. You must go! There is no debating it."

There was no further discussion and no debate.

Waitstill went home and told Martha. She was as shocked as he was but could see no way to refuse, as Waitstill recalled:

> But we agreed, all things considered, including our future in the denomination, that this was the only thing that could be done. And more than any other factor was the point that Dr. Eliot made that we could land in Europe as no one else could and begin with the connections that had only been temporarily severed by the fall and winter of 1939–1940. This appealed to us as the compelling reason for doing what he demanded; I cannot say requested.

When Dr. Eliot announced at the May meetings in Boston that the Sharps would be going to France, Martha burst into tears in the pew, even as their friends crowded around them to offer congratulations. She mumbled "thanks" through her tears. She had never fully agreed to go and leave the children again. Martha and Waitstill would not know it at the time, but looking back, Martha Content has said, "That was the beginning of when they began to lose each other."

——— · ———

It was a nearly silent drive back to Wellesley Hills. "We were hurt by Frederick Eliot's assumption that his command was all that was needed," Martha wrote, "and by his ruthless neglect of our right to decide what was best for our family. The implied threat to Waitstill's future in the denomination, threatening to side-track his success in Wellesley Hills or questioning his suitability for another pulpit, was frightening. And Waitstill wasn't the only one drafted. I was part of the package. The web was very strong."

When Martha and Waitstill arrived at the parsonage that evening, Martha Content ran to meet them at the door. "I hugged her so hard," Martha recalled, "she wriggled free as a few of my tears dropped on her dress."

The AUA's plans to send the Sharps directly to France were frustrated by the war's sudden acceleration. On June 3, the Germans bombed Paris, which fell eleven days later. France was sliced into two zones, a northern one occupied by the Axis powers and a southern one that was not officially occupied but was controlled by Germany. The reactionary Marshal Philippe Pétain, then eighty-four, known as the Lion of Verdun for his command skills in World War I, was installed as head of the puppet regime at Vichy.

Chaos reigned in France as a vast human tide—millions of civilians and soldiers—streamed south, immediately overwhelming the region's limited resources. Food and fuel were particularly scarce, as was potable water. Many of the refugees suffered bullet and shrapnel wounds as the Germans intermittently strafed and shelled the long lines of vehicles snaking slowly along the choked roads.

The Sharp family managed to shoehorn a two-day vacation into the brief and frenetic time that Waitstill and Martha were given to prepare for their mission. It was decided that Hastings would head to camp for the summer. His sister would spend part of her time with the Stebbinses at the family cottage on Lake Sunapee, in western New Hampshire, and the rest with Marion Niles, at her summer house on Martha's Vineyard.

With the fall of France, President Roosevelt issued an order prohibiting all US vessels from entering French waters. Percival Brundage, a senior partner at Price Waterhouse, the accounting firm, and a member of the new Service Committee board, used his influence to secure passage for Waitstill and Martha out of New York to Portugal aboard a Pan Am flying boat.

Martha Content accompanied her mother on several expeditions to purchase the numerous items unattainable in Europe. Martha tried to explain to her the purpose of all the activity, but Martha Content still was too young to understand.

"Hastings," Martha wrote, "hid his unhappiness by making believe he didn't care, absenting himself, or being difficult. At age nine, he felt he was the head of the family when his father was not at home."

No one on either side of the family thought much of the expedition. "Mine pledged to help the children in case of need," Martha reported. "Waitstill's brothers did the same. Privately, they all thought we'd taken leave of our senses. Of course, they knew that Waitstill was a fighting idealist, but who goes off into a war situation and leaves his two small children when he doesn't have to?"

On Sunday, June 2, Reverend Sharp delivered a farewell sermon urging war. He was so vehement that the *Boston Globe* devoted about four inches of column text to it. Under the headline "WELLESLEY PASTOR URGES U.S. TO DECLARE WAR ON GERMANY," the paper reported,

> Stating, "we have talked long enough of measures short of war," Rev. Waitstill H. Sharp, minister of the Wellesley Hills Unitarian Church, today in his sermon called for immediate declaration of war by the United States upon Germany. Rev. Mr. Sharp, who is to go to France this month, said German victory with a goal of mastery would upset our sources of raw materials, and give Germany naval domination of trade routes and a "whiphand over satellite currency systems." An immediate declaration of war would have the following five results, he said: "It would deter Italy in her dictator's course of cheap opportunism: inject hope into the Allies and the neutrals; discourage the Germans; warn the Fifth Column workers of South and Central America; and fix the status of the Fifth Columnists in our own nation, before their plans are refined any further. We desperately want the Allies to win, but so far we are not willing to secure that victory by any sacrifice or by running any risk of sacrifice. This is a very unhealthy dilemma."

Waitstill's stark oratory framed the issue succinctly, but in isola-tionist America he expressed a decidedly minority position. As for the Unitarians, perhaps a significant proportion agreed with him, however reluctantly, that war was the only possible answer to Nazi aggression. Others doubtlessly agreed with Reverend Leslie T. Pen-nington, the forty-one-year-old minister of the First Parish in Cam-bridge, Massachusetts, and a family friend who was nonetheless critical of Waitstill's war advocacy.

Leave-taking was once again painful.

"We tried to explain to the children that we loved them so much that we had to share our love with children in France who were in desperate need," Martha remembered.

"On the day Dr. Baker arrived to take us to the Back Bay Sta-tion, Martha Content stood in the library window, jumping up and down as she had sixteen months before, chanting, 'Mommy going bye-bye!' We kissed her and Hasty, who also shook hands with his father. Then we climbed aboard our old Ford with Ev Baker at the wheel and waved at the children until we turned the corner toward the turnpike to Boston."

That evening, the Sharps dined in New York with the Brundages. "E. P.," as he was known to his friends, steered that evening's conver-sation to a subject of personal concern—children. Brundage told his guests that he was on the board of the US Committee for the Care of European Children (USCOM). Although USCOM's initial focus was to remove children from the dangers of the aerial war raging over Britain, as the war progressed it went on to remove children, includ-ing Jewish children, from other countries.

"He thought that I might come across some children in France," Martha recollected, "whose families also might like to have them es-cape the danger and privations of the war. If so, we should advise him and he would be glad to try to arrange for the US committee to bring them over and find homes for them." His suggestion led to Martha's major endeavor during the fall of that year: the rescue of twenty-seven children from Vichy France.

—— CHAPTER TWELVE ——

In Lisbon

At three-thirty on the afternoon of Monday, June 17, 1940, the Sharps boarded the Pan Am Dixie Clipper at New York's newly opened LaGuardia International Airport, bound for Lisbon with a refueling stop in the Azores. Neither of them had much history with airplanes, and none with Pan Am's recently introduced four-engine Boeing B-314 flying boats. "My limited flying experience," Martha wrote, "was no preparation for the clipper, and any regular takeoff cannot compare to those old flying boats that needed a certain amount of surf, wind and speed to rise from the water. The noise in the cabin, the shaking of the ship, the long horizontal push when it seemed we couldn't possibly rise, and then up, up and away, the blue Atlantic below, and the ships getting smaller and smaller. For almost forty-five minutes we were beguiled by this new sensation."

The cabin's comfortable, upholstered seats were configured into sets of facing twins, similar to the seating in passenger train compartments. Across from Martha and Waitstill sat "a young Yalie," as Martha put it, who turned out to be Whitelaw Reid II, grandson of the famous *New York Herald* editor. Reid was en route to England on newspaper business. Next to him sat a heavyset middle-aged man wearing a name tag that read "Vice President, Nirosta Corporation."

The passenger may have been anonymous, but Nirosta was not. Part of the giant Krupp basic industries in Germany—essentially the flywheel of Hitler's war engine—Nirosta was a major international supplier of stainless steel sheets. Nirosta steel had been used in building both the Chrysler Building and the Empire State Building in Manhattan. Also on board the Clipper were a number of Britons, as well as Myron Charles Taylor, the former CEO of US Steel, who now served as President Roosevelt's special ambassador to the Vatican. Taylor, who did not look well to Martha, was accompanied by his wife, a personal physician, and a secretary. Two hours into the flight, the steward emerged from the cockpit with curious news. Due to weather conditions, he announced, they had changed course for Bermuda. "Mrs. Taylor," according to Martha, "already was knocking on the door of the cockpit, objecting to the decision. She insisted we go across according to the original plan, because the delay would not be good for Mr. Taylor's health. Meanwhile, I saw 'Vice President, Nirosta Corporation' across from me throw up his hands and mumble, 'It's all up with me.' Then he began to sweat. As the perspiration rolled down his face, I asked what was wrong. He didn't answer, but began to wring his hands until his knuckles were white. His face grew redder and redder."

They landed in Bermuda, in perfect weather, at about nine-thirty that evening. British officials met them as they disembarked. Since the United Kingdom was now at war, they explained, passengers, no matter what their nationality, were required to surrender all personal belongings: luggage, briefcases, wallets, purses, personal papers—everything.

Martha noticed that "the 'V.P.' had now perspired not just through his shirt, but also through his jacket. Whitelaw Reid whispered to me that he was going to the weather station to check on the flying weather." The passengers were taken by bus to the Belmont Manor, a seaside hotel where the Sharps were given a room with a lovely view of the ocean. At dinner they learned that two British passengers were members of Parliament, returning home from US lecture tours. Two others were Irish antique dealers, caught by the outbreak of war in the United States, where they had been hunting antiques to repatriate. Reid reported to the group that no one on the island seemed willing to discuss the weather with him, as if it were a military secret. The man from Nirosta said nothing at all.

The passengers did a bit of sightseeing the next day, then late in the afternoon boarded their B-314 for the Azores—minus the man from Nirosta. As they cleared Bermuda's hills, they saw a convoy of twelve ships lying at anchor. Martha learned that seventy-five vessels had assembled in Bermuda the previous week, then departed together for an undisclosed location. Above the clouds, they saw a rainbow, then the sea was lit by a full moon and stars bigger than any Waitstill and Martha had ever seen before.

Next morning they refueled at Horta in the Azores. Reid had excused himself to check on the weather once again and had not yet returned when the refueling was complete and reboarding for Lisbon begun. Once everyone but Reid was aboard, Mrs. Taylor imperiously demanded that they leave without the newspaperman. The captain demurred, explaining that some weeks there were but one or two flights in and out of Horta.

"So we waited," Martha remembered. "Fortunately, Reid soon made his appearance, only to be stopped at the doorway by Mrs. Taylor. 'Young man,' she scolded, 'don't enter this airplane until you tell me where you've been. Don't you know you've held us all up?' 'I was wiring my mother,' he answered meekly. 'You should have stayed home with your mother!' the ambassador's wife barked. With that, Reid slid into his seat, fastened his belt, and we took off."

——— · ———

The Dixie Clipper slowed, circled, and descended to lightly skim the waves of Lisbon's broad Tagus River, gliding to stop at its berth at just after seven on Thursday evening, June 20. Because hotel space in Lisbon was scarce to non-existent, the Sharps and most of the rest of the passengers were driven by bus to the resort town of Estoril, about fifteen miles away, where rooms awaited them at the Hotel d'Italia.

Trouble instantly erupted. National feelings were running high, and when the British passengers saw the name of the hotel, they refused to enter until they knew whether it was owned by Italians, the Italian government, or other Italian interests. "They said they would rather sleep on the street than in a hotel owned by their enemy,"

Martha recalled. The doorman spoke a little French, so the group was able to make him understand that they had to see the manager, who turned out to be a PR man par excellence. He swore up and down that "d'Italia" was just a name like "Britannia." The British were appeased, and after registering, they got to bed shortly after midnight.

Next day, they took a train into Lisbon to present themselves to US ambassador Herbert Claiborne Pell Jr. "We were beguiled," said Martha, "by the waving palms, the tropical climate, gaily painted houses, climbing vines and flowers everywhere. From the train windows we could see the bronzed bathers on the beaches, and their gay umbrellas. War seemed very far away."

The spell was shattered once they reached the US embassy, which appeared to be under siege. People were standing in long, slow-moving lines outside nearly every door. The letter that the Sharps carried from Cordell Hull had the intended effect on Ambassador Pell, who greeted them warmly, then led them to his office to brief them on the refugee situation. "Fourteen hundred are registered for ship space," Pell reported, "four hundred for the Pan Am clipper. The quota is filled until mid-August. The International Police of Portugal are only allowing people with guaranteed rooms in Lisbon to travel south of Oporto.

"In the north, they are sleeping in barns, schools or even on the ground. The English wine merchants have opened shelters in Oporto. We have so many Americans here in Lisbon trying to get home that we are seriously considering hiring a loft and filling it with cots to give them some place to sleep."[1]

With plans to open the USC office in Paris indefinitely suspended by the Nazi occupation, Martha and Waitstill had left Boston with AUA instructions to deploy themselves and their limited resources— about ten thousand dollars in bank accounts back in the States—as they saw fit, starting, they had understood, where the Red Cross left off. One of the first familiar faces they saw in Lisbon was that of Malcolm Davis, who had recently arrived from Paris, en route to Switzerland where he was to report on conditions in France to the League of Red Cross Societies, of which Davis was now *directeur-adjoint*. When the Sharps told him of their open-ended mandate, he didn't hesitate. Their old friend and mentor told them that the children of Vichy France were in desperate need of milk. Babies were dying. Local cows traditionally were not raised for their milk, Davis said, and what little there was of it was poorly handled, often not pasteurized, and largely unsuitable for consumption by children, especially very young ones.

Most of the French dairy herds, he explained, were in the north. As the Germans consolidated their hold on these regions—principally Brittany and Normandy—the cows were being slaughtered to feed the soldiers. As a consequence, milk shipments to the south had all but ceased. Canned condensed milk was impossible to find. The Vichy government was advising French mothers not to wean their babies but to continue nursing them indefinitely. "There is no milk in France," Davis told the Sharps over dinner at his hotel, the Avenida Palace. "If you have any funds available, I would advise you to put them into powdered and condensed milk and ship it to the children as fast as you can."

Several factors complicated the picture. One was the British naval blockade of France. Among the foodstuffs on the British Ministry of Economic Warfare's restricted list were potatoes, which could be used for distilling alcohol, and milk, because its main protein, casein, was a component in the manufacture of plastic. Also, at the US government's request, the Red Cross had agreed not to distribute food or clothing anywhere the Germans might appropriate the shipments for their own use.

Morris Troper of the Joint Distribution Committee, another acquaintance from their Czech mission, told them the same story the next night. "He felt that bringing milk to babies in France, where it was so desperately needed, would be the best possible initiation of our mission," Martha wrote. Troper also asked Martha to visit some of the internment camps in France and report on them.

They received similar advice from the French ambassador to Lisbon, Amé-Leroy, a staunch antifascist who so far had refused to yield his portfolio despite Vichy's repeated insistence that he do so at once. Madame Manoëlle Amé-Leroy was president of the Portuguese auxiliary of the French Red Cross. At his official residence, Amé-Leroy explained to Waitstill and Martha that the SS *McKeesport,* a Red Cross transport carrying milk for the children of the south of France, was stuck in Bilbao, Spain, indefinitely delayed by red tape. Moreover, under its agreement with the US government, the Red Cross could not move to distribute the milk into the region without ironclad assurances from the Germans that they would not confiscate it. Such promises so far were not forthcoming.

As the Sharps already knew, it was no longer possible in Europe to act simply out of charity, goodwill, or human kindness.

Madame Amé-Leroy also showed them a letter she'd received from Madame Saint-René Taillandier, one of the presidents of the French Red Cross, who lived in Tarascon, a fishing town on the Rhone, northwest of Marseille, not far from Nimes.

"Tarascon is filled with thousands of refugees," Madame Taillandier wrote.

> They sleep on straw, crowded together under any shelter. Many children and even babies among them are wounded by shrapnel and machine gun bullets. Some of these are without fathers or mothers. It is difficult to get food, even for ourselves. There is no milk for the babies, who are dying as a result. Everyone here applies to me, thinking that because I am President of the Red Cross I am accompanied by a Treasury. Alas, I have nothing to show them but my medal as president.[2]

The daily commute into Lisbon from Estoril was scenic but time-consuming, so the Sharps found a suite of rooms at the Hotel Metropole in the Portuguese capital, which also would serve as the USC office. As they were gathering their belongings at the Hotel d'Italia, Waitstill and Martha learned from their fellow Clipper passengers why the mysterious "man from Nirosta" had been so distressed, then vanished. It turned out that he was a US citizen who was suspected of working as a Nazi spy. Bad weather had only been a pretext for delivering him into British custody. When detained and questioned in Bermuda, he was found to be carrying certain sensitive documents.

Then still another old acquaintance from their first commission, Dr. Clayton Williams, minister of the American Church in Paris, arrived in Lisbon, bringing with him a carload of Americans eager to head for home. Williams's vehicle was a Matford, produced in France in the 1930s as a joint venture of the Mathis car manufacturing company and Ford, hence the name. When Waitstill and Martha told him they were planning to go to France, the reverend offered them the Matford, which had an international registration. However, the car's *carnet de passage* was set to expire on July 17. In order for the Matford to reenter France, they needed to beat that deadline.

When Williams agreed with everyone else that sustenance was the refugees' greatest immediate need in the south of France, particularly milk for the babies, no longer was there a question: the Sharps' first relief mission in France would be to find milk to feed the children.

The likeliest source was the Swiss-based Nestlé Company, which had available supplies of powdered milk, condensed milk, and Nestogen, a fortified baby formula. Madame Amé-Leroy set up a meeting between Waitstill and Jean Lanz, representative of the Nestlé Company in Portugal. She also arranged with the Portuguese and Spanish railroad companies for the train's free passage to the French border.[3]

Nestlé made Waitstill a very good bargain: twelve tons of condensed and powdered milk, as well as Nestogen, for about 141,000 Portuguese escudos, or approximately $5,450.

Reverend Williams also passed along the news that Don and Helen Lowrie were now refugees of a sort themselves. Dislodged from Paris by the German invasion, they had moved south as part of the mass migration and settled in the town of Pau, not far from the Spanish border, where they'd rented a four-room apartment at 2 Rue Darrichon. Don Lowrie was hard at work, organizing relief for demobilized Czech soldiers. He also was head of a loose federation of relief agencies headquartered in Nimes.

The Sharps were eager to renew their collaboration and friendship with the Lowries. They sent cables to them in Pau and to Malcolm

Davis, who was by now in Geneva, informing them that they were assembling a milk shipment for France. Don Lowrie cabled back that he would meet them at the Hotel Belvedere in the Mediterranean sea-coast village of Cerbère, just north of the Spanish border. Another wire went to Bob Dexter in Boston, explaining the reasons they had decided on the milk shipment and requesting five thousand dollars to cover the costs. It seemed a straightforward arrangement but would prove anything but.

———— · ————

In order to drive Clayton Williams's Matford from Lisbon into France, Martha and Waitstill would need international driver's licenses, which took them the next morning to the Royal Automobile Club of Portugal, the local issuing agency. Martha remembered standing before a Portuguese clerk at the information window, unable to make herself understood in English and then in French.

At that moment, a beautiful, expensively clothed American came over and introduced herself as Orlena Scoville. She said she was a Connecticut native, was now an expat residing in Portugal, and that she had overheard Martha. Scoville was very curious to know why a pair of Yankees were in Lisbon, heading for France. "Everybody else is going in the opposite direction," she said. "Why do you want to drive to France?"

There was a long and a short answer to that question. The Sharps settled on a brief personal history and then explained about the milk program. Scoville listened attentively, then said, "I'd like to help you."

She rose, walked over to a door marked "Private," and knocked. To the secretary who answered she explained, in Portuguese, that she'd like to introduce two American friends to the director. He soon appeared—"all smiles," Martha remembered him—and invited the three of them into his office. There, Scoville introduced the Sharps and explained that they needed driver's licenses for an upcoming trip to France. A secretary was summoned to bring the necessary forms, and it was arranged for them to take their driving tests at four that afternoon.

In a single gesture, Orlena Scoville had lopped hours of frustrating idleness off Waitstill and Martha's day. She told them that she wanted to do much more. A dinner date was agreed upon for the following evening. Scoville's car would come at about five, early enough for them to enjoy the lovely fifteen-mile drive to her *quinta*, or estate, near the village of Azeitao, in full daylight. "I want to discuss your work thoroughly," she said. "I believe there are ways I can help."

Lisbon's tumultuous traffic made Martha's road test an adventure. "I was so unnerved when I got my turn behind the wheel that I couldn't seem to remember anything," she later wrote. "The inspector spoke neither French nor English and simply gestured what he wanted me to do. Watching his directions, the weaving cars, the jay-walking pedestrians, translating the signs from Portuguese and the fear of failure made me break out in a cold sweat. I did everything wrong. The Matford stalled several times in a line of traffic when I had to jam on the brakes to avoid a collision. I drove the wrong way down a one-way street. All the cars blew their horns and the pedestrians gestured that I must be crazy. When the ordeal was over, I knew I had flunked."

Through it all, her instructor had remained calm and patient, a remarkable feat of self-control. Even more amazing to Martha, when they returned to the Royal Automobile Club, the friendly director was waiting with her brand-new international driver's license, all filled out and official, signed and stamped, with her photo affixed. There was never a chance that Madame Scoville's friends would not receive their licenses. The test simply was a formality.

CHAPTER THIRTEEN

Helping Hands

The following afternoon, Scoville's driver came for the Sharps at five as planned. Martha was charmed by the drive out to Azeitao, down dirt roads, past farms and vineyards. The Scoville estate was visible from quite a distance, "great walls with Portuguese-type round towers," as Martha described it, "convoluted like enormous, upside-down water lilies at the corners."

The driver finally reached the *quinta* and turned into an imposing entrance, framed with imposing wrought iron gates. He swept the car around an oval planting and stopped at an enormous, hand-carved entrance door. A liveried servant dressed in the ubiquitous Portuguese striped vest appeared and gestured for us to enter a magnificent hall. Orlena came forward to welcome us.

She led us up to the main salon, a great vaulted room, where another servant in livery took our wraps. Then she took us outside through French doors to an enormous covered veranda. An enormous tiled design of four great rivers gushing from huge urns in the arms of giant goddesses covered the two walls. The open side of the veranda faced terraced gardens with formal flower beds and groves of orange and lemon trees that seemed to stretch forever.

At the far end, about a quarter-mile away, was a huge swimming pool and bathhouse that faced the *quinta*. Orlena was pleased by our astonished delight. When she offered to take us down for a closer inspection we agreed enthusiastically. Down through the sweet-smelling citrus groves we went through the dusk to the bathhouse, where we examined still more tile art. Each room featured illustrated stories from the Bible! Then we returned as the lights came on inside the great house to have drinks and appetizers on the veranda as the setting sun bathed the terraces in a rosy glow.

The sumptuous dinner that followed turned out to be one of the few substantial meals Martha would enjoy for the next four months, when she would lose twenty-five pounds. As a parting gift, Scoville gave the Sharps twenty thousand French francs and several liters of gasoline for their trip to France.

———— · ————

It was now July. With the Matford's *carnet de passage* due to expire on July 17, the Sharps made plans to leave Lisbon no later than July 15. There was much to accomplish. As word got around Lisbon's refugee community that two American relief workers were in town they were besieged with pleas for help. As before in Prague, Waitstill and Martha began taking names and information.

Their food mission also expanded when Ambassador Amé-Leroy and Madame Amé-Leroy announced that they wished to sponsor a second train car, bound for the care of Madame Taillandier in Tarascon, carrying clothing for demobilized French soldiers, as well as food, including an abundant amount of very nutritious Portuguese sardines. They proposed that their car be attached to the Sharps' at least until they reached the French border.

As these preparations moved ahead, Malcolm Davis called to ask a personal favor. Davis said his friends, Ferdinand Rieser, former director of the famous Schauspielhaus theater in Zurich, and his wife, Marianne, whose brother was the Czech-born, antifascist writer Franz Werfel, were stuck in northern Portugal, unable to enter Lisbon without a confirmed hotel reservation. Since the Sharps seemed to have the right contacts, would they be on the lookout for a room for the Riesers?

A week later, Martha and Waitstill secured a reservation for the Riesers at the Metropole and learned in the process from Marianne Rieser that Franzie, as she called her brother, had gone underground somewhere in the south of France with his extraordinary wife, Alma, whom he had married in 1929. Beautiful, vivacious, and an accomplished musician and composer, Alma had been married to the composer Gustav Mahler and then to the architect Walter Gropius before marrying Werfel.

Werfel, a poet and playwright as well as a novelist, was best known in the United States for two plays, *The Goat Song* and *Juarez and Maximilian*, both of which were produced on Broadway. Because he was Jewish and an ardent enemy of the Reich, the Nazis had destroyed all but three of Werfel's works in the infamous book-burning of 1933. He and Alma had subsequently fled the *Anschluss* in his adopted city, Vienna, for Paris, where he'd suffered a heart attack.

From Paris, Franz and Alma had made their way to the south of France. They had lived since 1938 in Sanary-sur-Mer, a haven for anti-Nazi artists and thinkers, about thirty miles from Marseille. His sister said that Werfel recently had been unreachable, and she was worried. She reported that her brother had not answered multiple telegrams from producers in the United States eager to stage what was then his best-known novel, *The 40 Days of Musa Dagh.*

The Riesers finally received word from the Werfels a few days later. Marianne learned from Franzie that with the fall of Paris to the Germans on June 14, he and Alma had decided to flee through Spain for Portugal and ultimately the United States. They made it as far as Hendaye, France, on the Spanish border before being forced back. As they fled, Franz Werfel lost most of his manuscripts, some that were originals of which he had no copies. He would only ever recover a few of them.

Franzie and Alma now were hiding in the shrine city of Lourdes, not far from Pau, inexplicably living under the name of Mahler.

"Marianne made me promise to look for them," Martha remembered. "We gave her the Lowries' address to use until we knew where we were going to be. She said, 'Franzie is so impractical! He can write great books, but he can't even get on a train without someone boosting him from behind. Please, Martha, *boost!*'"

———— · ————

All portents for the milk mission to France were positive until just before Martha and Waitstill's departure, when they received a wire from Robert Dexter:

CABLING FIVE THOUSAND, CABLE IMMEDIATELY AS-SURANCES MILK WILL REACH STARVING CHILDREN STOP WITHHOLD FURTHER COMMITMENT PENDING ADVICE WHY NOT RED CROSS RESPONSIBILITY.

Then came a second cable from Dexter.

ADVISED AMCROSS LANDING FIFTEEN THOUSAND CASES MILK MARSEILLE SUNDAY COMMITTEE SENDING NO ADDITIONAL MILK RECOMMENDS NO FURTHER MASS FEEDING OR GENERAL RELIEF FRANCE SUGGESTS DESIRABILITY DEVOTE EFFORTS EVACUATING WHERE POSSIBLE THOSE IN DANGER. ROBERT DEXTER.

The cables were a shock. Waitstill and Martha were assured when they left for Lisbon that they were free to choose their commitments as conditions dictated, just as they had after the Einmarsch in Prague. That Bob Dexter had authored this repudiation of their judgment was particularly hurtful.

Dexter was an old friend and influential Unitarian who had pushed hard for both the creation of the USC and the Sharps' designation as its first commissioners. Where was his loyalty and support now?

The rebuff did not stop them from carrying on. At six on Sunday morning, July 14—Bastille Day—they pointed the Matford north for France, via Spain. They loaded it with several liters of gasoline in jerry cans, courtesy of Orlena Scoville, as well as packages for internees in the camps and rounds of cheese that Scoville hoped they could share with the children of France.

They lashed a one hundred fifty-pound bag of sugar to the roof. On either side of the car flew makeshift cotton flags, Old Glory and the French Red Cross ensign. Martha and Waitstill also carried identification as certified representatives of the French Red Cross, into which Ambassador Amé-Leroy had inducted them.

The first day on the road was carefree. The car performed smoothly, and they enjoyed the verdant Portuguese countryside as would any pair of tourists. They crossed into Spain the next morning and proceeded again without incident until they passed through Avila, where they saw the first signs of destruction from the recently ended Spanish Civil War. "However," Martha noted, "this did not prepare us for the devastation to come."

As they headed on toward Madrid, Martha remembered,

We passed piles of bricks, masonry and rubble, obviously the remains of houses, blown up or shelled, surrounded by outbuildings and trees that were scarred and broken. The road was filled with so many holes that navigation was difficult. As we topped the crest, we saw what must have been a string of pillboxes which had been blasted into twisted steel and concrete.

Now we found every dwelling or shack on either side of the road had been blown up. Nothing moved, not even chickens or goats, all the way to the horizon. There were only vultures, flying and swooping overhead, as we picked our way down the mountainside.

At the base of the Guadarrama Mountains we drove through San Lorenzo de El Escorial, where seven or eight thousand people once lived. It was now deserted, completely devastated, every home a shambles. Someone had erected a lean-to against the single standing wall in the village. We thought we saw eyes as we passed. It was like driving through a skull.

The car developed a troubling motor noise on the afternoon of the second day. When they reached Madrid, the Sharps stopped at an old office building that had been turned into a pension, or boardinghouse, and asked about a room, as well as directions to the closest Ford dealership.

"The owner offered to reserve us a room only if we could pay in pesos," Martha recalled. "He drew a map to the nearby Ford agency which we were able to follow. Most of Madrid's squares had been renamed for civil war heroes or battles, and some streets were impassable. But we actually found a Ford sign on a half-demolished building and, miracle of miracles, a mechanic who not only could diagnose the Matford's problem, but also was able to produce the part with which to fix it! Perhaps there weren't so many Fords being fixed just then. But we were in luck."

Since the car wouldn't be ready for a couple of hours, the Sharps took a taxi back to their pension. They paid the cab driver in cash. Their change came in the form of scrip, supposedly applicable to their next taxi ride.

The bill of fare was limited that night. The pension owner said he could make them an omelet with bootlegged eggs, "since you are special friends." Butter, he told them, was four dollars per pound. Tea was not available, but he had some bootleg coffee. Martha found a piece of hair in the black bread. "They're sweeping the floors of the granaries now," he shrugged.

After paying in cash for the meal, the room, and a parking space on the street in front of the café, Waitstill and Martha cabbed back to the Ford agency to retrieve the Matford.

They settled up with the mechanic, filled the Matford's tank at five dollars per liter, accepted another handful of scrip in change—everything was redeemable at the border, they were assured—and headed back for the pension for a night's sleep against another tough day on the road.

Next morning, the mountainous leg from Madrid to the ancient Catalonian city of Lerida brought them face-to-face with more misery. "We were so occupied with seeing everything and watching the road that we hardly realized we had crossed four mountain ranges that same day, many of them mist-clad," Martha wrote. "We even tied our raincoats over the bag of sugar to prevent it from melting. But we could never forget the sight of people living in caves in abject poverty and children foraging for food in refuse piles and cans like animals. Only in the big cities did we see people able to forget the daily horrors and think of something beyond their human suffering. The frightened peasants without seed, tools, work, homes or hope were a nightmare for us."

The final push to beat the clock began early on July 17 in Lerida and took the Sharps through Barcelona, where they met briefly with the US consul general and picked up their messages, then north along Spain's Costa Brava to Portbou, where they would cross the frontier into southern France.

"It was like life after death," wrote Martha. "Behind us were the black mountains, red and white boulders, cold swirling winds[,] clouds and circling birds of prey. The sunlight and the incredible blues of the Mediterranean picked up our spirits. We might reach the frontier by nightfall we thought, then over the border where a dear friend and our French work waited!"

But there were serious, last-minute scares.

In addition to the papers being out of date, there were currency problems at Portbou. "The notations of exchange and our numerous paper slips didn't tally," she recalled, "and there were no refunds anyway. However, a very cooperative officer changed our remaining pesos into French francs and let us go."

They drove the short distance to the frontier only to encounter a barricade across the road. Dozens of people were milling around. When the Sharps asked what was going on, they were told that the frontier was closed. In fact, it had been closed for two weeks.

"We couldn't believe it! We drove on to the little house beside the barrier and spoke to the guard. 'The frontier is closed,' was all he'd say. 'Nobody may enter France.'"

When Waitstill inquired when the border would open, the guard shrugged. "Who knows?"

When they asked his best advice in the circumstance, the guard suggested they get a room, then turned and disappeared into the guardhouse.

The prospect of being stuck indefinitely in Portbou with their milk shipment who knows where was profoundly distressing, particularly since there seemed to be no way out of the predicament.

Then Martha's intuition for just how to finesse such moments kicked in. She'd first surprised herself with this talent when she had successfully slipped Mr. X past the Gestapo agents at the British embassy in Prague.

She remembered Don Lowrie saying a year before that logic ruled the French more than did the law. She was now ready to put Lowrie's theory to the test. She thought about the logic of children starving while the milk was on its way. Then she gathered the letters of introduction they'd received from various French officials in the United States. She explained to the soldier on duty that she and her husband had come to France to feed starving children; in fact, the milk they wanted to distribute might already be in the country, waiting for them. She asked if he'd take their documents to the commandant and explain to him why they needed to enter France at once. Obviously moved, thinking perhaps of his own children, the soldier took the papers and set off for a small house in a hill.

After ten or fifteen minutes, he returned with a uniformed officer. "Madame Sharp," the guard said, "I should like to present my commandant."

The commandant was all French gallantry. After bowing over Martha's hand, he asked about their "errand of mercy." After she explained, the commandant spoke: "Madame, your papers and letters from distinguished members of our Ministère des Affaires Étrangères are all void. They are dated before the armistice. Those who wrote them are no longer representatives of our country. Even your *carnet de passage* is no longer legal. But to me, as a father and a Frenchman, your desire to feed our starving children at the very earliest date is of the utmost importance. I agree it is essential that you are given every assistance to start your work as soon as possible. Therefore, I will personally take responsibility for speeding your way into France and a thousand blessings go with you."[1]

Lowrie's theory about French logic and, in this case, mercy trumping legalities proved true. Martha's beauty and disarming, dimpled smile might well have helped.

They drove the thirty miles to Cerbère, arriving there past midnight, grateful to be, at last, in France.

— CHAPTER FOURTEEN —

Reunion in Cerbère

Friday morning, July 19, 1940, began with breakfast with Don Lowrie at the Cerbère train station café. Then all three climbed into the little Matford for the drive north to Perpignan. There, Lowrie introduced Martha and Waitstill to the mayor, who favored them with a "*bon,*" or permission, to buy gasoline, which was strictly rationed. Then on to Nîmes that same afternoon to see the two-thousand-year-old Roman temple, the Maison Carrée.

The next day Waitstill, Martha, and Lowrie drove on to Marseille and took rooms at the Terminus Hotel, directly adjacent to the Gare de Marseille Saint-Charles, the city's huge old train station, which soon would figure large in their lives. They also made an appointment for Monday to see Richard Allen, local head of the American Red Cross.

Marseille challenged Waitstill's sturdy New England rectitude. It was, he pronounced, "one of the most dangerous and picturesque great cities in the world," whose old main street, the Canebière, was "the stamping ground of drug-pushers, swindlers, prostitutes, gamblers, and men with commission to commit murder—a more diversified gamut of criminals than any other city of the world." As he also noted, it was the center in France for people fleeing the Nazi juggernaut.[1]

The rest of the weekend was given over to relaxation. Although food shortages were critical and growing worse all over Vichy France, fish of all sorts were still abundant in Marseille. "Vendors sold a har-vest of the Mediterranean catch in stalls along the waterfront," Mar-tha wrote, "shrimp, oysters and other fish that were strange to us. Don suggested we go to the world-famous Pascal's for bouillabaisse. Afterward, we walked back to the hotel. All of a sudden, all of the lights went out—our first blackout. With Don's expert guidance we found our way to the Terminus, and with the aid of candles gratefully went to bed."

Richard Allen was another acquaintance from Paris in the sum-mer of 1939, not a good friend but a respected colleague with whom the Sharps enjoyed cordial relations. It was therefore a surprise for Waitstill to find the Red Cross man stiff and distant at their meeting that Monday, July 22. They'd known one another by their first names in Paris. Now it was "Mr. Sharp" whenever Allen addressed his old acquaintance.

"I inquired of myself, *What is wrong?*" Waitstill remembered. "I am not the most sensitive person in the world. But I can discern, I believe, a certain frigidity in the atmosphere."

Allen evidently registered Waitstill's unease. "All right," he said at length. "Mr. Sharp, you might as well know what has happened." Producing a folder, he said, "I have to tell you, sir—I have no choice—that something has happened that bears upon your work here and particularly bears upon any requests that you would make of me."

With that, Allen pushed across his desk a letter written on fa-miliar AUA stationery and carrying at its bottom Robert Dexter's equally familiar signature. According to Waitstill's memory, the let-ter read: "This is to inform you that Mr. and Mrs. Waitstill Sharp are shortly arriving, if their plans hold up, in Marseille, as the newly-chosen representatives of the Unitarian Service Committee. I must say to you that they come without any approval from me. In fact, I actively disapproved of their candidacy for this post and their selection to do this work. I regret conveying this word to you, but I have no choice."

Waitstill's characterization of the letter, which has been lost, might have been too harsh. Dexter had wired the milk money, albeit with misgivings. Although the United States was not yet in the war, Robert Dexter was. An ardent Anglophile, he unequivocally supported the British sea blockade of Germany and the occupied areas as necessary to defeat the Nazis. Denying the Nazis products or materials they might exploit in their war effort was a point of principle.

Whatever Dexter intended to accomplish with his letter, its effect was to stoke Waitstill's angry astonishment, precipitating a permanent estrangement. "I have never been more amazed," Waitstill said almost forty years later, "and I have seen some amazing turns of events. Nor have I ever, at age seventy-six, encountered any denouement like this."

He kept his remarks brief that day in Allen's office, explaining that he and Martha had been told by none other than AUA president Dr. Eliot himself that it was their moral obligation to come to France. He would otherwise keep his own counsel until he next met up with Dr. Dexter. "I am not going to let this matter rest here," he said. "You can be assured of that."

And he did not. In at least two lengthy written reports to Dexter, Waitstill explained the rationale behind the milk delivery, reminding his colleague that he and Martha were sanctioned to do what they deemed best in whatever circumstances they might encounter.

In their official joint report to the AUA, the Sharps also made it a point not just to justify the milk delivery but also to celebrate it. They emphasized not only the project's success but also its key importance in establishing their credentials with skeptical French officials, whose vital help included precious and scarce supplies of gasoline. The French officials' trust, they wrote, would have been "absolutely impossible to gain if we had announced ourselves as interested only in the rescue of distinguished refugee intellectuals."[2]

Waitstill told Allen he would gladly answer any questions he had about the matter. "I agree with you that it appears incredible," Allen answered. "Now each of us can do his best for our common cause, the relief of need and suffering in unoccupied France."

Hugh Fullerton, the US consul general in Marseille, mentioned at his meeting with the Sharps the next day that he too had heard from

Dexter. Fullerton, whose previous posting had been Paris, where he also had been among Waitstill and Martha's network of friends and contacts, knew their work in detail. More important, Fullerton realized from personal experience how urgently needed their milk program was, especially in view of the Red Cross's distribution problems. Fullerton was prepared to extend any help he could.

Over the next few days, the Sharps' relationship with Richard Allen warmed considerably. "Keep in touch," he told them, "and when you come to the end of your milk shipment I'll be glad to try to help you get more milk from the International Red Cross." Allen also issued them both an *ordre de mission* on Red Cross stationery, a useful document to establishment credibility with wary French officials as well as to gain priority access to gasoline.

With the matter of the milk delivery settled, Waitstill and Martha turned their attention to the welfare of Czech refugees. Don Lowrie introduced them to Vladimir Vochoc. A onetime college professor and former chief of the Czech foreign service's personnel division, Vochoc had been his country's consul in Marseille at the time of the Einmarsch. Since then, the ex-diplomat and academic had wittily restyled himself consul of "Czechoslovakia in liquidation," and in that capacity happily issued precious Czech passports to any and all enemies of the Reich.

They weren't legal, of course, but they usually worked, and they saved an untold number of lives. When his supply of blanks from Prague ran out, Vochoc had his own passports printed in Bordeaux, in the Occupied Zone.

Of immediate concern to Vochoc—and Don Lowrie, who was local delegate for the American Friends of Czechoslovakia—was a group of about a thousand Czech soldiers and their families, at that moment encamped at Agde, on the Mediterranean coast near Perpignan. When the Nazis had taken Czechoslovakia, these men had all joined the French army. After Paris fell, they were led south by their general, Sergej Ingr, who later became minister of defense of the Czech government in exile in London. Ingr hoped to put them on ships to North Africa, where they might regroup and join the Allied

Portrait of Waitstill Sharp, 1936.

Waitstill and Martha Sharp standing in the doorway of Hotel Pariz in Prague, Czechoslovakia, 1939.

A photograph from Martha Sharp's collection showing children escaping on a Kindertransport organized by Trevor Chadwick, March 14, 1939.

American ambassador Lawrence A. Steinhardt (left) addressing audience in Prague on March 9, 1939, inaugurating the child-feeding program of American Relief for Czechoslovakia. Waitstill Sharp is third to the right of Ambassador Steinhardt.

Martha Sharp presents a trainload of powdered milk to the mayor of Pau, France, 1940.

Martha Sharp and a group of twenty-seven children before their journey from France to New York City, 1940.

A woman believed to be Martha Sharp (middle) in a nursery in Pau, France, during the Milk Distribution Project run by the Unitarian Service Committee, 1940.

Portrait of Martha Sharp from her congressional campaign, 1944.

From left: Martha Sharp, Hastings Sharp, Waitstill Sharp, and Martha Content Sharp, 1944.

Martha Sharp during her congressional campaign, 1944.

armies. It was critical to evacuate the Czechs. The Nazis considered them deserters, a crime for which the penalty was execution.

In the meantime, the refugee Czechs' predicament was exacerbated by new, anti-immigrant laws from Vichy that made proof of French birth a requirement for obtaining a work permit. Not even naturalized citizens could legally obtain the vital documents.

Waitstill, Martha, and Lowrie visited the Czech camp at Agde with Vladimir Vochoc on July 25. Martha, who had been given a small amount of discretionary funds by AmRelCzech, found that some of the men's relatives were staying near the camp. One was Anna Pollakova, trained and experienced as an interpreter and a secretary, who appeared in rags. She told Martha that her brother, a Czech soldier, had escaped to join the British army. Pollakova was down to her last thousand francs, about twenty dollars. Fortunately, she had an address for her brother in Great Britain. Martha agreed to wire him and also arranged for the woman to go to work in Vochoc's office. AmRelCzech would subsidize her salary.

Ella Adler, whom Martha found in a hospital, also had a brother, named Ladislav, fighting with the British. She was nearly penniless and had been so distraught that she'd slit her wrists. Martha paid her hospital bill and arranged a weekly stipend for her after her release. She also offered to cover Adler's fare to England, if it were possible for her to reunite with her brother. If not, Vochoc promised to find her useful, remunerative employment of some sort.

"There were many variations of these cases," Martha wrote.

Most of them could be helped temporarily by a small sum of money and some time spent assisting them with their problems.

Elizabeth Steiner came to me in happy despair. Her husband had just been demobilized. His only clothing was a pair of army pants—not even a shirt to his name! Yet they'd just learned that they both had been granted U.S. visas. Their relatives in Chicago, according to letters they showed us, promised to pay all their expenses for the trip, as well as give them a place to stay until Mr. Steiner found work.

The Steiners' only problem is that they had no money whatso-ever; none for food or clothes or even to get to Marseille to pick up their visas, much less pay for steamship tickets to the U.S.

We joyously gave Mrs. Steiner the money to cover everything. They agreed to return the sum to Vladimir Vochoc when they reached their family in Chicago, thus allowing him to use the money to help another family in need.

In another instance, Martha remembered, "Just before leaving the camp I stopped to talk to a woman carrying her infant child in her arms. The baby was sickly yellow, the mother emaciated. When I asked her what was wrong with the baby, she burst into tears and said, 'I can't nurse her! I have no milk. I have no money to buy food for her. We live on scraps from garbage and my husband is lost somewhere in France. My baby is dying in my arms!' I took mother and child to the army hospital, arranged for medical care and a regular stipend for food and clothing and rent. I also took her husband's name, and would give it to Don and Vladimir, to see if they could find him."

On July 27, Martha and Waitstill parted with Lowrie in Marseille and drove to Tarascon to see the aged Madame Saint-René Taillan-dier, where she awaited word of the Red Cross shipment to which the Amé-Leroys in Lisbon had entrusted her. "Madame's maid greeted us with the sad news that Madame was ill and could not see us in the salon," Martha remembered. "However, she would receive us in her bedroom."

No French queen at her levee could have been more elegant. This indomitable aristocrat, frail and elderly, wearing a lace boudoir cap over her white curls with matching peignoir, and supported by numerous lacy pillows, received us with great dignity. She held out her hand to be kissed. We bowed, introduced ourselves and felt as if we should be kneeling.

Formalities over, her first question was, "Where's my wagon?"

We gave her letters from the Amé-LeRoys, the bill of lading for "her" wagon and a list of its contents. As she read, tiny tears of joy welled up in her eyes. She looked up and explained to us how a simple pair of work pants would bring dignity to demobilized French soldiers, most of whom were still wearing their tattered old uniforms and blue armbands that denoted their demobilization. These old rags were demoralizing reminders that France had fallen in defeat.

We explained to Madame that the Red Cross car and our car, filled with milk for the babies of Unoccupied France, were attached and stuck somewhere in transit from Lisbon. Waitstill was headed back for Portugal the next day, and [he] would search for the cars on his way. Our question for her was once the cars finally were released, where did Madame wish hers sent?

"Montpellier!" she answered vigorously, then added that the Sharps should advise a Colonel Cros of the French Red Cross in Montpellier of the shipment date. Waitstill agreed to do so and promised to wire her the moment he knew anything firm about arrival dates.

Before they left, the maid served coffee, which was brought on a silver tray with an antique silver pot, sugar bowl, creamer, and fine china, "worthy of a museum," Martha thought. After coffee, they rose, kissed her hand again, and bade her a speedy recovery.

Martha knew that Madame must have been saving both coffee and sugar for months. As she had so often before in Czechoslovakia and here in France, Martha marveled at the human ability to live "as usual" in the midst of chaos.

CHAPTER FIFTEEN

Dividing Forces

Waitstill departed for Lisbon from Perpignan on Monday, July 29, 1940. As they had in Czechoslovakia, he and Martha would divide their responsibilities. She continued onto Pau with Donald Lowrie to organize the milk distribution, while Waitstill returned to Lisbon to check on the progress of the milk train, begin the immigration work, and help get the Czech soldiers out of Agde.

"I miss you dreadfully already," Martha wrote him two days later. "It seems a shame to be separated when all these new things are happening, but I suppose it multiplies the family experience and is more efficient. With all my love to the dearest boy in the world, Martha."

Martha and Don Lowrie set out together in the Matford. Lowrie didn't drive, so with Martha at the wheel they headed for the Lowries' apartment at 2 Rue Darrichon in Pau. Ordinarily a community of about forty thousand, Pau had swollen to twice that population or more with refugees and demobilized soldiers. Accommodations at the Lowries' apartment were cramped. During the day, all four rooms were used as offices. At night, Don and Helen shared the premises with Irina Okunieff, his secretary, who also had fled Paris, plus Irina's husband, Alexis; their son, Nicholas; and Irina's mother, Madame Stepanova. To Martha's deep delight and gratitude, the Lowries found her a room of her own, with a bath, nearby.

Helen Lowrie happily surprised her by volunteering to help with the complicated work of figuring out how many babies there were to feed and how best to get the milk to them. She would prove an able and amiable compatriot for the next four months and an important part of the USC enterprise.

The necessary first steps were to visit the surrounding towns and villages of the Basses-Pyrenees in the Lowries' Peugeot. Martha and Helen Lowrie met and conferred with local officials, as well as medical and health workers, especially midwives. Now that most doctors and nurses were away at war, midwives were often the only locals with any medical training at all.

Word of the mission spread quickly. In the village of Lembeye, the women were greeted by the town crier, who played a flute, banged on a drum, and loudly announced the arrival of the American "Humanitarian Service Committee." Martha decided not to correct him. *It is not such a bad thing,* she thought, *for "Unitarian" and "humanitarian" to be confused.*

On one of those forays, Martha and Helen reached the town of Nay, about ten miles from Lourdes. Martha took advantage of its proximity to search for Franz and Alma Werfel, as she had promised Werfel's sister, Marianne Rieser, she would.

The Werfels indeed were in Lourdes, famous for a series of miraculous apparitions of the Virgin Mary in 1858. The Virgin is said to have appeared fully eighteen times at a local grotto before a fourteen-year-old French girl named Bernadette Soubirous, who reported that Mary spoke to her. The site became one of Christendom's most popular pilgrimages. Waters from the grotto are believed to have supernatural healing powers.

"I was quite surprised to see Franz Werfel," Martha said. The nervous, disoriented Werfel, forty-nine, was "a short plump man with sort of a lot of wild grey hair," she recalled. "He was wearing a sweater, and his pockets were stuffed with telegrams."

Martha asked, "Why didn't you answer all those telegrams?"

"I couldn't decide what I should do," Werfel replied.

Martha found Frau Werfel, sixty, to be "an ample perky blonde" with an extraordinary thirst for crème de menthe, as well as another cordial, Benedictine, which she consumed from huge containers called carboys.

The Werfels registered at their Lourdes hotel as Herr and Frau Gustav Mahler, an odd choice if their intent was to avoid attention. Martha explained to Werfel that he and Alma needed to go to Marseille, where she would try to get them visas. Martha thought that he seemed confused; she wasn't sure he was taking anything in.

Then Werfel turned to her and asked, "Have you seen the grotto?" No, she hadn't.

"Come, I'll show it to you." he said.

> So we walked out arm in arm. Mrs. Werfel and Helen followed us, and we walked down to see the grotto, the place where Bernadette had her vision. Hanging around the statue of the Virgin were little arms and legs made of gold or silver, according to the wealth of the person who'd received the miraculous healing power of the Virgin.

Werfel recounted Bernadette's story to Martha, then purchased for her a cupful of grotto water from a nearby vendor.

> "Drink and anything that's wrong with you will be cured," he said.
>
> I went over every part of my body. I couldn't think of anything that was wrong, but I drank the water. I never tasted anything so terrible in my life. Then we watched people being brought before the statue of the Virgin in the grotto, on stretchers and in wheelchairs, all of them praying with the most amazing expression of faith and hope. Others were crawling on their knees at the steps of the church, hoping and praying for the indulgence of the Lady for them, and the cessation of their illness.
>
> I then looked at Werfel's face and I realized that he believed. I knew he was Jewish. "You believe this really happened, don't you?" I asked.
>
> "Oh, of course," he answered. "I believe in miracles, don't you?"

In less than two years, Werfel was to become well known in the United States for his book on the miracle at Lourdes, *Song of Bernadette*, which became a popular film the following year. In the preface he wrote, "I vowed that if I escaped from this desperate situation and reached the saving shores of America, I would put off all other tasks and sing, as best I could, the song of Bernadette." He sent Martha a signed copy of the first edition.

—— CHAPTER SIXTEEN ——

The Emergency
Rescue Committee

As Martha continued preparations for distributing the shipment of milk, Waitstill made two stops on his way back to Lisbon, meeting with US and British military attachés in Barcelona and Madrid to share some ideas that he and Don Lowrie had worked out with Vohoc for rescuing the Czech troops at Agde. The soldiers had been slipping out in small groups on French fishing boats to Spain, from where they had to find their way to Portugal and then Britain. Some had escaped by foot over the Pyrenees. To exfiltrate them in greater numbers, Lowrie had proposed two plans. The first would be to commission about a dozen French fishing boats that would each take twenty men to meet up with a British destroyer. The second, more ambitious plan would put six hundred soldiers on a Yugoslav ship, then in the harbor at Marseille, for transport to North Africa. Because Yugoslavia was neutral at that time, the Czechs could reasonably expect that the inspection of a ship from a neutral country would be perfunctory. The harbor inspectors agreed to the deal provided Lowrie could get authorization from Vichy. After weeks of negotiation, he was able to get authorization, but within hours of the ship's planned departure, the Petain government changed the rules. Henceforth, ships leaving Mediterranean ports would have to be inspected by French, German, and Italian officials.

While the trickle of escapes continued—about four hundred of the soldiers eventually made their way out—a significant number of the rest melted into the surrounding countryside to work abandoned farms. Some of them trained members of the French resistance in the use of firearms.[1] It is not known how many survived the war.

As he retraced the milk shipment's route from Lisbon, Waitstill discovered that the two railroad cars had been halted at the Portuguese-Spanish border because the shipment Madame Amé-LeRoy had facilitated lacked a full and detailed manifest, as the law demanded. Back in Lisbon, when (with not a small amount of annoyance) he gave the news to the embarrassed woman, she immediately set about correcting that oversight.

——— · ———

It was time to set up the Unitarian Service Committee refugee office, and after three weeks away, Waitstill found a mountain of cable traffic awaiting his attention. A selection of the messages from individuals and organizations such as the USC, AmRelCzech, and the Joint Distribution Committee suggests the breadth of problems and issues that the would-be émigrés faced and aid workers such as Waitstill tried to solve:

KINDLY LOOK FOR LOTTE BRAUN WITH SON
EIGHT YEAR.

UNITARIAN SERVICE COMMITTEE REQUEST DELIVERY
FIFTY DOLLARS GEORGE POPPER PALAIS DU FOIRE
LYON OR AMERICAN CONSUL LYON AND ARRANGE
TRANSIT LISBON AFFIDAVITS SECURED QUOTA
NUMBER UP.

WATCH FOR OTTO BOSTROM SWEDISH PASSPORT
FURTHER INFORMATION FOLLOWS DEXTER.

To help with the ever-increasing paperwork, Waitstill hired Ninon Tallon, an actress and a refugee from the south of France. She was the niece of Édouard Herriot, leader of France's Radical Party, who served three terms as France's prime minister. Waitstill found her efficient and intelligent.

In the pile of correspondence was a wire from Marion Niles, their friend and a member of the church in Wellesley Hills who was writing to inform them that Martha Content had developed a bad strep infection. Dr. Lyman Richards, the family physician, recommended that Martha Content's tonsils be removed at once. Waitstill cabled back authorization for Richards to immediately perform the procedure and sent a copy of the correspondence on to Martha. In truth, their daughter also had contracted pneumonia and was in far more serious condition than Waitstill knew. What he did know, however, was that her condition was further indication that a potential war zone was no place for a couple with responsibility for young children. As he later wrote to Frederick May Eliot, only childless people should be considered for future overseas work.

There was, as well, a note from Frank Kingdon, president of the University of Newark. It would profoundly impact Waitstill's work. Kingdon was executive director of the newly organized Emergency Rescue Committee (ERC). Formed at a June 1940 meeting in New York City's Commodore Hotel just after the French capitulated to Germany, the ERC proposed to rescue anti-Nazi artists, writers, and political and labor leaders who were trapped in unoccupied France. Erika Mann, daughter of novelist Thomas Mann and wife of poet W. H. Auden, was a founding member. ERC's sponsors included distinguished public figures such as journalist Dorothy Thompson, writer Elmer Davis, *Commonweal* editor George Shuster, and three college presidents besides Kingdon.

The committee's first steps were to solicit names of the imperiled in southern France and then compile dossiers that included identifying information, such as occupation, place of origin, and, most important, the individual's last known address in France. This effort had the strong support of Eleanor Roosevelt, Interior Secretary Ickes, and others in the Roosevelt administration.

Unfortunately, all visa applications for potential rescues required approval of the anti-Semitic, xenophobic Breckinridge Long, an assistant secretary of state whose self-appointed task was to keep Jews and anyone who might, because of nationality, be a Nazi spy or sympathizer, out of the United States.

Kingdon, with whom Martha and Waitstill were acquainted, informed Waitstill that the ERC's new representative, thirty-two-year-old Varian Fry, would arrive in Lisbon from the United States on August 6 and that the ERC would appreciate any assistance Waitstill could extend him since Fry had no experience in relief work.

———— · ————

Fresh off the Pan Am Clipper from New York, with a list of two hundred people who, Breckinridge Long notwithstanding, had been given emergency visitors' visas, Fry was much in need of mentoring by seasoned veterans of the work, which would have included members of the Joint Distribution Committee, the Quakers, and HICEM, a Jewish refugee aid organization.

As Waitstill explained in a letter, "For three days I tried to teach Fry the fundamentals of finding people in hiding without exposing them, and how important it was for a refugee worker to keep a low profile. I tried to help Fry work out a plan to find and help each of his intellectuals to escape. I also gave him introductions to Richard Allen, Hugh Fullerton and Don Lowrie."

Waitstill told Fry of the milk shipment for the children of Pau.

"Sharp asked me to follow it up, and I agreed," Fry later wrote. "He gave me letters to the shipping and forwarding agents all along the line and a card making me a delegate *pro tem* of the Unitarian Service Committee. I was glad to get those credentials: they promised to be useful camouflage to my real activities, more useful by far than my other letters."[2]

In addition, Waitstill taught Fry about Spanish and French money regulations and the intricacies of moving cash across international borders. In Spain, Fry would have to declare every cent of foreign exchange that he took into the country and account for it all when he left. It would all be written down in his passport. If he left the country with more foreign exchange than when he had entered, he'd be arrested at the frontier.

The French, Waitstill advised, would confiscate Fry's money at the border, then reimburse him several weeks later with francs pegged artificially high at forty-three and a half to the dollar. The only solution was to ask the French chargé d'affaires in Lisbon for special permission to take his money into France for relief work.

"I sat up all night that night writing my last reports to New York and making a list of harmless pseudonyms for every one of the refugees on my long list," Fry wrote. "I left one copy under Sharp's door and mailed another to New York. The third I folded in a tight wad and put in the little front pocket under the belt of my trousers. Now I could safely cable from France without letting the Gestapo know I was trying to save the men and women it was looking for."[3]

On August 20, 1940, five days after he first arrived in Marseille from Lisbon, Fry sent Waitstill a note on Hotel Splendide stationery. The hand-delivered message arrived five days later back in Lisbon. "Dear Sharp," it read, "I followed the milk through, and am glad to be able to tell you that it crossed the French frontier last week and ought by this time to have reached its destination. I telegraphed Mrs. Lowrie as soon as I was sure both wagons were over the border."

The rest of the typewritten letter reflects how quickly the two men had come to trust and rely upon one another. "We have had no news from you so far," Fry continued,

and so we have no information about developments in Lisbon. I have asked Mr. Aisenberg, who brings this letter, to speak to you about this. We are naturally all very eager to have news of our friends, for living in France today is rather like living on the moon.

I am also asking my people in New York to authorize you to give out relief funds to anyone on our lists who is in need there. Persons of Hebraic origin may of course be referred to HICEM and it is better that they should be, for our funds are very limited. But I am counting on you to take care of the others. I hope you will also keep New York informed by frequent letters, such as I wrote before I left Lisbon. I am also asking New York to get a man to Lisbon as quickly as possible; so that there will be someone to replace you when you have to leave.

Good luck. Give my warmest regards to the Riesers, and tell them that I hope their relatives will soon be with them. Yours most warmly, Varian Fry.

By the time Fry left Lisbon, his list of people to be rescued had swelled to perhaps as many as three thousand. With Waitstill—and then with the Rev. Charles Joy, who replaced the Sharps in August as his liaison in Lisbon—Fry would spend thirteen months directing a bold, high-risk, and much-celebrated refugee-smuggling operation in the south of France that included an all-star cast of Kulturträgers, among them artists Marc Chagall and Max Ernst, writer André Breton, and philosopher Hannah Arendt.

———— · ————

In early August, Waitstill also heard once more from Robert Dexter, who telegrammed that Ernest Swift, a US Red Cross official, had complained to him by letter that with the milk shipment the Unitarians were wandering onto Red Cross turf. "It seems to me and to Mr. Gano, with whom I talked after receiving this letter," Dexter went on, "that we must not tangle things up by going into relief, and particularly the sending of goods. You ought to be able to arrange to use Red Cross supplies or any others that are available, but we will get both you and ourselves in trouble if we attempt to ship goods. . . . I am sure that it was only because you saw the urgent need that you went into the relief business, but hope you can straighten things out with the Red Cross, and that we won't have to do it again. Also, I do not see any way by which we could ship much in the way of supplies without crippling our other work."

Waitstill wrote back in exasperation, reminding Dexter, "Martha and I came over on this commission with the clear understanding that we held a roving commission. Over and over it was said, 'We will back you in whatever you decide is the best course of action on the spot.' The general idea is that we began where the Red Cross left off, with services of a personal nature AND with the material relief which the Red Cross was unable to administer. AND THAT IS PRECISELY JUST WHAT WE HAVE DONE, if both you and Swift will let up on the anvil chorus long enough to learn the facts."

CHAPTER SEVENTEEN

The Milk Arrives

Martha spent the first weeks of August 1940 working in Pau and surrounding villages with Helen Lowrie to prepare for the arrival and distribution of the milk. The more time Martha spent among the French villagers, the more deeply she understood how acute their children's plight truly was. At the time, the local weekly milk ration was one-half liter per family, when available, no matter the number of children to be fed. Many of the refugee children received no milk at all.

Nor were their medical problems confined to malnutrition. In one clinic, she later recalled seeing "a boy with a shattered knee, a premature baby in an incubator and another child, found just the day before, abandoned. He was covered with eczema from head to foot." A case of typhoid was diagnosed in nearby Oloron during her visit.

Martha's conversation with Percival Brundage was never far from her mind. When she began to ask, informally, if French parents in the area would support the idea of sending their children to the United States for the duration, she was referred to Madame Hyacinthe Loyson, head of a Protestant women's auxiliary, who was herself a refugee in Montauban, north of Toulouse, along with a daughter and granddaughter.

Martha wrote Loyson of her interest in taking French children to America. On the morning of August 15, they met together over coffee. "She showed me the letter she had sent to all the French Protestant women leaders," Martha wrote. "I was surprised that she had broadcast what was a simple request on my part without sending me a copy. Fortunately, she had not included too many details. But when I saw the piles of replies, and read the queries of anxious parents she had received in response, I knew that giving United States hospitality to French children for the duration of the war was a vital and necessary program which many French parents felt would be a godsend."

Martha met later in the day with *pasteur* Marc Boegner, de facto leader of French Protestants, who worked tirelessly to rescue Jews, particularly Jewish children. The minister strongly urged Martha to take as many French children as possible to the United States.

"He was especially worried about the plight of some of his outspoken young ministers who had been arrested and imprisoned for preaching resistance," she remembered. "He asked me if I thought we could accept emigration for the children of these leaders fighting totalitarianism from the pulpit. Their emigration would free the children from persecution and potential starvation and would lessen their fathers' sense of guilt for their plight."

Martha left the meeting determined to push ahead with a children's emigration program. But with her long-range objectives now settled, she was increasingly alarmed about the present. Communications between Pau and Lisbon suddenly and mysteriously stopped cold. Day after day she wrote and cabled Waitstill and heard nothing in reply. He, meanwhile, was writing and cabling her as well, with the same results. Nothing was moving in either direction.

There were multiple causes. The Germans capriciously held up all outgoing mail from the Pau post office in order to destroy its time value to any potential foe. More generally, there was an unexplained weeklong interruption in cable traffic between France and Portugal. Not knowing any of this at the time, Waitstill glowered and seethed while Martha fell into a chronic state of panic that gradually deepened until August 18, when mail from Lisbon finally caught up with her in Toulouse. It was, she recalled, a bittersweet moment.

The first letter from Waitstill brought the first news of any kind from home, and so Martha at last learned how Martha Content had developed a badly infected throat requiring a tonsillectomy more than three weeks earlier. "My first impulse," she said, "was to leave France at once to reach my daughter's beside. I called the US consulate in Toulouse to get their advice on how long it would take to get visas for Spain and Portugal. They replied that visas were possible, but the French frontier again was indefinitely closed. Nobody could leave France.

"Then I read the date on my husband's letter. It had taken fourteen days to arrive! I thought, *Martha Content must already have had the operation. She* must *be better, or somehow I would know.*"

She cabled Waitstill at once, asking for news. She felt helpless and perhaps a bit guilty but comforted by the fact that the child was in good hands.

Three days later, the much-delayed milk shipment finally arrived in Pau.

"Thanks to American generosity, our babies will not lack milk!" announced *Le Patrie des Pyrenees,* largest of the local newspapers, in its August 23 edition. The paper described a grand ceremony in Pau presided over by the local prefect, or police chief, as well as the mayor and numerous other dignitaries. "In symbolic recognition of the participation of the mayor," *Le Patrie* reported, "Madame Sharp expressed in the purest French, and in a most eloquent manner, the profound feelings of affection that unite the great American people with the great people of France."

In all, the twelve tons of condensed milk and milk products that Martha and Waitstill brought to the lower Pyrenees would feed eight hundred babies and toddlers for about two months. Beer trucks were used to haul the precious cargo from the railhead to its various destinations.

Martha had sent a full description of the needs for milk that she and Helen had documented to Malcolm Davis in Geneva. In response, Davis said that the International Committee of the Red Cross (ICRC) was shipping seven more carloads of milk to southern France, and he indicated that more would come. Martha believed all her life that the children of the Basses Pyrenees received monthly deliveries of milk for the duration of World War II. Tragically, that was not the case. It is possible that there were sporadic shipments to the area, perhaps from supply ships like the *McKeesport*—at least until November 1942, when the unoccupied zone came under Nazi control. There is no evidence, however, of regular Red Cross deliveries. Records of the ICRC in Geneva paint a cruel and depressing picture of the relief situation. ICRC efforts to get supplies to starving civilian populations met the harsh resistance of the military on both sides. The ICRC shipped just over 280 tons of milk to all of France for the balance of 1940, Davis's seven carloads presumably among them, and four million liters of milk, total, over the next four years of fighting. The supply did not begin to meet the need.[2]

CHAPTER EIGHTEEN

Refugees' Odyssey

In Lisbon, Waitstill's world was about to become considerably more complex. As he later recounted, Erika Mann paid him a surprise visit one day with news that her uncle, Heinrich, sixty-nine, and her thirty-one-year-old brother, Gottfried, known as Golo, were hiding from the Nazis in the vicinity of Nice. Also with them, Erika said, was Nelly Kroeger, forty-one, Heinrich's longtime companion, whom he'd married the previous year. Nowhere in his surviving papers does Waitstill mention when he learned that Heinrich and Nelly in fact already had made their way from Nice to the Hotel Normandie in Marseille, and that Golo was hiding in the villa of Hiram (known as Harry) Bingham IV, the US vice consul in Marseille.

Though not a Jew, 1929 Nobel laureate Thomas Mann (*Buddenbrooks, Death in Venice, The Magic Mountain*) was as prominent as any of the literary Kulturträgers. The Thomas Mann Societies in Europe, such as the one J. B. Kozak chaired in Prague, led the intellectual resistance to Hitler. Mann's older brother, Heinrich, was also a leading antifascist. With the rise of Hitler, he fled first to Prague and then to Nice, with his new wife and nephew.

According to Waitstill, the meeting with Ericka Mann fundamentally reordered his priorities, yet at the same time he deeply yearned for home. When Dr. William Emerson, chairman of the Unitarian Service Committee, inquired whether he and Martha would consider extending their stay in Europe, Sharp declined emphatically. "We feel we must come home now," he wrote Emerson on August 16.

> Our little daughter was seriously ill this July with a streptococcus throat which will necessitate a tonsillectomy. She has never been a strong child and must have her mother's constant care during this coming winter.
>
> That rules Mrs. Sharp definitely out of a return to Europe. Before we parted she said that she was returning for good on September 19. Our son needs both of us for his guidance. And thirdly, there is my church at Wellesley Hills which I am most loath to leave at this time with my full service not rendered there so far. If this decision were coming before me at the end of say a ten-year pastorate, I might much more easily break the very happy pastoral connection than I am able now. Fourthly, I do not wish to live for a winter in Europe separated from my wife and children.

As sincere as Waitstill was in his determination to get home with Martha according to schedule, fortune was about to intervene.

The Werfels and the Manns presented a novel and complex set of challenges. All five were "hot," in Waitstill's term, and in clear peril of arrest and deportation to Nazi concentration camps if they weren't able to escape. Helping them also entailed major risks.

Then arose another complication in the person of the popular German Jewish novelist Lion Feuchtwanger, fifty-five, who in the summer of 1940 was at the top of the Gestapo's hit list. "Now, he's a Jew and anti-Nazi," noted Holocaust scholar Mordecai Paldiel, "so when the Germans entered France they really wanted to lay their hands on him so Feuchtwanger was quite in jeopardy."[1] He was, according to historian Deborah Dwork, on "a list of German-Jewish refugees they wanted to incarcerate. The clock was ticking."[2] In 1933, the Nazis had burned all available copies of Feuchtwanger's books. He had earned the Reich's undying enmity in February of that year with a speech at the Hotel Commodore—later birthplace of the ERC—where he satirically disparaged Hitler's prison manifesto, *Mein Kampf,* as a 140,000-word mess containing 140,000 mistakes. "To speak with absolute exactness," he told his audience, "the book contains 139,900 mistakes. For, in the earliest editions, there were about a hundred words which were quite correct both as to subject and form."[3]

A month later, storm troopers raided the writer's Berlin residence, ransacking the place. They stole documents and an unfinished manuscript, and even drove off with his car.[4]

The Feuchtwangers, like many of the Nazis' opponents, did not foresee how fast and far Fascism would spread. Instead of departing for the United States or Latin America and safety, they chose to join many like-minded friends, colleagues, and coreligionists in Sanary-sur-Mer in the south of France, where they expected to wait out the madness in Germany in safety. By the summer of 1940 it was clear that none of them had run far enough.

In 1939, panicky French officials rounded up thousands of stateless aliens, including Feuchtwanger, and sent them to detention camps. In his case, that was a derelict brickyard in the village of Les Mille, near Aix-en-Provence. Although the writer was quickly released with apologies from the government, which explained that there had been a mistake in his case, it was clear to Feuchtwanger that the French were at best deeply ambivalent toward prominent German antifascists. Anger and disappointment quickly shaded to dread, however, when without explanation he was refused an exit visa.

On April 9, 1940, Feuchtwanger learned from radio newscasts that the Germans had invaded Denmark and Norway. In May, after the Panzers rolled into the Netherlands, Luxembourg, Belgium, and France, he wrote, "I was alone, listening to the news reports. Things did not look good either in Belgium or in the Netherlands. . . . Suddenly, the following came: 'All German nationals . . . men and women alike, and all persons between the ages of seventeen and fifty-five who were born in Germany but are without German citizenship, are to report for internment.'"

On May 21, Feuchtwanger reentered the camp at Les Mille as prisoner No. 187. His wife, Marta, reported to the women's camp in Gurs.

The brickyard at Les Mille was "indescribably ugly," he wrote in *The Devil in France*, a memoir of 1940, comprising "two buildings surrounded by earthworks and brick walls inside a barbed wire fence on which the detainees, anywhere from one to three thousand men, customarily hung their wash."

The facility was crowded and filthy, was covered in brick dust, and stunk of excrement. By day, the men were required to haul the crumbling bricks around the open yard, stacking and restacking them to no purpose. At night, they slept on the second floor of the main building in a bare room lined with brick racks made of lathes. "We were given a little straw for our bedding," Feuchtwanger wrote, "and the rest was left to us. There were no chairs, no benches, no tables, nothing but piles of defective bricks. Out of these we tried to build seats and tables, but they would always fall apart."

Potable water was scarce (only a single faucet in the camp was safe to drink from), diseases such as dysentery were chronic, and not a few of the older detainees (some in their seventies) fairly quickly descended into various stages of dementia.

Feuchtwanger spent about a month at Les Mille, each day more dreadful than the previous one, as the Germans continued their push south. Unaware that the Nazis would momentarily halt at the Loire River, leaving the south of France unoccupied and under nominal Vichy control until November of 1942, he and all the rest of the antifascists in the camp expected advance units of the Wehrmacht to march into Les Mille, round them up, and either shoot them on the spot or ship them back to Germany for imprisonment and execution.

Walter Hasenclever, the German expressionist writer, finally broke under the strain. On Saturday, June 22, the day the German-French Armistice was signed—and two days after Martha and Waitstill first landed in Lisbon—Hasenclever apparently "took his own life with an overdose of the barbiturate Veronal so as not to fall into the hands of the Nazis" at Les Mille, just hours before a French freight train arrived at the camp to take internees who were at highest risk to an allegedly safer camp. After an interminable, "hideous, torturing trip," as Feuchtwanger described it, he and the others were deposited at their new home, "San Nicola," an abandoned farm near Nimes.

He was tempted to escape; getting away would be relatively easy. Yet the writer also knew that to be caught by the regular French police with no identification papers or travel passes meant an immediate and probably lengthy stay in a regular jail or prison, where the risks were even higher.

Marta meanwhile was all right, considering the rigors of camp life in Gurs, and had returned to their house in Sanary. She had slipped away from Gurs by creeping under a fence. She knew Lion had been moved, but had no idea where. By the middle of July, discreet inquiry finally led Marta to Lion at San Nicola, where she found him, racked by dysentery. She stayed with him for several days. In the meanwhile, a scheme to rescue them both was beginning to take shape.

It began with a photo of the haggard, ragged novelist, taken at Les Mille. Somehow the picture made its way to the New York editorial offices of Viking Press, where Ben Huebsch, Feuchtwanger's editor, knew precisely what to do. Working through intermediaries, Huebsch brought the picture to Eleanor Roosevelt's attention.

The next problem was to find Feuchtwanger.

Marta solved that difficulty. Desperate for help, she headed directly from San Nicola to Marseille and the consulate, where she spoke to Harry Bingham's colleague, Miles Standish, who had visited the Feuchtwangers in Sanary some months before.

Enlisting the aid of a Madame Lekisch, a regular visitor to the camp, where her husband, an Austrian physician, was interned, Standish arranged a rescue. Knowing Feuchtwanger's routine, Madame Lekisch was able to direct Standish to a swimming hole where the author regularly bathed. There she handed him a note in Marta's handwriting that said simply: "Ask nothing, say nothing, go with him." In a waiting car, Standish had a woman's overcoat and shawl and a pair of sunglasses, which Feuchtwanger put on. Disguised as an elderly woman, Feuchtwanger left the camp for the safety of Hiram Bingham's attic, where he and Marta would wait to take a journey out of France.

—— CHAPTER NINETEEN ——

Escape from Marseille

Waitstill explained in an August 27 "Dear Friends" letter to his parishioners that on September 1 he and Martha would attend a "final conference" in Carcassonne, about sixty miles southeast of Toulouse, where presumably the subject was relief schemes to assist the Czech soldiers still marooned in Agde. Also, he wrote, "Our Unitarian co-workers in Boston have been joined by Erika Mann (Mrs. W. H. Auden), the Belgian Minister and his wife, and by the former French Minister and his wife in asking us urgently to stay. . . . The inducement to stay and to have a hand in a movement of intellect as historic as that of 1848—this is very strong." Evidently, the Belgian minister and former ambassador Amé-Leroy were in on a rescue mission, hinted at in the letter.

Waitstill signed the letter for both himself and Martha, with whom he was reunited in Toulouse on August 29—"unexpectedly," as Martha put it in her datebook.

They had big news for each other. Waitstill told Martha about Erika Mann, the three Manns then hiding from the Nazis, and presumably something about the plans to rescue them, as well as the Werfels. At this point he was unaware of Lion Feuchtwanger. Martha for her part announced that her return to Wellesley Hills would have to be delayed because she had resolved to put together a transport of children at risk in Vichy France.

Waitstill did not try to dissuade her or question Martha's decision.

— · —

After spending another day in Toulouse, observing and participating in a local Quaker feeding program, Martha and Waitstill headed east along the Mediterranean coast for Marseille, stopping about halfway at Agde, where the Czech soldiers were billeted. The plan to get them out on the Yugoslav ship hadn't yet been mooted by the abrupt change in Vichy regulations.

In Marseille, on September 2, Martha met Varian Fry for the first time. The ERC representative already was committed to a September 8–18 expedition to locate Kulturträgers on his list, so Waitstill agreed to stand in at Fry's Marseille office, Secours Américain, in his absence.

As temporary head, Waitstill held interviews and tried to get necessary papers from local authorities, as well as from contacts overseas to whom he sent cables that he hoped would get through.[1] Martha and Waitstill met with Fry on September 8, probably to finalize the plans for getting the Manns, Werfels, and Feuchtwangers out of the country. Since the Feuchtwangers, Manns, and Werfels were all wanted by the Gestapo, they had no chance of securing legal exit visas. This meant that an illegal clandestine operation would be necessary. The group agreed that the single most important figure in such a scheme would be Leon (known as Dick) Ball.

Ball was exactly the right choice for such operations. An American who owned a pig farm and a lard factory in the south of France, he had formerly driven for the American Ambulance Corps, a volunteer group that helped evacuate French casualties during the military disasters of May. He also had assisted any number of British pilots to escape by boat out of the Old Port of Marseille and escorted others over the Pyrenees and across the Spanish border. Ball was now working with Varian Fry.

Waitstill remembered walking out onto the terrace of their room at the Terminus "and looking out by night at the twinkling lights of this magnificent harbor and the shadow of the Cathedral of Notre Dame de la Victoire standing on a promontory across a reach of water. And after what I hoped at least in Unitarian terms was prayerful consideration, I went back in and said to myself, 'Sharp, you can't take any more risks here than you did in Prague.'" And with that he flushed all his notes down the toilet, just as he and Martha had destroyed every shred of evidence the year before at the Hotel Atlantic in Prague.

Fry and Waitstill decided to split the group. Fry and Ball would take the Manns and Werfels. Ball would then return to Marseille to help Waitstill, if necessary, with the Feuchtwangers and three other émigrés. One of the three was the Reverend Blahoslav Hruby, a Czech Protestant minister who had worked with the French underground. Another was a lawyer, and the third possibly was the lawyer's wife.

Before Fry and Ball left with the first group, Waitstill had a run-in with the flamboyant Alma Werfel, whose legendary appeal was lost on him. He found her narcissistic, frivolous, and far too fond of alcohol. But it was the flowing outfit in which she had chosen to make her escape that crossed his line.

"Madame," Waitstill fumed, "this is an extremely taxing climb. Wear low shoes. Throw away that summer reception hat; it makes you appear as if you're heading for a Viennese garden party. And please come in some other dress than your all-white dress. And what *is* that white dog with the red leash?"

The lecture didn't make much of an impact. "I think she'd had an extra nip of Benedictine," he said, "which made her somewhat resistant to this life-saving counsel."

Dick Ball explained to the émigrés that they likely would have to trek over smuggling trails and that the journey would be both arduous and risky. French border guards were apt to pop up anywhere and were trained to shoot at anything suspicious. The comparatively underpaid Spanish sentries usually were amenable to bribes, plus many of them detested the Germans. Nonetheless, this would be no garden party.

The first group of protégés, as Fry and Waitstill sometimes called them, made the train trip from Marseille to Cerbère with no problems.

They arrived at 5 p.m., hoping that security would be lax enough for them to catch another train to Portbou in Spain. If all went well, they would be in Spain later that evening.

It was a vain hope. Police were everywhere. Without exit visas, the band of fugitives would not be allowed to travel farther.

Taking a chance that the officers on duty that night could be bribed or cajoled into waiving the regulations, Dick Ball took the passports to the police commissioner, who proved immovable. He said the group was welcome to spend the night in Cerbère, period.

Thus, lacking exit visas, the only way out was on foot over the mountains into Spain.

Ball led them in two groups, first the Werfels, then the Manns. Despite a heart condition, Franz Werfel made it. So did Alma, white dress billowing in the wind, visible for miles. The challenging climb was almost too much for portly Heinrich Mann, whom Ball, Golo, and even Nelly had to carry for most of the way.

Golo was traveling on an "affidavit in lieu of passport" that listed both his correct name and his ultimate destination, his father's house in Santa Monica. A curious Spanish guard looked over the document, then addressed him.

"So you are the son of Thomas Mann?" he asked.

"Yes," Golo replied, fearful that his personal journey to freedom was about to be aborted. "Does that displease you?"

"On the contrary," the Spaniard answered. "I am honored to make the acquaintance of the son of so great a man."[2]

———— · ————

Back in Marseille, Waitstill, with Lion and Marta Feuchtwanger and the three others, prepared for the journey. Frau Feuchtwanger later recalled that the first obstacle to boarding the train at the Gare St. Charles was the military guards who carefully scrutinized everyone's identification. Since neither she nor Lion carried the required travel permits or exit visas, Martha and Waitstill needed a plan to sneak them aboard.

The answer lay in a highly convenient architectural feature of the Terminus Hotel. The Sharps discovered that hotel guests could avoid a long trek with their luggage to the appointed track by the simple expedient of a small tunnel that led directly from the hotel to the trains.

Since Waitstill and Martha already were staying at the Terminus, they brought the Feuchtwangers to their room. At the appointed early-morning hour on September 18, 1940, they escorted them through the tunnel to board the 5:05 train to Cerbère without incident. The soldiers posted at the terminal gates never saw them. Marta remembered that her fashion-conscious friend Martha had convincingly disguised herself as a fisherwoman for the occasion.

Martha and Waitstill and Lion looked on as Marta boarded the train alone and took a seat at one end of the second-class car. Then Waitstill and Lion sat down together at the other end and enjoyed the lovely Mediterranean scenery as the train chugged southwest toward the Spanish border.

———— · ————

They were well on their way to Narbonne when a stranger approached Waitstill with the warning that just ahead government agents were waiting to search every passenger to see if they were *en regle*—literally, in order. Waitstill faced a serious dilemma. Was this man a friend or foe? Could it be a trap?

He decided to take the stranger at his word. Quietly, Waitstill moved through the train, speaking briefly to each of his five charges. "We have been reliably informed that this train is going to be stopped and searched at the next station south of Narbonne," he told them. "We must get off."

The émigrés responded brilliantly, casually disembarking and then moving in random order to a small monastery garden, planted with espalier trees and vines, where they patiently waited for the next Cerbère-bound train. Once in Cerbère, they checked into a hotel to rest overnight for the next day's climb.

In the meantime, Waitstill went on a six-mile excursion to Banyuls-sur-Mer, historically a major smuggling center, perched on the border between France and Spain. He had an appointment in the seaside town with Dr. Otto Meyerhof and his wife, Hedwig.

In 1922, Otto Meyerhof had won the Nobel Prize in Medicine for his work in muscle physiology and metabolism. With the help of the president of the Marseille Academy of Sciences, Meyerhof secured a position at a biology laboratory in Banyuls, hoping to position himself and Hedwig for an escape over the border into Spain. He then sought out Varian Fry. Although the Meyerhofs were not on the original ERC list, Fry was pleased to accommodate them.

Waitstill went over the details of the flight over the Pyrenees that the Meyerhofs would be taking with Dick Ball. Waitstill also took a collection of Meyerhof's papers which he successfully transported to a Professor Malinsky in London. The couple left Banyuls on October 4 with Ball and were soon on their way to Philadelphia where a professorship awaited the Nobel laureate at the University of Pennsylvania.

From Cerbère the next day, Lion and Marta started out on foot, passing through the village and past vineyards into the high country along the border. Waitstill went by train with their belongings to wait for them in Portbou.

"It was very hot," Marta remembered of the climb up and over into Spain. "But we both were used to mountain climbing, and it was no difficulty. The only thing we knew which was absolutely necessary was to find the customhouse. If you didn't and one of the border guards saw you, he would immediately shoot without asking."

The Feuchtwangers successfully crested the high hill—along the path Lion came across his picture on a wanted poster, which offered a hefty reward for his capture—and spotted the Spanish customhouse about fifty yards below. Since he had the superior identification, a US visa—Marta had only an old identification card—they decided that Lion should go first.

Marta couldn't see him actually enter the structure, but she did see her husband walking away "with a good pace."

She exhaled. He'd made it!

Harry Bingham had insisted that Marta bring a big supply of Camel cigarettes, and she soon had reason to thank him for his foresight. As she later recalled,

> I came into the customhouse and said, "I wanted to take these cigarettes with me to America, but I heard the customs are so high that it's not worthwhile. So I'd rather leave them here."
>
> I threw all those packages on the table, and they jumped on the cigarettes and didn't even look at me. They just gave me a stamp on my paper, which said Feuchtwanger, and just let me go. They didn't even open the door. I opened it myself. You know, I had never run down a mountain so fast!

Their ordeal wasn't over. Lion Feuchtwanger also was wanted in Spain. From Portbou, the three of them rode to Barcelona, where they arrived on a Sunday. Short of cash with which to book the next leg of the trip, to the Portuguese border, Waitstill found the US consul at home that day and secured sufficient funds for them to keep going.

He installed Lion in first class, where train guards were less likely to check identities, and also gave him his briefcase with a bold Red Cross symbol painted on it. "You are to go nowhere without this briefcase," Waitstill ordered.

He booked Marta in third class, where a polite Swiss gentleman noticed her frailness and secured for her an empty compartment. The Spanish railroad police showed up moments later, announced the compartment was reserved for them, and ordered Marta out. Suddenly her Swiss benefactor began shouting at the guards in German. "He did absolutely sound like Hitler," Marta recalled. "They were so afraid of the German sounds, the German bellowing, that they ran away and let us alone. I could at least sit down and rest a little bit."

Up front in first class, Lion had a close call of his own. "My husband went into the bathroom," Marta explained, "and from the other side somebody opened the door and came into the bathroom. This was a German official. He said to my husband, in English, 'Ah, you are from the Red Cross.' He spoke with a Prussian accent. And my husband, in his Bavarian English, said, 'Yes, I'm from the Red Cross.' So they exchanged some polite words and left. It was dangerous and comical at the same time."

Their last brush with discovery came at the Portuguese frontier. As they waited for a new train to take them to Lisbon, an American reporter approached Marta. "Is it true that Lion Feuchtwanger is on this train?" she asked in a loud voice.

"Who is that?" Marta replied

Waitstill walked up.

"What do you want from her?" he asked.

"I'm from the newspaper and I want a scoop!" the reporter answered, almost shouting. "I heard that Feuchtwanger was on the train. I want to send a telegram to my newspaper."

"Be quiet!" Waitstill snarled. "Don't you know it's dangerous, something like that? You should know as a reporter."

She apologized and said nothing more.[3]

———— · ————

Waitstill and the Feuchtwangers at last arrived safely in Lisbon, where Waitstill then had to do battle on Lion's behalf with the local US vice consul. Relations were not nearly so cordial as they were with Harry Bingham. Not even a slow recitation of Feuchtwanger's many published titles could convince the vice consul that here was a major Kulturträger, worthy of every consideration. Exasperated, Waitstill finally pulled out a document provided him in Marseille by Bingham. Under the US secretary of state's letterhead, it read: "American Consular Foreign Service officials are directed to extend every aid for the emigration to the United States of the German writer Lion Feuchtwanger. Signed Cordell Hull."

The letter, Waitstill remembered, "had its effect, and his papers were put in order and secreted by me."

Waitstill and Feuchtwanger, who would use Martha's ticket, were scheduled to depart three days later aboard the SS *Excalibur*. In the interim, Madame Amé-Leroy summoned Waitstill to the embassy, where she introduced him, as he recalled, to "a somewhat emaciated couple, pale and worried and apparently underfed. . . . I took pity on them before Madame l'Ambassadrice said a word."

They were the Doctors Anet, a French husband-and-wife team of physicians; he a general surgeon, she a pediatrician and also a surgeon. They were bound for some remote corner of Africa on a church-sponsored mission to minister medically to the locals. However, a short time prior to this, while working together in a French field hospital, a German bomb had hit their operating theater. Luckily, the Anets had not been hurt, but all their surgical instruments were destroyed. Now, in Lisbon, their steamer about to leave port, the Anets needed to replace their implements for use in Africa. They told Waitstill that they'd gone to the Rockefeller Foundation to apply for help but been told that they did not qualify for financial assistance under foundation rules. Could *Monsieur*, in his capacity with the Unitarians, perhaps help? They produced a complete list of their needs. Waitstill was deeply moved. "I will do my best," he told them.

Waitstill controlled AUA's funds in what he called the Bank of the Holy Spirit. He checked the balance, considered what his successor, Reverend Charles Joy, would require to continue the AUA's work, and "took the decision that they would have the maximum of what they wanted in surgical equipment." Then he consulted the Rockefeller Foundation's local office for recommendations where to buy the instruments and proceeded accordingly with the Anets' shopping list.

When he'd fully assembled their equipment, he called the doctors to his hotel room.

"One of the great rewards of my life was the look on the faces of each of these two doctors," he said, "and the large, slow tears that ran down their faces. We exchanged grand *abrazos* and kisses on both cheeks and they walked out like new people."

The next day, Waitstill recalled, "Lion Feuchtwanger appeared just before the gangplank was going to be lifted, and walked those last steps on European soil. His wife stepped forward, threw her arms around him, said some words of endearment and farewell, and they parted, a pair of stoics. And that ended my tour of duty."

———— · ————

Aboard ship, finally safe, Feuchtwanger asked Waitstill a question that had been on his mind for several weeks.

"Mr. Sharp," he said, "I am a novelist. I am more interested in human motivation than any other question. Why do people do what they do? May I address you as though you were a character in one of my novels and ask, Why are you here doing what you are doing? How much are you paid per carcass? Is there a payoff from some agency?"

"Not one escudo, Mr. Feuchtwanger," Waitstill answered.

"Are you paid a large salary, then, because this is dangerous, difficult, exacting work?"

"I'm not paid a salary at all. I am a Unitarian minister. My salary to maintain my wife and my two children and my home is paid for by my church."

Waitstill then explained the missions to Czechoslovakia and France. "And now I'm getting out you Kulturträgers," he said.

Feuchtwanger said he didn't often encounter such altruism.

"I'm not a saint," Waitstill answered. "I'm capable of any of the many sins of human nature. But I believe the will of God is to be interpreted by the liberty of the human spirit. So I do what I do without any piety at all but *ad magna gloria libertatis humani spiriti.*" (To greater glory, freedom of the human spirit.)

"Well, this is a surprising answer," said Feuchtwanger. "You get enough reward out of that?"

"Yes, I do," Waitstill answered. "As my friend Dick Ball said, 'I don't like to see guys pushed around.'"[4] (Waitstill had to explain the terms "guys" to Feuchtwanger, who nodded his understanding.)

"I hate it," Feuchtwanger agreed, "and I'm going to do whatever I can to stop it and to sustain freedom, by which you mean the liberty of the human spirit."

At the conclusion of an uneventful voyage, the *Excalibur* docked in New York on October 5. Waitstill recalled mixed emotions. "Finally, we arrived in New York Harbor, steamed past the Statue of Liberty, and it had never meant as much to me as it did then. But my elation was short-lived. I knew that Martha was still in peril. How would I tell our children that their mother hadn't come home?"

———— • ————

After seeing off her husband at the dock, Marta Feuchtwanger made her way immediately to Estoril, where she went in search of the grandest hotel, correctly assuming that this was where she'd find the Werfels in residence. Marta had but five or six dollars total and was in need of help.

On the way, she also had her single serious encounter with the authorities. Walking along an estuary in the afternoon heat, Marta stripped down to her two-piece bathing suit and dove in. A local policeman noticed and was waiting for her when she climbed out of the water.

"He said it [was] a crime against public morals to wear a two-piece French bathing suit. He had to arrest me. I spoke a little French and a little Spanish. I asked, 'Is there a fine?'"

She thought the policeman said yes, and she tried to hand him her few dollars, which he refused. Instead, he instructed Marta to appear at the nearby courthouse.

Meantime, she found the Werfels, strolling together. When Marta explained her predicament, Alma reached into her stocking and produced sufficient cash for her to book a steamer to New York.

Then Frau Feuchtwanger headed for the courthouse, where she convinced the Portuguese authorities that the policeman was mistaken—she had not meant to bribe him. It was a minor misunderstanding but one that might have had cataclysmic consequences for her. "I wasn't afraid to go to jail," she later said, "but that they would send me back to Germany again."

She rejoined her husband in New York two weeks later.

CHAPTER TWENTY

The Children's Journey

In late August, before her reunion with Waitstill, Martha had composed a letter to Hastings to explain why she would be staying in France a while longer. She was recording, as well, her own rationale for prolonging her absence from him and Martha Content for yet another extended period of time.

"I have some very important news for you," she wrote.

Here in France today the children do not have enough food. They do not have enough milk. There is not enough soap left to wash the clothes. I have seen *no* butter since I came here in July. There is no chocolate. There is not enough wool to make them sweaters and there are no more factories making woolen cloth to make trousers and skirts—and there is no coal to heat the houses for the winter.

So the children will be hungry and very cold and some of them will be sick. These children would like to have good food and warm houses. Some families in America are inviting these children to come to spend a year or so with them in their homes. They must come soon before winter, so I am going to wait until I can arrange for them and bring them to America myself. This means that I shall not return home with Dad. I must wait until I can make all the arrangements for the children. So I must give up seeing you until about your birthday! Then what a celebration we will have!

She signed the note, "Lovingly, Mommy."

The children's emigration project had seemed well on its way just three days earlier, when Martha was notified that fifty blanket immigration visas, which the US State Department originally had earmarked for British children, had been redesignated for French children and soon would be available to her at the consulate in Marseille.

In fact, the visas would be delayed until November. The second bit of news was more solid. She learned that the US Committee for the Care of European Children had officially agreed to include children of different nationalities in the group, rather than only French as originally had been planned. Brundage's group would also pay the children's transportation costs from Lisbon to the United States.

Now all she had to do was find the right candidates, secure their French exit visas as well as exit and entry visas for Spain and Portugal, gather all of them together, then transport the group to Lisbon and onto a ship for New York. Among the few people available to provide her regular, practical assistance was Helen Lowrie, who once again volunteered her services.

Martha did not wait for anyone's approval to get started. On August 27, two days before her reunion in Toulouse with Waitstill, she visited the internment camp at Recebedoux, near Toulouse, where she encountered a pair of brothers, Joseph and Alexander Strasser, eight and six respectively.

Their father, Paul Strasser, a Viennese physician, had been sent by the Nazis first to Dachau and then to Buchenwald. After two years in the concentration camps—the systematic exterminations hadn't yet begun—his wife, Madeline, had sold her jewels to purchase Strasser's freedom. The family had then moved to France where Frau Strasser died of metastatic breast cancer, and her husband and sons were interned.

"We left money with the staff to get the boys photographed," Martha wrote. "Their father begged us to make it possible for the boys to go."

Now that the children's US entry visas and transportation costs were guaranteed, she approached the prefect for the *département* (state) of Bouches des Rhone, whose office was near Marseille, to ask if he would cooperate in granting the necessary exit visas. "He was most gracious and cooperative," Martha later recalled, "and expressed himself as delighted by the possibility of this French-American collaboration. He promised me that he would give the exit visas to all the children in his prefecture within 24 hours whenever I gave him the names."

The one part of her work she knew would be little problem was finding émigré recruits. Since Hyacinthe Loyson had spread word of Martha's project countrywide in August, Martha had received hundreds of letters and postcards from parents all over France, pleading that she take their children with her to America.

Some were even smuggled south from the Occupied Zone in hay carts, tucked inside midwives' instrument bags, and even secreted under loaves of bread. All her correspondents wrote that they feared that soon there would not be enough food in France to feed their children, and many openly wrote that they wanted their children to attend schools free of Nazi ideology.

Martha then confidently visited the Portuguese and Spanish consulates in Marseille. Both countries at that point still regularly issued visas. The Portuguese only required a valid US visa and a fully paid ticket from Lisbon to anywhere outside the country. The Spaniards asked for Portuguese and US visas, nothing more.

It all seemed straightforward, but it was deceptively so.

Martha opened a joint office with the Lowries in Marseille. Irina Okounieff came over from Pau to serve as their shared secretary. Before Waitstill left Marseille by train with the Feuchtwangers on the morning of September 18, he had run a lawyerly eye over the registration form Martha was creating, a complex document that needed to address not only the immigration laws of four countries but also potential civil matters, such as lawsuits should any of the children die, be physically injured, or suffer some other sort of harm or disability.

Details were important. Under French law, for example, only a father could legally pass responsibility for a child to another individual. It was therefore of paramount concern to secure the fathers' signatures.

By September 25, the registration and related documents were completed, and Martha, along with Helen Lowrie, had collected affidavits from the parents or guardians of fifty children, all of whom were ready to emigrate at once.

Then came her first reversal. It was suddenly decreed that exit visas no longer could be issued on a prefect's sole authority. Permission had to come directly from the top, Vichy.

So instead of taking her list of names to the friendly regional police commissioner, Martha headed instead for the seat of Marshal Pétain's collaborationist government. She grimly guessed it would take at least three days to secure the proper approvals in Vichy—wildly wishful thinking, as it turned out.

Martha later called Vichy "the city of lost hopes." Because the old spa lacked proper governmental office space, Pétain operated out of a hotel. So did several of his ministries. The Ministry of Interior, for instance, was headquartered at the abandoned casino. The spa itself was reserved for the Foreign Ministry.

"The former bathing areas, where you could take showers before you went into the swimming pool, were all used as offices," Martha said. "They all had these spigots on the side and the top and the bottom so that if you happened to touch one of them you would have inundated the person sitting there in front, facing out with the linen curtain pushed back, because it was the shower, you see. You were allowed to sit on something that normally had been the place where people sat when they dressed after they had their shower. It was a sort of bench. It was very interesting because they had a little sign on all of these *robinets* [faucets] which read, 'Do Not Touch.'"

She pulled every string she could. In Vichy, Martha called on Robert D. Murphy, the interim US ambassador, who said he would like to help her, but since hers was a private program, not a national one, there wasn't much he could do.

There ensued a frustrating string of meetings with officials in various Vichy ministries. The routine never varied. Most appointments had to be rescheduled several times. If one of Pétain's bureaucrats actually was in at the appointed hour, the drill began in the lobby, where Martha would be handed a pencil stub with which to write her name, the identity of the person she wished to see, and a description of her business.

Then, along with everyone else, she waited, sometimes for hours, before a uniformed soldier would walk among the crowd, calling out the names of those who had at last been summoned to their meetings. Martha strained for recognizable syllables.

Most of the "offices" Martha visited were converted bedrooms, minus the beds. Typically, she found an office supplied with some sort of filing cabinet and two or more chairs. Desks seemed to be at a premium. The interviews with Vichy officials invariably concluded with a pronouncement either that her plan was impossible or that she needed to speak to somebody else, often multiple somebodies.

Slow seemed to be the only speed the bureaucrats knew, but they actually did conduct some due diligence. In the Pau municipal archives are several letters written by local officials in October 1940, all in response to Vichy inquiries about Martha and her milk program.

"Her generosity was greatly appreciated," wrote a welfare inspector to the prefect, who was collecting a dossier on Martha, "as well as her tact, particularly: She met with the various directors of maternal and infant care organizations in the unoccupied zone . . . so as to precisely gauge their needs and it is thus, in my humble opinion, that it was possible to assure an equitable and judicious distribution of the milk products (thirteen tons) thanks to American generosity."

A "special commissioner" under the prefect also remembered Martha with fond respect. "She has not, in any circumstances, manifested any hostile sentiments toward France, and actually seems to have good intentions toward our country," he reported. "She has thus rendered a real service to the children and has warranted our thanks."

But the warm reviews did not seem to advance her cause in any substantive way. After eleven days of traipsing around Vichy and getting nowhere, Martha wrote Waitstill, who by then had returned to Wellesley Hills.

> My darling Waitstill, I have been thinking of you all day and wishing I were at home to hear that first sermon—and see the church full of friendly faces—greeting you at the door—and tying Martha Content's ribbons for Sunday School and hearing from Hastings' new teacher. How dear and familiar it all sounds.
>
> I am still in Vichy—trying to get consent for the *visas des sorties*. The difficulty seems to be that they don't want French children to grow up in America, where they will find the life so easy and delightful that they will want to stay. As a matter of principle, they want French families to stay together to take what comes together.

She explained that Vichy also had refused the Argentine and Mexican governments after they offered to take children.

The bureaucrats told Martha they feared that the children would learn English, forget their French, lose touch with their culture, and therefore wouldn't really be French anymore and would never be able to completely readjust and re-assimilate. They were concerned that British propaganda might even make the children anti-French. They raised the possibility of French boys growing to young manhood in America and then possibly facing conscription into the US armed services. If French boys were to be soldiers, Martha was informed, they would be *French* soldiers.

She disclosed that she had been reading D. H. Lawrence's *Lady Chatterley's Lover*. "The parish would disown me if they knew that book!"

Martha closed the letter, "All my love, Martha," then resumed writing again: "I couldn't resist taking another page just to say I love you and miss you dreadfully—really one of us is less than half as efficient alone—at least I feel that way—I need your vitality—either for or against things!"

She went on. "I really must stop and send you my love—and tell you how I wish you were here—or that I was there. I think you made the right decision in August—we must be together—but perhaps we can be sent over here together after the war—at any rate we ought to begin to improve our French from now on. It is important to speak well. Love, again all of it, Martha."

Over the next two weeks she would continue to battle the Vichy bureaucracy as well as a variety of digestive and respiratory problems. Martha spent October 10 sick in bed with "aches all day in legs and arms," according to notes in her datebook. Doctors put her on six different medications.

Martha even underwent "fire cupping," a folk remedy for a number of ailments, in which alcohol-soaked wads of cotton are placed on the skin and set afire. A glass cup is then placed over each burning wad, which is extinguished. As the hot air inside the cup cools, a vacuum is created that allegedly relieves "stagnation" under the patient's skin. There is no reliable evidence that fire cupping works, as Martha attested, and it can leave ugly marks, as she also discovered. "They draw the blood to the surface and make you look perfectly awful," she wrote.

Martha soldiered on until October 18, when she at last capitulated to the bureaucrats' intransigence—or seemed to. "It is with much regret that we write to say that the project for the children invited by American families to stay in the U.S.A. for the duration of the war must be given up," she announced in a typed memorandum.

The plan was started with definite assurance from French Government officials that the exit visas would be given. Since that time, the regulations have been changed. [Mrs. Sharp] has now been advised by the Ministry of Foreign Affairs that the sending of French children to America under present circumstances is contrary to the policy of the French Government.

We are keenly sorry that this link in French American friendship cannot be forged, and that these young ambassadors cannot carry out their mission to keep alive in so many American homes and committees, sympathy and interest for France. We had hoped that the interchange of customs and ideas might still further strengthen the ties between our two countries.

We know that you will share our keen regret—

The unfinished note was meant either as a surrender or a ruse. Whether a finished copy ever was completed is not known. However, the Vichy government soon and suddenly reversed itself. Since the Unoccupied Zone was burdened by thousands of homeless French children—particularly Alsatian children—who'd been driven from their homes by the Nazis and weren't likely to reunite with their families any time soon, it was decided that Martha would take these children to the United States, as long as she could find relatives there who'd take care of them. In practice, this meant that her best choice would be children with an American parent. One of the children joined his father, a physician, in the United States.

She also would be allowed to take the children of foreign and stateless refugees from Germany, Austria, Czechoslovakia, and elsewhere, whose citizenship had been revoked by the Nazis—provided that none were more than sixteen years of age.

To assemble a group under these restrictions would be a challenge. Besides Joseph and Alex Strasser, Martha would select the six daughters, aged six to fourteen, of Edouard Theis, the liberal Protestant pastor in Le Chambon-sur-Lignon whom she'd met in August.

There were thirteen-year-old triplets from Czechoslovakia, Amélie, Eveline, and Marianne Diamant, and three-year-old Mercedes Brown, the youngest of the children, and her seven-year-old brother, Clément. Irina and Alexis Okounieff joined the group with their seven-year-old son, Nicholas, as did the Vakar sisters, Catherine and Anna, thirteen and eleven, the French-born daughters of Russian émigrés whom the Okounieffs had befriended in Pau. Andre du Bouchet, sixteen, the oldest child, came with his fourteen-year-old sister, Helene. Their father and mother made the trip as well.

At the eleventh hour, Catherine and Anna Vakar, thirteen and eleven, also made the trip. As Catherine remembered it, "My father said to Mrs. Sharp, 'If you could only include my girls in the group of children to go to America,' and she said, 'Well, the group is full.' And as it turned out, at the last minute, two boys did not show up. And my sister and I were included." Accompanied by their mothers were Helene Vincent, nine; Germaine Triscos, ten; and Gerard Fuchs, six. Traveling with neither parent nor sibling were Wolfgang Fleischmann and Pierre Garai, both twelve; Hans Frank, eleven; Tes Huger, ten; Stephen Hawthorne, five; and Eva Feigl, fourteen.

All the children's histories were remarkable but none more so than that of Eva Feigl, who would later take her mother's name, Rosemarie. She was a native Viennese like the Strasser boys and an only child, born into a life of privilege and ease only to see her world shattered by the Nazi *Anschluss* of March 1938. Eva remembered the Austrian sky turning black with Nazi warplanes, "like flies over Vienna." Eight months later came the terrors of Kristallnacht.

Franz and Rosemarie Feigl harbored no illusions about the Nazi agenda and taught their only child to fear for her life. As it happened, Franz, an attorney, previously had served as court-appointed counsel for a young Nazi who'd been arrested at a demonstration. Feigl had won the case, and his client had gone free. Soon after the *Anschluss*, the same young man came to the Feigl house with a warning for Frau Feigl that her husband was among those Jews already marked for arrest.

"We're going to come to get Dr. Feigl," he said. "When we come I don't want to find him here."

Eva's father fled at once to Genoa, where his brother worked in the Austrian consulate. Eva remained in Vienna with her mother until January 1939. By then, the Nazis' overt campaign against Jews had intensified to the point where people threw stones at Eva and other Jewish children each day as they walked to their religious school. Her maternal grandparents, who like most members of the family would not survive the Holocaust, sent her and her mother to join Franz in Genoa.

The Feigls left Italy on a forged Belgian visa. In time they made their way to Marseille, where, by the summer of 1940, they were running out of money and hope. Franz, prevented from working, spent every free moment making the rounds of the foreign consulates in Marseille, searching without success for some avenue of escape before the Nazis came for him. It was in the course of these daily visits that he met Martha and arranged with her to save his daughter from the Gestapo. "My father," remembers his daughter, "went from trying to get visas to go anywhere that was plausible. That's how he met Martha Sharp who saved my life."

After returning to the United States, Martha would get both Franz and Rosemarie out as well.

—— · ——

As late as October 20, 1940, Martha hoped to have the children on a boat for New York by the end of the month. No such luck, however. Not only were their US entry visas still held up, but complications now arose with the Spanish and Portuguese too.

First, Portuguese authorities changed their rules to require that all visa applications be sent to Lisbon rather than be handled in Marseille as before. Then the Spaniards decided that they would not issue transit visas unless both Portuguese and US visas already were affixed to each applicant's passport.

At Harry Bingham's personal request, the US ambassador to Spain successfully interceded with Madrid. Herbert Pell in Lisbon wired to report—incorrectly as it turned out—that the Portuguese would issue visas without requiring direct application from Martha and Helen Lowrie in Marseille. A new sailing date of November 22 was set but then postponed as before.

Martha was repeatedly back and forth between Marseille and Vichy by airplane and train, each time forced to secure a series of official permissions to simply make the journey. She took sick again and again. But she never forgot her priorities. Right in the middle of her hectic and sketchy daily notes appears a notation that on

November 11, in Vichy, Martha went shopping for Christmas stocking stuffers for the whole Sharp family.

Finally, in the early morning hours of November 26, Martha, together with twenty-seven children (seventeen girls and ten boys) and ten other adults, boarded a passenger train at the Gare St. Charles in Marseille on the first leg of their journey to freedom. For the nine Jewish children among them, it was a matter of life and death. One can imagine the feelings raging through the parents as they saw their children off. Holding the application form many years later, Mercedes Brown mused: "And this is the paper that obviously was filled out so we could start our journey. And it must've been very painful for my mother to do this." Yehuda Bauer, noted Holocaust scholar, noted: "Heartbreaking as it was for the parents, they wanted to rescue their children first and foremost so they handed them over to strangers rather than endanger them by keeping them with them."[1]

Just before departure, Martha issued each of the children a beige beret in order to more easily identify them as members of her group. For most of the trip to Portugal, three-year-old Mercedes Brown, who was not as yet toilet trained and was covered with impetigo sores, would occupy Martha's lap.

One of the parents on the trip suffered recurrent psychotic episodes.

This was not going to be simple.

Beginning with their first stop, in Narbonne, the entire party would be taken off the train to be questioned fourteen times. Their sixty-seven articles of luggage likewise would be closely examined each time. Alexis Okounieff, the single able-bodied adult male aboard, carried the bags off and on at every stop.

Martha later described their stop in Cerbère in a letter to Helen Lowrie:

> The station agent called me to say that Thomas Cook's man in Portbou wanted to speak to me. This conversation, confirming the fact that tea and supper waited for us at the Spanish frontier,

cost me my place in line for the passports—and necessitated an hour's wait in line. When their turn came, each child had to be passed in review—Mercedes was passed with Clément, but refused to leave until Tes Huger and Dr. Dubouchet accompanied her. She started to wail. The passport officer was adamant: No. Tes Huger came with the H's he said. Finally, however, he could bear it no longer and took Tes and Dr. Dubouchet before the others. Then those two led the weeping child into the next torture chamber—the customs inspection. Meanwhile, [one of] the Strasser boy[s] lost his lunch and howled and a scene was had by all.

They reached Barcelona at eleven that night, went sightseeing the next day, then boarded the Madrid train at 10 p.m. "It was a terrible night," Martha wrote. "Mercedes woke every hour and cried and kicked me." The train pulled into the Spanish capital at about noon. They boarded another one that night at ten-thirty and reached the Portuguese frontier at seven the next morning.

A customs inspector discovered a small package of dishes Martha was bringing home for Martha Content. When he asked her about them, she explained that she had purchased them in France for her daughter in America—just children's toys.

"Oh no!" he replied excitedly. "You're bringing them to the ceramics market in Portugal!" he accused. "Open up! You'll have to open up everything else!"

Martha protested. "These are just for my children to play with."

"Madame," he answered. "How many children have you?"

At precisely that moment the passport officer approached with the group's papers. "Señora Sharp," he said, "all your twenty-seven children are in order."

"My God!" shouted the customs inspector. "You have twenty-seven children! That's marvelous! You know, I have twenty myself. I'm not going to make your exit any more difficult. Put back all the packages. You take anything you like, and I bless you for the rest of the journey!"

Martha delivered the children in time to make their scheduled departure that day. However, in Lisbon, Ninon Tallon met the train with bad news. The steamship company, not believing that anyone could move such a group across three countries in three days, had released all their tickets to other passengers. The good news, Tallon went on, was that she had arranged for the children to be taken as a group to an agricultural school outside the capital, where they would be housed and well fed until new trans-Atlantic accommodations could be found for them.

Transportation of any sort out of Lisbon for America was of course very scarce and dear. After several days of intense discussions with a US company, the American Export Lines, Martha found berths for herself and a couple of the children on the SS *Excalibur*—the ship Waitstill and Lion Feuchtwanger had taken in September. The *Excalibur* departed Lisbon for New York on December 6. The balance of the group, including Ninon Tallon, would come a few days later aboard the SS *Excambion*.

Getting Madame Tallon out was yet another victory for Martha against a stubborn bureaucrat. Ambassador Pell was reluctant to issue the woman a visa because he disapproved of her leftist leanings. Martha somehow prevailed, and Tallon received her visa.

——— · ———

On board the *Excambion,* the crew covered a dining room floor with mattresses to create a dormitory for the children. Anna Vakar remembered trying to rest while Clément Brown and some of the other boys stomped over the mattresses playing tag. A steward taught them English words using fruit as prizes. The child who correctly said the name of each piece of fruit as it was held aloft received it as a reward.

Many of the children remembered being seasick.

Clément Brown and Hans Frank looked for German U-boats, so that they could wave at the captains, thinking they would wave back. The *Excambion,* in fact, would later be torpedoed and sunk by a U-boat.

Tes Huger was frightened by the imagined sound of bombs and planes in the night. In letters never mailed, Josef Strasser reported to his father that he and his brother were upset because their grandmother had not met them in Lisbon. He begged for his father and grandmother to come quickly to the United States.

When the *Excambion* docked in Jersey City on December 23, 1940, Martha was there on the pier, waiting to greet her young charges and to pass around mugs of hot chocolate. Newsreel cameras recorded the happy scene as the New York press paid extensive attention to the extraordinary and uplifting story.

Although they were safe, the children now faced a new world vastly different from what they had known. Most would be in the company of strangers, at least for the time being, and many would have to begin by learning a new language.

Frustrated by her lack of fluency in English, Anna Vakar hardly spoke for three months. Her sister, Catherine, adapted more easily.

Mercedes Brown continued to fear the Nazis and cried inconsolably at the sound of any siren.

Tes Huger, who went to live with a young childless couple in Iowa, also struggled to master English. But she quickly adapted to her new home and later reported that her new family had spoiled her.

Some of the refugee children were reunited with parents or relatives. Others, such as Huger, went to live with utter strangers. Hans Frank joined his mother in New York. Wolfgang Fleischmann was reunited with his father, a physician at Johns Hopkins Medical Center in Baltimore. The Brown children stayed with their mother's sister in Virginia. Anna and Catherine Vakar were welcomed into the family of Kerr and Elsie Atkinson, members of the Wellesley Hills Church. Their parents arrived the following year, but the children stayed with the Atkinsons for several more months until Mr. and Mrs. Vakar were settled in their new lives. The Vakars repaid the Unitarian Service Committee for their passage.

Dr. Rudolph and Charlotte Diamant, Pierre Garai's father, and Mrs. Brown emigrated during the war, as did Tes Huger's parents.

The children's lives proceeded as lives do. They married or remained single, raised children, divorced or didn't, worked, and traveled. Anna Vakar would teach French, then work as a technical translator before moving to Canada, where she wrote and published haiku. Catherine Vakar stayed in the Boston area, raised three children, and earned a PhD at Harvard. She was a professor of Russian studies at MIT until her retirement in 1994.

The Strassers settled in New York State. Josef Strasser became a successful businessman; Alexander, a physician in Rochester, New York.

The Diamant triplets and their parents traveled across the United States to settle in Oregon, where they had relatives. All three of them would marry and raise families. Amélie taught for forty years. Eveline became a dentist like her father. Marianne worked as a legal secretary and court reporter.

Nicholas Okounieff went on to work for a large electronics and defense firm for several years and then for a security company. Clément Brown joined the US Army, took graduate degrees from schools in Tennessee and Georgia, and became an educator. His sister, Mercedes, known as Dee, would travel to France regularly as an executive in the cosmetics business. She settled in New York, where for years she lived just down the street from Martha.

Tes Huger raised three children and eventually moved to the seaside community of Rockport, Massachusetts.

Jeanne Theis became Jeanne Whitaker and a language professor at Wheaton College in Norton, Massachusetts. Her sister, Jacqueline, would teach elementary school in Philadelphia. Cécile, Louise, Françoise, and Marguerite Theis went home to France, where three of them became teachers and the fourth, Marguerite, studied psychology. Their father, Edouard Theis, died in 1984.

Pierre Garai became a professor at Columbia. He went through a period of disillusionment and distraction that led to a midlife suicide.

Wolfgang Fleischmann became dean of the School of Humanities at Montclair State College. Fluent in seven languages, he edited the first edition of *Encyclopedia of World Literature in the 20th Century*. Fleischmann died suddenly in 1987.

---- CHAPTER TWENTY-ONE ----

The Home Front

During the six months she spent on her second mission abroad, Martha had traveled thousands of miles within France by car, train, bicycle, and on foot, as she and Helen Lowrie set up the milk distribution program and simultaneously wrestled with bureaucrats for the official papers that would make French children's emigration a reality. She made the two-hundred-mile round trip to Vichy three times and suffered the disappointment of being able to use only twenty-seven of the fifty visas she had originally acquired. Despite bouts of illness she kept going with single-minded intensity. Dr. Charles Joy, her USC successor in Marseille, likened her to a mother bear fighting for her cubs.

Waitstill too had spent his summer in feverish activity, trying to rescue a thousand Czech soldiers who were stranded in Agde, organizing refugee relief and emigration from the USC's new office in Lisbon, and getting the Feuchtwangers safely out of France to refuge in the United States. It was time, the Sharps seemed to agree, to head for the harbor, pull down the sails, and resume life as it had been two years earlier. They both felt that their most important work was, as Martha put it, "to grow souls together"—a reference not to the ministry but to child rearing.

AUA leaders had other ideas, however, and continued to use the Sharps as prime publicists. For Waitstill, combining parish duties with speaking engagements would have been particularly onerous.

Nonetheless, he was so successful at speechmaking that the AUA offered a recording of one of his talks to interested constituents. Martha meanwhile gave seventy talks between December 1940 and June 1941.

There was another factor. Both seemed unable to leave the overseas work behind. A *Christian Register* article noted that Waitstill "is continuing to work on individual and group cases of refugees still abroad whose papers and problems he has brought home with him." Martha too kept up her efforts for the refugees they had been unable to help while in France. While on her speaking tours, she missed no chance to solicit the precious affidavits without which there was no chance to secure visas. She was quite successful at this. The Case Work Committee reported that 30 percent of the people who expressed interest actually did sign affidavits, saying that "we are hopeful to get more affidavits for these, technically, enemy-alien cases. As an illustration, we may mention the instance where we were in desperate need of a sponsor for an urgent case—a wire to Niagara Falls following up one of Mrs. Sharp's leads produced an affidavit in 24 hours."

She took time to publicize the situation of refugees by penning two articles for the *Christian Science Monitor:* one about the Czech soldiers in Agde and the other about the thousands of people languishing in internment camps with no country willing to take them.

Despite their increasing separations and the attention each gave to their work, Martha and Waitstill were bound in marriage by more than love, respect, friendship, or faith. They believed that they completed each other, that their union was greater than the sum of its parts. When tested in the crucibles of their two European aid commissions, this sense of shared purpose gave them the strength to succeed in courageous and daring enterprises. As Martha wrote Waitstill from France in October of 1940, "We must be together."

But they drew very different lessons from their experiences, which in time would help push them in different directions. They would never lose the intensity and commitment that carried them through all adversity in Prague and France, but their bond began to fray and ultimately broke.

Waitstill returned home from France disillusioned, in part by the shabby treatment from a trusted friend, Bob Dexter, but also more broadly at the appalling rise of barbarism and collapse of civil society across Europe. "It is almost certain," he wrote to Livingston and Edna Stebbins in a long, introspective letter from Lisbon,

> that I'm going to consider this summer's trick at the wheel the last one until something like civilized order arises here in Europe.
>
> This is a lot worse than Prague in some ways, because it is wartime, and everything is out of joint. At least in the Prague experience we were able to leave the region of lawlessness and find a stable area outside, a place in which promises meant what they said and letters were delivered when they were posted. But here all the rules are off. This is the end of the Europe that we of this generation have known and loved and hoped would continue and would save itself by gradual reform, the liberal tradition. Now the revolution of nihilism has swept over all but this hospitable, generous little land [Portugal]."

For the time being, at least, Waitstill wished only to take up his old life in Wellesley Hills. Despite the bare-knuckle treatment he and Martha had received from the AUA, and the bitter estrangement from Dexter, Waitstill had not lost his calling, and he never would.

Martha, for her part, kept trying to rescue more Kulturträgers and other victims of the Nazis, such as Eva Feigl's parents, whom she and Waitstill had been unable to help while in France.

Martha was no less affected than Waitstill by the chaos, misery, and danger that had surrounded them in Czechoslovakia and France, yet she derived considerable satisfaction and self-assurance from what she had accomplished, much of it by herself. "I developed a sense of my own power," she explained. "I had been an extension of Waitstill. Here were things I could do on my own."

What had begun for her in early 1939 as an acquiescent errand of conscience and mercy—if she did not go, Waitstill would not go—

would now evolve into a more personal agenda and inevitably a political one. In Prague, she'd been forcefully exposed to the ghastly plight of the Jews, and she'd made imperiled children her core concern in France. Not surprisingly, when she returned to the United States, Martha not only worked hard through the AUA—whose board she joined in 1941—to extend and consolidate what she had achieved in Europe. She presented papers at academic and policy conferences and wrote articles on refugee issues for the popular press. As well, she soon was out fund-raising for Youth Aliyah, a program of Hadassah, the women's Zionist movement founded by Henrietta Szold. Youth Aliyah was founded by Recha Freier in 1933 to rescue European Jewish children from the Nazis and bring them to Palestine.

Martha was especially adept at accessing an audience's wallets through their hearts, as evidenced by a memorable fund-raising excursion in Flint, Michigan, in the early 1940s, with Hadassah executive Annabelle Markson. Asked to address a roomful of well-to-do men, Martha proceeded to tell them about the orphaned Holocaust survivors she had seen in Europe. With a rare gift for storytelling, she brought the children to life, making their suffering palpable to the audience. By the time she finished, Mrs. Markson and some of the men were in tears.

One man rose to ask, "How much do the children cost?"

Mrs. Markson answered, "Three hundred and sixty dollars apiece, and we hope to leave here today with fifteen children."

The leader of the group promised that "the men of Flint will do their duty," and that Youth Aliyah would have its fifteen children.

The next day, Annabelle and Martha met with the leader and some of the men who had been unable to attend the previous day's meeting. They wanted to hear some of Martha's stories. The women left Flint with enough money to rescue thirty children.

Martha proved just as skillful in front of Unitarian audiences. In May of 1941, Helen Ansley, a Unitarian living in Cleveland, wrote to USC president Emerson after attending one of Martha's presentations. According to Ansley, their guest speaker hadn't appealed for money during her remarks, but the crowd of 250 had anted up $275 anyway. "A group of women entirely unconnected with the Church offered her their services," she reported.

> I write you all of this so you may know of what inestimable value to the Unitarian Service Committee Martha Sharp's trip to Cleveland was.
>
> Martha would be the ideal person to coordinate all the women's work for the Committee. . . . I feel sure that all the women of the denomination and many others as well would be grateful for the opportunity to rally under her splendid leadership.
>
> To the women of Cleveland, therefore, the Unitarian Service Committee will be symbolized by Martha Sharp, and the question will come many times in the future, as it did to me last week, "What does Mrs. Sharp want us to do?" I hope you can persuade her to accept some title or office that would give her the right to answer this question and direct this splendid enthusiasm which she engenders whenever she speaks.

CHAPTER TWENTY-TWO

The Family

Thirteen-year-old Catherine Vakar, newly arrived from France aboard the *Excambion* with her little sister, was hired at five dollars a week in the summer of 1941 to serve as a mother's helper at the Sharps' vacation house on Lake Sunapee. Despite her growing list of commitments, Martha was determined to begin work at the lakeside house on the memoirs she would never manage to complete.

The pace that summer was hectic, Vakar later recalled. She found Martha "full of Yankee ingenuity and thrift." Catherine learned how to put up preserves that summer and also how to light the Sunapee house's balky kerosene stove, which was apt to explode if not treated with care.

Hastings, who had turned nine the previous November, could vaguely recall bits of his boyhood dating back to the days of his father's first ministry, at the Unitarian Church in Meadville, Pennsylvania. For example, he remembered a huge Mayflower moving van coming for their furniture and how his father joked about Mayflower taking them back to New England.

But Hastings's active memory, like that of his little sister, Martha Content, who turned four in September 1940, dated to the return of their parents from France in 1940.

Brother and sister recalled that their mother was away giving speeches much of the time. The household refrigerator was always full of orchids and corsages that she brought home from her various speaking engagements. There often wasn't much else in the fridge, barely enough from which to make a meal.

"I would say our parents were so caught up in what they were doing, what they felt *had* to be done," Martha Content recalled, "that we were sort of incidental."

She recalls the great care that Martha took with her personal appearance. "Mother was always very elegant," she says. "I can remember seeing an upper shelf full of hats with feathers, hats with veils, hats with bows. She stood up straight and was always very well dressed. She was an excellent seamstress and made many of her own clothes, as well as mine. Her shoes were immaculate. She had a dressing table with three mirrors. She really enjoyed what little she did to make herself up."

Waitstill treated the children in the manner he was raised by his own stern mother and in much the same way he managed parishioners: he was precise, judgmental, and unyielding. His children remembered him for the most part as a rigid, remote, and often forbidding figure in the household. He did not read to Hastings and Martha Content, unless it was from the Bible at breakfast around the kitchen table. Waitstill rarely hugged or touched them with affection. Martha Content recalled that he always shook hands with her. Waitstill was one of those Victorian fathers who was restrained in his ability to express his feelings directly to his children. But, as in many of his love letters to Martha, he was easily able to write out those feelings. In a personal letter of August 12, 1940, from Lisbon to friends Helen and Curtis (no last names are given), he writes:

> The news about your talk with Martha Content was reassuring. Since her two illnesses I can hardly get enough news of her, to know that she is recovering enough to go through with the tonsillectomy as soon as Lyman Richards [the doctor] says she is ready. Do spread the good word to all who write that they try to insert some news of that darling child. The very thought of her purity and grace just keep me on the job and make everything worth the effort here.

Hastings would recall attending Boston Braves games with his father and only a handful of occasions when they ever played catch, usually "to humor Mother," as Waitstill would tell him.

Martha Content and Hastings remembered how each Saturday the Reverend Sharp worked at home, polishing and practicing his sermons. The next day, Waitstill would expect them to discuss his message after church, over Sunday dinner at the parsonage. Martha Content frequently forgot what the sermon was about, which would earn her a stern lecture.

Neither would ever forget their father's injunction: "What have you done today to justify your existence?"

Casual familiarity was not the Sharp way either. "It was always 'Father' and 'Mother,' never 'Daddy' and 'Mommy,'" Martha Content remembers. "No diminutives. Their personal love was really sublimated too. It was never allowed to shine. I think I've seen one picture of my mother and father holding hands. We never saw them in the bedroom. We never saw them wild, running around the house after each other. We never heard giggles. It was all very formal."

Martha Content particularly resented that she was sent to stay with friends or neighbors whenever her mother was away—that is to say, frequently—and retaliated by embarrassing Martha with temper tantrums. One of these families was the Beckers, members of Waitstill's congregation. When Martha came to fetch her at the Beckers after being away for a long time, Martha Content hid under the piano.

"Where's my little girl?" her mother asked.

"I'm *not* your little girl," Martha Content insisted. "I love Mrs. Becker. She's my mother."

Hastings got into considerable mischief too. When Martha Content was quite young, he eviscerated all her plush toys (on the pretext that they were made in Japan) and tried to push her, with the toys, in a box out the second-floor window of the parsonage. Another time, at Sunapee, he had to be prevented from shoving a dish mop down her throat. "It's just as well we were apart so much," Martha Content reflected. "He would have killed me."

Hastings also had what he called "numerous failures" with his chemistry set, and he once shot out a few streetlights on Washington Street in Wellesley Hills with his BB gun.

Sometimes the children worked as a team. The family dog, an Airedale named Mack, suffered from eczema, which was treated with what Martha Content described as a "nasty, creamy purple silver nitrate." Once or twice while their father performed a wedding, Hastings and Martha Content brought Mack into the back of the church, slathered him with the ointment, then let him go, knowing that Mack would make a tail-wagging beeline for the altar, smearing everyone with globs of the purple gunk as he brushed past them.

When Martha later reflected on these years, she acknowledged that she had been forced to make sacrifices. She explained, "This kind of life work for a woman has its very expensive side in the home." But she also felt that her children's reproaches were not entirely fair.

> I was away for two weeks of every month, and spent a minimum of four to six weeks abroad every summer. In some ways, I feel that I concentrated more on my children when I was at home and tried not to neglect anything which had meaning for them.
>
> However, I realized that they felt neglected because they heard it from others and used my absences from home to excuse whatever went wrong in their personal lives. Thus I became the scapegoat for their own failures.
>
> They were proud of my achievements. They were thrilled by the publicity in the papers. But they really gave me a hard time when I came home. Psychologically, this caused me to be always apologizing at home. No matter what I did, I was always wrong. But the work I did underwrote private schools, camps, clothes for the children and, for myself, a housekeeper, and many other privileges which otherwise would not have been ours.

CHAPTER TWENTY-THREE

Back to Europe

In the spring of 1942, the USC sent Martha on a West Coast speaking tour. She also was tasked by her fellow directors to report on the impact of President Roosevelt's infamous Executive Order 9066 of February 18, 1942, signed in the aftermath of Pearl Harbor and over the objections of both Mrs. Roosevelt and J. Edgar Hoover, the unlikeliest of allies, that empowered the US Army to relocate those of "foreign enemy ancestry" to assembly centers and then internment camps.

The practical effect was to uproot approximately 110,000 Japanese Americans—more than 60 percent of whom were US citizens—and ship them to prison camps in the name of national security. It is one of the sorriest blots on America's human rights record. Nearly half a century later, President George H. W. Bush signed legislation that authorized reparations of $20,000 apiece to the surviving internees, plus an apology to each.

Martha visited a Japanese American "assembly center" at the Puyallup, Washington, fairgrounds and similar facilities set up at the Tanforan and Santa Anita horse-racing tracks in Northern and Southern California. "Race tracks and fairgrounds have been the easiest to adapt," she noted in her report of the trip, "since they usually comprise wide areas surrounded by barbed wire fences."

There were seven thousand internees crammed together at Santa Anita. Martha noted that hymnals printed in Japanese were forbidden, that one seventy-year-old disabled person had a quarter-mile walk to the nearest toilet, and that in one case five hundred people shared a single shower.

Her report, published in the *Christian Register,* described how

hysteria and suspicion of the Japanese rose to such heights . . . that the order for evacuation came as a relief to all on the Pacific Coast. A local clergyman told me, "Right after Pearl Harbor there was no widespread antagonism against Japanese-Americans here. It was not until two weeks later when the Fruit Growers Association organized a campaign for deportation of their Japanese competitors that feelings began to rise."

Irresponsible radio commentators jumped on the bandwagon with stories of suspect sabotage. Politicians, catering to mass prejudice, added their fuel to the fire. Extremists of all kinds, led by the Hearst newspapers, raised apprehension to such a pitch that bewildered, and honest, patriots felt forced to join them.

Two Filipinos made violent attacks on Japanese. Loyal and disloyal alike became fearful for their lives. Until it was too late, the mass of intelligent people never believed the evacuation would take place. When it did, they deeply regretted their inactivity in not following down rumors and acting on their own findings.

Unitarians as a group responded to the internments with aid and support to the hapless victims. Some of the Pacific Coast Unitarian congregations provided ministry to the camps. Churches collected books, equipment for nursery schools, layettes for babies, and other supplies. Teenagers provided a shopping service, and ministers made regular visits to the assembly centers to see where the churches might be useful as well as to give spiritual comfort.

Toward the close of the war, the USC opened hostels in Boston and New York where relocated Japanese Americans could find transitional housing, hospitality, and help with making their way around a new city. The opening of the hostel in New York, jointly sponsored by the USC and Community Church (Unitarian), was celebrated by an intercultural and interracial open house that reflected the neighbor-hood's melting pot. It was organized by one of the people USC had helped emigrate from Lisbon in 1941.

Martha returned to Boston in June 1942 and prepared to deliver a comprehensive presentation on her seven-week trip before the AUA's annual board meeting. Instead, Bob Dexter limited her to a ten-minute summary. She was furious and denounced Dexter's "un-concealed ill will" in a letter to President Eliot, prime mover behind the Sharps' two commissions to Europe.

Dr. Eliot responded with much the same argument he had used dispatching Waitstill and Martha to France over their stated objec-tions. The "job is so big and so important," he wrote Martha, "that even wholly justifiable feelings of having been unfairly and discour-teously and unreasonably dealt with are beside the point."

Martha henceforth kept her own counsel, but another threshold had been crossed. In 1944, she accepted a temporary USC posting to Lisbon, but by the end of that year she would resign from the com-mittee altogether. Aside from a single special mission to Iraq in 1949, she was finished with the USC.

So too was Waitstill. Proud as they were to have successfully launched the committee, which would enjoy a vital and exciting fu-ture, henceforth neither of the Sharps would be part of it.

—— · ——

By 1944, Martha's speaking and travel schedule—for USC, Youth Aliyah, and the National War Fund (a kind of United Fund, admin-istered by the US government, which helped support about twenty agencies, USC among them)—took her further and further away from the life of the Wellesley Hills Church.

On May 7, 1944, one month before the D-Day landings at Nor-mandy, Waitstill resigned from the pulpit at Wellesley Hills to accept a yearlong commission with the Displaced Persons Division of the Middle East Mission of the United Nations Relief and Rehabilitation Administration (UNRRA). The division had been established the previous autumn by the Allies to manage the repatriation of refugees once the war was concluded. It was another decisive moment for the Sharps. With the exception of brief interludes, the four of them would not reside together under the same roof again for three years.

Waitstill wrote,

I proceeded to College Park, Maryland, for four weeks' training, and flew June 28th to Cairo via Miami, Belem, Ascension Island, Accra, Maiduguri and Khartoum.

This was a paradoxical year. It was rewarding for a lifetime as an experience in world travel and social observation; the Mediterranean World—Egypt, Palestine, Italy—came alive with all its poverties, its diseases and its promise.

Promise there is in the Middle East, if reason and conscience can gain a foothold, first for education, social service and the formation of labor unions, and then for a social revolution.

As an administrative experience, the year in this vast, cumbersome, paper-cluttered machine called "Middle East Mission, UNRRA," was as deep a disappointment as could follow two such exciting and rewarding adventures as were 1939 in Central Europe and 1940 in the Iberian Peninsula and Southern France. The Middle East Mission was bedeviled by months of idleness, the oversupply of personnel, black market corruption with supplies, drunkenness, the result of frustration and boredom, and hatreds and rivalries between Americans and Americans and between British and Americans.

The prince of devils was the British military intent to prostitute the whole UNRRA program in the Middle East to serve Churchill's political enterprises in Greece, Yugoslavia and Albania. Scores of us did not accomplish one single act in that whole year; we sat about rustling papers, or ran about wangling military orders for travel to see refugee camps (and also Palestine). This was my first intensive experience with the species *bureaucrat,* the little man with the glossaries of official lingo and his eyes on the next stage of the climb up the administrative chart; he shines apples for the higher brass the while he plants flyspecks on the names of his competitors for the next salary level. The female of this species is more deadly than the male.

——— · ———

Martha arrived in Lisbon for her final USC assignment on February 11, 1945. Before she returned home that September, she worked hard to help Republican "illegals" who had fought against Franco in the Spanish Civil War and now faced imprisonment and death if they returned home. She managed to help twenty of them immigrate to Venezuela and helped another seventy-five immigrate to Mexico. She also saved the life of Albert Assa, a Jewish language teacher from Turkey who was under sentence of death in Spain. She organized an international, interfaith protest, including through her connection to Eleanor Rathbone, MP, one of her contacts during the mission to Czechoslovakia. With the help of the British Foreign Office, Assa's sentence was commuted, and he and his family eventually immigrated to Mexico.

Waitstill joined Martha in Lisbon on May 29 after finishing his one-year commitment to UNRRA. He was on hand to watch the first twenty Spanish Republicans sail off to freedom, and he spent six weeks in Lisbon with Martha before sailing for New York in late June. On July 13, he sent her a postcard from Washington, DC. "I miss you with all my heart," he wrote, "on this my 17th wedding day! Love even greater, Waitstill."

Martha completed her assignment on September 3, then traveled to Czechoslovakia for an eleven-day visit before flying into LaGuardia on September 15. The family was reunited in Wellesley Hills for just eight days before Waitstill would depart aboard the *Queen Elizabeth* for yet another extended deployment abroad. He had accepted a position as field director for AmRelCzech and was on his way to Prague to oversee a program for re-equipping Czech hospitals that had been bombed and looted by the Nazis.

Hastings and Martha Content, now thirteen and seven, had seen their father just three out of the previous sixteen months. They would not see him again until the spring of 1947, another eighteen months away.

In Prague, Waitstill found echoes of the dangerous days of 1939 in an exhausted city, with the country trapped in the shadow of yet another foreign conqueror, the Soviets. Jan Masaryk had returned to Prague to continue serving as foreign minister, now in the coalition National Front government formed the previous April.

Karl Haspl had replaced his murdered father-in-law as minister at Unitaria. Ruzena Palantova had survived the Nazis too. Most everyone else the Sharps had known had either perished or escaped abroad.

One exception was the young woman dressed in a British Royal Air Force uniform who approached Waitstill one afternoon as he was having tea in the lobby of the Hotel Alcron. "You don't remember me," she said. "You couldn't. But I remember you because after an interview you gave me ten thousand korunas that made it possible for me to escape."

She was a Czech Jew who'd followed the underground escape route through the coal mines, under the border into Poland, then up to the Baltic Sea, and onto a British submarine that took her to England. It turned out that she possessed both a fine mind for math and an encyclopedic memory of southern Bohemia and Moravia, as well as Slovakia.

Within an hour of arriving in England, she told Waitstill, she had been put to work in an RAF calculating room, helping British fliers calibrate their bombing attacks on military targets in these regions.

She found the work both satisfying and redemptive. Of eighty-eight people in her family, she was the only one to survive. "I've just been back," she explained. "Nobody can find them."

———— · ————

As Waitstill prepared that autumn to go back to Prague as a field agent for AmRelCzech, that organization offered Martha a position in Prague too. The USC also asked her to coordinate a medical mission to Czechoslovakia. She and Waitstill thus had the opportunity to team up again, as they had often discussed, possibly placing their son and daughter in Swiss boarding schools so they could be near. It might have been a way to resume family life and recapture the shared responsibilities they had executed so ably a few years ago. But again Martha and Waitstill went their separate ways, as she decided to stay in the United States to work in support of Hadassah. This decision contravened all the plans they had made for reuniting the family and is inexplicable except in terms of Martha's commitment to Youth Aliyah. Perhaps she felt, as she had when she had stayed on in France to complete the children's emigration, that to abandon the work would be like watching children drown and doing nothing. Martha watched Waitstill board the *Queen Elizabeth* in New York to begin his trip to Prague at eight on Sunday evening, September 23, 1945, then immediately threw herself into an exhausting public-speaking tour.

It began the next morning with a five-day trip around New Jersey, after which Martha returned to Wellesley Hills in time for a Saturday night dinner with the children. She then left immediately for a National War Fund meeting in New York and then was off on a five-week tour that took her to Pennsylvania, Ohio, Michigan, and Iowa. Her speaking schedule eased through the Christmas holidays, when she spent as much time as possible with her children. Since she had given up their rented house when she flew to Lisbon in February of 1945, there was no "home" for the three of them. In December, she would rent an apartment at 31 South Russell Street in Boston, but until then Martha and Martha Content stayed with friends and Hastings boarded at the private Fenn School in Concord, Massachusetts, where he was now an eighth grader.

It is hard to imagine that the irony of her situation—devoting herself to the cause of displaced children while neglecting her own—was entirely lost on Martha. On the other hand, as she had written, she was providing perks like private schools that the children could not have had on a minister's salary, and she might have told herself, as she did in the letter to Hastings from France in 1940, that her children were being well cared for and well educated while thousands of others were in desperate need of her help.

In mid-November she wrote to Waitstill that family finances were now firmly in the black. There was $4,500 in the bank, and she intended to invest $4,000 of it "as soon as the market goes down" at the end of the year, she said. She also said that she'd received eighteen speaking invitations in the mail on the same day. Eight were from Hadassah, which paid Martha $50 per appearance, plus expenses. But she was exhausted. "I just feel I can't refuse them," she wrote, "but really I am at the end of my rope." She reiterated the complaint to him a few days later. "I need a rest dreadfully. I find that my mind is so tired that I can't remember anything." But she didn't stop.

In Concord, Hastings earned four A's, four B's, and three C's that term. French, Latin, and Conduct were not his strengths. "Examination marks weren't as good as we had hoped they would be," wrote Hastings's housemaster, Mr. Frothingham, "but I feel somewhat encouraged, having the impression that Hastings is reaching out a little more in some directions. He is getting along better socially, having largely dropped his habit of making caustic remarks about personalities."

"My chief impression right now," he wrote, "is that Hastings has surprised himself once or twice by really learning a Latin lesson. I hope the experience will be like the olives in a bottle. Now that the first has been finally pried out, the rest will come easily in a steady stream."

Martha Content, now a third grader at Kingsbury Elementary in Wellesley Hills, had been staying with the Becker family. "It has been a very trying experience for me, as well as her," Martha wrote to Waitstill on November 18. "I wish you would come home," Martha Content wrote her father. "I see all the other fathers home, so you can come home. Couldn't you come home, please? You should have been here this Sunday. Yes, you should have. I cannot write any more."

She enclosed a sketch she'd done of herself and Waitstill. "Picture of you and me," she wrote, signing the letter simply "Martha."

— CHAPTER TWENTY-FOUR —

A Run for Congress

Martha celebrated the first postwar Christmas with the children in 1945. All that was missing was Dad. She took them shopping and to a performance of the Ice Capades. Christmas Day was spent with the Dickies, her paternal aunt and uncle who lived in Providence, Rhode Island.

Then on January 12, 1946, she dropped what she later called a "bombshell" in a letter to Waitstill, announcing that she'd been approached to run for Congress by leaders of the state Democratic Party. The Republican candidate in Massachusetts's 14th District would be eleven-term incumbent Joseph W. ("Joe") Martin Jr., a hard-line conservative and adamant foe of most New Deal measures. Martin was in line to replace Texas Democrat Sam Rayburn as Speaker of the House if, as was widely expected, the GOP won a majority in the lower house for the first time since 1932.

The run for the popular Martin's seat would be one of the key races in the 1946 congressional campaign and among the sternest challenges for the Democratic Party. Martha looked like cannon fodder.

Martha explained to Waitstill that John Cahill, chairman of the state Democratic Party, had promised her full support. "Mr. Cahill has asked me to come to the Jackson Day dinner tonight," she wrote. "There I am to sit with Mrs. Louis McHenry Howe of Fall River, who is Postmistress, and to meet Mr. Hannigan, Postmaster General. If they agree tonight, I have the nomination. I have not yet decided to run. But they are lining up money and people, and if I am offered the CIO PAC [political action committee], and the Citizens' PAC and the nomination of the Independent Voters of Mass., I think it is my duty to do it. But I shall cable you beforehand and ask you. It is a great honor and a great responsibility."

She signed the letter, "Love, Martha."

Electoral politics was a natural next step for Martha. She had seen how Neville Chamberlain's failure of political will in Munich in the autumn of 1938 had led inevitably to the Einmarsch of the following March. Martha and Waitstill had been appalled in 1939 by the failure of the US Congress to enact the Wagner-Rogers legislation that would have granted asylum to twenty thousand German Jewish children. Three years later, Executive Order 9066, which incarcerated thousands of Japanese Americans, amply demonstrated to Martha, as she said, how critical vigilance is to protecting and preserving the ideals of a free society.

Joe Martin, sixty-one, was just the sort of politician whose voice Martha would have liked to supplant in the national political dialogue. FDR had mockingly lumped Martin and two co-isolationists, New York congressmen Bruce Barton and Hamilton Fish, as "Martin, Barton, and Fish" at the 1940 Democratic convention. Barton and Fish lost their seats in 1941 and 1945 respectively, but Joe Martin persevered, even thrived, while nearly every other Roosevelt foe was steamrolled by the FDR political juggernaut.

Now the war was over, however, and FDR was dead. The Republicans were on the rise, and Joe Martin had all the advantages of incumbency. He worked his district tirelessly and enjoyed high name recognition plus the support of an ascendant national party eager to retake the House. The GOP would strive at all costs to make certain its Speaker-apparent was victorious. Joe Martin also was Catholic in heavily Catholic District 14.

Martin was an indifferent orator, however, while Martha was an articulate speaker who might offer energy, youth, and glamour to the race. Her liberal politics might not go down easily around Wellesley, in the far northern precincts of the 14th district, but the fact that she spoke French and some Portuguese (which she had studied in her short stay in Lisbon, in 1945) would serve her well in the industrial areas, the working-class, ethnic southern cities, such as Fall River, which made up the bulk of the 14th.

Waitstill did not respond to Martha's letter of January 12 until February 23.

When he did, Waitstill detonated a couple of bombshells of his own. He broke his response into two parts:

(1) Practicality—probability of winning. *Can* you?
(2) Desirability—propriety of winning. Do you *want* to?

Given the political climate and the opposition, he began, "I should rate your present chances at about 3 out of 100. This may sound like a rather austere calculation, when one figures that you have succeeded so far at practically everything you have ever tried. But this man is Joe Martin of the famous trio 'Martin, Barton and Fish.' Just recall that FDR successfully 'put away' *two* of those three men, but *one* survived even the landslides."

Waitstill then went on at length on how Republican demagoguery over the issue of American troops still garrisoned overseas ("All the Boys Home—Now" was one slogan he said came to mind) could "sweep the House from stem to stern, women voting their anxiety and loneliness and compassion for their men."

Waitstill saw it as part of a gathering conservative assault on internationalism, a return to the politics of the thirties, and warned: "If that gets going, you will not be able to stop it. You won't get a rational vote. You won't be able to face a single pre-primary or pre-election crowd without having to come clear on that in the first five minutes."

Regarding the other issue, the "desirability" of Martha's running for office, Waitstill opened his heart, uncharacteristically. It must have been an agony for him to write.

"Suppose you could sweep the District?" he began.

Do you want to? Apparently you do. OK by me, if that is the thing you want to do. I would help in any way I could, with as much of our small hoard as you wanted to chuck into the pool—and a candidate is expected to do a very generous part himself—and in any other ways.

As for me, I am beginning to wish to put down roots again. . . .

I want to go on, for what there is left of life, *with* you. Either here, or in the USA, *with* you. Not in either place in a house or a job whence you will fly whenever you can escape.

Waitstill had put it on the line.

"Seven years ago tonight we stepped off the train into Wilson Station—and into a new world," he concluded and signed the letter, "Love, Waitstill."

———— · ————

In Martha's response to Waitstill's *cri de coeur,* a surviving March 25, 1946, letter, she told him that "after you wrote me that you approved of my running I began seriously to work in the district." Their friend Marcia Davenport, who had visited Waitstill in Prague, "comes back to report that you are not happy about my running," Martha acknowledged. "But I can't back out now. It is unfortunately too late."

Waitstill would not return for the campaign.

———— · ————

In April, Martha reported that Hastings required glasses and that Martha Content's eyeteeth were coming in with no place for them to grow, "and her lower teeth are all severely out of place." She'd already been fitted for braces. Most of the rest of the letter was devoted to their housing situation. The little apartment on South Russell was not working out, so Martha was looking at a three-story, four-bedroom house on Eaton Court in Wellesley Hills. The asking price was twelve thousand dollars—"an extraordinarily low price for anything in Wellesley Hills," she wrote. A mortgage could be arranged that brought their monthly payments below the total of ninety dollars she was paying for rent and to store their furniture.

"If I win the election . . . the house will be handy," she continued. "If I lose, then we can decide if you want me to come over with or without the children, and we can rent the house. If you decide to return, you have a place to stay while you decide what you want to do. I should think it a wise move in any case, and surely no loss for the next three years."

"Tonight," she concluded the letter, "we sat in front of our tiny fireplace & MCS said, 'All the family together but Daddy. How I wish he were here. He would find it too small and cramped I'm afraid, but we are happy once again to be together.'"

———— · ————

In June, Martha reported to Waitstill that she had won her Democratic primary handily—7,128 votes to 2,232—but that she remained a long shot in the general election. "The possibilities of winning are small," she wrote.

> Martin has done favors for 20 years. He is liked as a person, and very few people have taken the trouble to look up his record. He has the businessmen scared to come out for me, because he already has threatened some of them. The silver manufacturers need his help on silver prices, the Jews on Palestine, etc. They are scared to death to even be seen talking to me.
>
> The big manufacturers are all for him. The local newspapers are all Republican-run. The Unitarian Mr. Reed who owns the Taunton *Gazette* is really very cooperative, but the Fall River *Herald News* and the radio station are owned by Republicans.

The Wellesley *Townsman* declined to print her press releases.

Her best chance, she said, was with the predominantly ethnic vote around Fall River, but Martha complained that she would have to do it all on her own. "The Massachusetts Independent Voters Assn., the

Citizens PAC and the CIO all promised help," she told him. "I got *nothing* from any of them, and the *liberals* are so wishy-washy that their help is NIL."

She nevertheless was hard at it. "I spoke 14 times last Sunday," she wrote, "in Portuguese, French, Italian, Greek and Polish clubs and in a Portuguese Protestant Church where they took up a collection of $49—for your work! All the Protestant ministers so far are for me. Now I start organizing 'Republicans for Martha Sharp,' and go to clambakes and picnics all summer. The fighting doesn't begin until Labor Day."

She signed off, "Love all of it, Martha."

———— · ————

Early in the campaign, Martha was advised by a Harvard lecturer, Dr. Jerome S. Bruner. His polling in the 14th District suggested that her liberal, internationalist positions were more in line with the voters' attitudes than were Martin's conservative positions. Her decision to run was based, in part, on the assumption that she could run a campaign of ideas and that her ideas carried more weight and currency in the electorate than did Martin's.

Arthur H. White, one of Bruner's students, later produced a comprehensive look at the election, "Martha Sharp for Congress 1946: A Case Study." White's analysis isolated several problems that prevented Martha from keeping the campaign focused on legitimate issues. Important among the difficulties was a lack of money. Martha raised barely a third of the fifty thousand dollars she needed to wage an effective campaign, White said. Also, the muscle, money, and foot soldiers she counted on from organized labor did not materialize. The zeitgeist was against her, not for her.

Whether Martha might have overcome these obstacles is not known. As White pointed out in his thesis, her run for Congress was ultimately doomed by an old-fashioned smear, for which a paper trail survives.

The North Attleboro *Chronicle,* owned by Representative Martin, referred to Martha as "the little lady who sometimes wears a red dress," which was consistent with the paper's general preoccupation with Communism.

One of the earliest documents pointing to a campaign to discredit her, however, is a September 16, 1946, memo from FBI director J. Edgar Hoover to "Mr. Tolson, Mr. Tamm and Mr. Ladd." In it, Hoover described a meeting with an unnamed acquaintance who informed him "that a legislative counsel from the Hill was injecting himself into a congressional campaign in Massachusetts. The story is going around up there that MARSHA [sic] SHARP, the democratic candidate who is running against representative Martin, is a communist."

Hoover added that "this legislative counsel is now in Boston looking into her record. It has been rumored that Marsha Sharp, who is the wife of a Unitarian Minister, aided the communists when she was in Europe for several years in connection with Unitarian relief." The director wrote that he had assured his source "that I would check our files on this woman and let him know what I found."

The "legislative counsel" was Ernest (Ernie) Adamson, chief counsel to the House Un-American Activities Committee (HUAC), which had been investigating the alleged communist ties of the Joint Anti-Fascist Refugee Committee, which had funded some of Martha's work with Spanish Republican "illegals" on her second assignment to Lisbon.

As part of his investigation, Adamson had been granted access to the AUA records and encountered Martha's extensive file therein. This had been in June. Adamson's interest then extended to Waitstill. It probably didn't help Martha's case when HUAC staffers discovered that in 1943 Sharp had signed a petition calling for the abolition of HUAC.

On October 18 the *Boston Traveler* reported: "Representatives of the Unitarian Service Committee, which has headquarters in Boston, have been invited to appear before the House Committee on Un-American Activities in Washington, it was learned today. Ernie Adamson, chief counsel of the House committee, said that the Unitarian officials would be questioned regarding their affiliations with the Joint Anti-Fascist Refugee Committee, which has been branded a Communist front by the House committee."

Next day, under the headline "Asks Inquiry on Mrs. Sharp," the Fall River *Herald News* reported that the local Admiral Nelson Navy Club had passed a resolution calling for the Fall River War Veterans Council to investigate Martha. The author of the request was Father Ambrose Bowen, a Catholic priest who had written Adamson four days before J. Edgar Hoover's September 16 memo, asking if Martha's name had come up in connection with any HUAC investigation. How Father Bowen might have known that the House committee was looking at the Sharps, or that Ernie Adamson was leading the probe, was never addressed in the press reports. There had been nothing about it in the papers at that time.

Martha responded immediately on radio station WSAR. "One of the oldest tricks, as everyone knows, is to yell 'red,'" she said. "When everything else fails, that is the technique they dust off. No matter that it has no basis in fact, if it beclouds the real issues and takes attention away from an office holder."

She also angrily demanded that this investigation be held immediately, in order for her to "meet face to face with my accusers."

That did not happen. Instead, on November 4, 1946, the night before the election, Joe Martin's campaign paid for time on WSAR for Father Bowen to expand on his suspicions and allegations, which extended even to inferences that Martha, because she distributed relief funds provided by the Joint Anti-Fascist Refugee Committee, approved of Yugoslavia's communist Marshal Tito.

In the voting on Tuesday, Joe Martin swamped her by more than thirty thousand votes, a margin of nearly two to one. As Waitstill (and nearly everyone else) predicted, the GOP reclaimed the House, and Martin became Speaker in January of 1947. Martha's political career was at an end, but she exited the public arena proudly, with a well-honed bit of valedictory. "I have never," she told the Boston *Herald* later that week, "seen anything more un-American than the House Committee on Un-American Activities."

————— CHAPTER TWENTY-FIVE —————

Palestine

Bitter as the loss to Joe Martin had been, Martha barely broke stride. By the middle of December 1946, she was back on the lecture circuit, appearing before audiences in Buffalo, Rochester, and Great Neck, New York. When Hadassah offered to send her to Palestine, she readily accepted. The organization wanted to familiarize Martha, one of their top fund-raisers, as well as a leading liaison to the liberal Christian community in the United States, with the programs that her inspirational fund-raising supported. It was also a chance to cement her commitment to Zionism, which began with her work with Hadassah, which Martha theretofore had embraced enthusiastically but mostly in the abstract.

At 7:15 on the evening of January 16, 1947, she boarded a multi-stop, three-day flight to Cairo. After what she had seen in Europe, the idea of a safe homeland for Jews, particularly their children, struck Martha as a solidly sensible and desirable goal. Now she would see the ideal made real. Witnessing the as-yet-unborn state of Israel as it began to flower in the desert had a profound impact on her.

"A great powerful stream of sacrifice and idealism is bringing about the birth of a nation," she later wrote. "We are witnessing an epic like that of America. The pioneers are giving their lives and are challenging us to share enough to help in time."

————— • —————

Martha was shown the length and breadth of Palestine, from the Dead Sea, where she bobbed about with the rest of the tourists in the inky, super-buoyant water, to the Syrian border. The tour included, it seemed to her, every kibbutz and Youth Aliyah program that could be crammed into a six-week visit. She also met David Ben-Gurion, who would become Israel's first prime minister the following year, as well as many other of the nation's founding leaders. Among these was former Milwaukee schoolteacher Golda Myerson, who would soon become Israel's first minister of labor. After she Hebraized her name to Golda Meir in 1956, she would eventually serve from 1969 to 1974 as Israel's first—and to this date only—female prime minister.

There was also a poignant reunion with Yehuda Bacon, a sixteen-year-old Czech she had met in 1945 in Czechoslovakia on her way home from Lisbon. Bacon, then emaciated and haunted looking, was among a group of children recently rescued from Nazi death camps.

Of Bacon's immediate family, only a younger sister had managed to escape, to Palestine, before the Germans began implementing their so-called Final Solution. In 1942, Yehuda, his parents, and an older sister had been interned first at Terezin, then transported to Auschwitz. His mother and sister later were moved to another concentration camp, where they died two weeks before its liberation. Yehuda's father was gassed and cremated at Auschwitz.

Yehuda himself was spared by the Nazis to work in the death camp. He remembered hauling wood for the ovens and being told by a guard on one particularly cold day, "If you want, you can warm yourself in the gas chambers." These were built below ground level. "Not all the boys dared to do it," Bacon remembered, "but I was a very curious boy."

He wanted to see where and how his father had been murdered. "I went in and I asked like somebody who goes to a museum, 'What is this? What is that? What is the purpose of it?' Somehow I wanted to remember everything and I kept it very sharp in my memory."

He committed the scenes at Auschwitz to paper, producing numerous drawings that he somehow preserved and kept safe. Some of them later would be introduced as evidence at the 1961 trial in Israel of Adolf Eichmann, a chief architect of the Final Solution. Bacon would also testify personally at Eichmann's trial. Martha took many of Bacon's drawings with her back to the United States and shared them with her horrified audiences. In one of the most powerful, the boy depicted his father's image rising huge above the landscape from one of the crematorium smoke stacks at the camp. There was a common term for this: "human smoke."

In Czechoslovakia, Bacon had given Martha the yellow Star of David he had worn, the emblem of faith that the Nazis ordered sewn onto the clothes of all Jews. (Martha would preserve the piece of cloth, which survives today.) Bacon told Martha at the time that his single greatest desire was to immigrate to Palestine.

His wish came true in May of 1946, and the following spring, when they met again in Jerusalem, he was studying at the Bezalel art school, laying the foundation for a long and successful career in Israel as an artist and a teacher. At this meeting, he gave her a self-portrait as a token of gratitude.

Thereafter they would remain in touch, mostly by mail. When Yehuda Bacon visited the United States in the 1960s, Martha restored all his artwork to him, including some pieces that are now in the permanent collection at Yad Vashem, the Holocaust memorial in Jerusalem.

———— · ————

In the spring of 1947, Waitstill's quest for "rootage" brought him home from Czechoslovakia, where he had administered a $1.5 million relief program, largely for undernourished children. The four Sharps finally were reunited, if only intermittently, at the new house Martha had bought at 18 Eaton Court, which would be Waitstill's home address for the next two years. Over that time he would work as a freelance consultant, preach on occasion, and travel relatively infrequently.

From July 18 to August 19, the family vacationed for the first time in years at Lake Sunapee, where Martha made curtains and applied two coats of paint to the guest room sashes.

Martha remained the family breadwinner when in September 1947 she signed a yearlong contract with Hadassah. She agreed to combine fund-raising for Youth Aliyah with certain administrative responsibilities for Children to Palestine, an organization she helped found in 1943 along with Waitstill and others. Its goals were to raise funds for the housing and maintenance of Youth Aliyah children, to publicize Zionism in the Christian world, and to forge interfaith links. Much of the activity was directed to Sunday schools, where children were encouraged to fill collection books for new housing. After a speech-making trip Martha made to Tulsa, Oklahoma, in 1948, the secretary of the Hadassah chapter there wrote: "The entire Jewish community has been revitalized by her visit and reinspired by her devotion to our cause. In addition, she accomplished worlds of good with our Christian neighbors, most of whom had never heard the story of the concentration camps, let alone of Youth Aliyah or Children to Palestine."

Not long before she died, Henrietta Szold wrote to Martha commending her on her work toward the advancement of interfaith understanding. "I want to leave you with the impression," she wrote, "that your Inter-Faith undertaking strengthens faith and consecrates hope."

Through the efforts of Martha and Gisela Wyzanski, one of her Hadassah friends, Children to Palestine later became Fellowship in Israel for Arab-Jewish Youth, making grants to integrated projects such as a theater-training program at Oranim College in Haifa and Neve Shalom/Wahat al Salam, currently the only integrated Jewish-Muslim-Christian community in Israel.[1] After she returned from her first trip to Palestine, Hadassah immediately sent her out on a three-month national tour that paid her twelve hundred dollars per month. She also received one hundred dollars for each appearance she made on a number of local and regional fund-raising forays.

When she resumed her national speaking schedule that autumn, Hadassah began booking her on numerous joint appearances with Eddie Cantor, the popular comedian and singer who had been an early and vociferous opponent of the Nazis. Cantor also campaigned for the National Infantile Paralysis (Polio) Foundation, which was begun in 1938 by FDR, who had come down with polio in 1921 at the age of thirty-nine. Cantor coined the foundation's informal name, March of Dimes.

Martha made many friends in the entertainment industry, including Murray Silverstone, head of international distribution for 20th Century Fox studios. In November of 1947, Silverstone and his wife, Dorothy, invited Martha to their house in Scarsdale, New York, to celebrate the opening of *Gentleman's Agreement,* the Academy Award–winning examination of anti-Semitism based on Laura Z. Hobson's novel of the same name.

The movie, directed by Elia Kazan, had special resonance for Martha. Its producer, Darryl Zanuck, was moved to pursue the project after Congressman John E. Rankin of Mississippi, a prominent member of the House Un-American Activities Committee, uttered a series of anti-Semitic slurs on the floor of the House. Rankin is mentioned by name as a bigot in the film.

Martha brought eleven-year-old Martha Content with her to the Silverstones' party, where she danced with the star of *Gentleman's Agreement,* Gregory Peck, whom she found to be very shy.

The Sharps all celebrated Thanksgiving in Wellesley Hills on November 27. Two days later, Waitstill and the children cheered along with Martha when the United Nations voted to partition Palestine, paving the way for the birth of Israel the following May 14, as the British Mandate expired.

The first Arab-Israeli War broke out in Palestine immediately after the UN vote. In May of 1948, armies from Egypt, Syria, Transjordan, Lebanon, and Iraq invaded the new nation. By July, a UN truce was in effect, but bullets were still flying in Jerusalem when Martha arrived in August on her second trip to the area. A bullet almost hit her in the head one night as she walked in the Old City. She stayed only a couple of weeks on this trip. At the request of the American Jewish Joint Distribution Committee (JDC), on the way home Martha flew to Casablanca, where for several days she worked in the *mellah,* or ghetto, to recruit impoverished and disease-ridden Moroccan children for emigration to Israel.

—— CHAPTER TWENTY-SIX ——

Civil Rights and Chicago

In the spring of 1949, Waitstill was appointed executive director of the Chicago Council Against Racial and Religious Discrimination, one of the seminal civil rights organizations in the United States. He was recruited to the job by two Unitarian ministers. One was Reverend Leslie T. Pennington, who had criticized Waitstill's declaration of war against Hitler in June of 1940. Pennington had accepted the pulpit at Chicago's First Unitarian Church in 1944 when Waitstill went to Cairo for UNRRA. The second was the Chicago council's previous executive director, Homer A. Jack, a Unitarian minister with ties deep to the budding civil rights movement.

Taking the Chicago job meant a radical refocus for Sharp, although it certainly was consistent with his announced purpose of putting down new roots in his native country. Whatever his motives, Waitstill clearly saw the struggle for civil rights as yet another battle for human rights and human dignity. In 1947, long before the stirrings of a national civil rights movement, he gave a sermon, "The Colored Man Waits," which shared his biblical passion for civil rights and equality. Referencing the book of Amos 9:7, "'Are ye not as children of the Ethiopians to me, O children of Israel?' saith the Lord," Waitstill asked: "When shall white men really believe the vision of Amos, 750 BC? . . . Here is one of the key tasks of World Commonwealth," he continued, "the development of a maturity and a compassion resourceful enough to control racism. A Christianity brave enough, gallant enough, wise enough to develop these resources, is the only Christianity fit to survive. The Judgement Day is upon us of the other white races."

Martha helped him hunt for a house that May. Then she sent Martha Content and Hastings to camp for the summer before packing up the family belongings in Wellesley Hills and heading by car for Chicago in early July. From July 7 to 14, according to her diary, she and Waitstill settled into the new house at 4523 South Greenwood Avenue. Then Martha boarded a plane at Midway Airport for New York and headed to Israel once more.

This third mission to Israel, in July 1949, was another of her exercises in multitasking. She combined touring for Youth Aliyah with coordination of a short film, *The Magnetic Tide*, produced by her friend Dorothy Silverstone. The film expresses the core of Martha's vision for the nation of Israel: a multicultural society where Jew, Muslim, and Christian would live in peace as they built the new land together. With music by the Palestine String Quartet as well as Jewish orchestral groups, the film presents a glowing picture of interfaith cooperation including the sharing of technology that brought water to dry places and integrated life in places like Nazareth and Beersheba. It features the village of Ben Shemen in central Israel, an agricultural settlement led by Dr. Siegfried Lehmann. Lehmann was a friend of philosopher Martin Buber and lived a life committed to Buber's concept of dialogue rooted in the biblical idea that in each human being is the image of God. Lehmann's friendship with Arab neighbors was the decisive factor in the safe removal of his wards from Ben Shemen during the war the previous year. The neighbors warned him of the impending attack. Children to Palestine sent funds to rebuild destroyed buildings and construct new ones. Over the years, it provided a new school, community house, and library, as well as several houses, including the Martha Sharp House.

Expressing pride in the land, in the new life that it was giving to child survivors of the Holocaust, and in the promise that Jew, Muslim, and Christian could live together in peace, the film reflects much of Martha's faith that the new country would become a beacon of democracy and interfaith cooperation. Its closing phrase, "The Fatherhood of God and the Brotherhood of Man," could not be more Unitarian.[1]

During this trip, Martha visited Palestinian refugee camps in Gaza. Quakers working there asked her to bring the plight of the refugees to the attention of Israeli government officials. In the Quaker tradition of "speaking truth to power," she raised the issue with Moshe Sharett, the foreign minister. As she recalled the meeting, Sharett, one of the more dovish members of the government, was "interested" but "overwhelmed" by the need to deal with the tidal wave of immigration unleashed by the establishment of the Israeli state. She called his attention to international sympathy for the displaced Arab population, and he agreed to increase the number of Arabs allowed to stay in their own homes in Gaza. He could do no more, she wrote, because of the housing shortage that was relegating thousands of new arrivals to crowded transit areas where tents were the only shelter available.

Another of Martha's projects was to supply the Youth Aliyah settlements with games and sports equipment. Working through Children to Palestine, Martha had persuaded Mel Allen, the legendary New York Yankees radio play-by-play announcer, to act as honorary chairman of Operation Sports, a campaign to collect the equipment, both new and used, with the help of children in American Sunday schools. In all, several tons of balls, sticks, gloves, helmets, nets, and other gear were shipped from the United States to Israel.

She wound up her visit to Israel in mid-August, but this time there was an additional stop on the way home: Iraq. The USC, which had made health and medicine its major international aid priorities at the close of the war, wished to open a dialogue with Iraq and asked Martha to visit the country as their representative.

Her four-day visit to Baghdad, the capital, and Basra, a major river port city to the south, began on August 27. Discussions with Iraqi doctors and state health officials led to plans for a cooperative campaign against a debilitating parasitic disease called bilharzia (also known as schistosomiasis, or snail fever). Martha also spent time quietly gathering information on the plight of oppressed Iraqi Jews, who were forbidden to travel.

Some of Martha's meetings with secret informants were conducted at night on the roof of her hotel, a page out of her clandestine days in Prague and the south of France. She would report on her mission directly to Abba Eban, then the Israeli ambassador to the United Nations. Ultimately, a deal was worked out whereby 124,000 Iraqi Jews—practically the country's entire Jewish population—were allowed to immigrate to Israel as long as they left all their material possessions behind.

—— · ——

Hastings and Martha Content spent that summer of 1949 in Chicago with their father. Hastings would begin his senior year at Hackley, a private college prep school located in Tarrytown, New York. Hastings was by then serious about his schooling, or at least serious enough to be accepted the following year at Harvard, where he would study chemistry.

On Labor Day, September 5, Waitstill and the children drove the current incarnation of Lizzie, the name the Sharps gave to all their cars, to Midway to meet Martha's plane. The next morning, Martha escorted Martha Content to her first day of eighth-grade classes at a local public school. By September 12, however, Martha was back in New York. According to her diary, she did not return to Chicago until October 4.

Life in Chicago was hellish for Martha Content, she recalls. With her big brother Hastings away at boarding school and her mother only occasionally in the house, she had to contend with more than any thirteen-year-old should have to face.

The house, located in a marginal neighborhood, had a large backyard, where she and her father kept a couple of ducks as pets. Martha Content mowed the grass for a dollar a week. Waitstill had no domestic skills and apparently no intention of acquiring any. His daughter remembers serving as de facto cook, laundress, and maid.

She clashed with him on questions of makeup and wardrobe. Sharp saw no need for the former and sought to severely circumscribe the latter. Oxfords and dresses to the ankle were his idea of appropriate teen fashion. Martha Content finally resorted to petitioning him in writing. When that didn't work, she took her case to their church, where elders counseled the reluctant Sharp to let his daughter dress and look like other girls her age.

The neighborhood could be dangerous, and her father's work was perilous as well. The council against discrimination was focusing much of its attention on fair housing issues for blacks, who were then excluded from much public as well as private housing in Chicago.

There was violence. Waitstill twice came home covered in blood. On the second occasion, Martha Content had to drive him to the hospital at night in Lizzie the car, struggling to operate the unfamiliar standard transmission. Afraid for her well-being in the neighborhood and at school, Waitstill enrolled her in a private school, the Faulkner School for Girls, in Chicago, which she attended from 1950 until her graduation, in 1954.

———— • ————

The four Sharps spent the Christmas holiday together in Chicago. Martha appears to have been ill most of the time. Her notes indicate that she took a painful fall down a staircase, requiring X-rays, which showed no broken bones. Then she came down with one of her frequent acute upper respiratory infections before leaving, January 5, for Los Angeles, where in just under three weeks she would raise approximately seventy-five thousand dollars.

Martha still was Hadassah's hottest ticket, yet the work's constant demands were getting to her. She was exhausted and more prone than ever to the wide variety of medical problems that seemed to be a routine part of travel for her. Travel itself had long before then lost most of its magic, especially the long speaking tours when the days melted into one another and the only thing she looked forward to was getting into a hotel room bed each night.

That summer of 1950 she made one final trip to Israel, with Eddie Cantor, and returned in mid-July for one last family summer vacation at Sunapee. Martha expected to hit the road for Hadassah that autumn, as usual. Then came a telephone call from India Edwards, vice chair of the Democratic National Committee and a personal friend since her congressional campaign of 1946.

Edwards told her that Stuart Symington, chairman of the National Security Resources Board (NSRB), had asked her to find for him a woman with international relief experience, broad knowledge of the United States and women's organizations, and the ability to engage in effective public speaking and writing. The NSRB was a Cold War civilian preparedness agency that Symington had taken over after stepping down as the first US secretary of the air force. The job he needed to fill, preferably with a woman, was director of civil defense for women and children.

India Edwards appealed to Martha's patriotism, particularly the hostile unease that most Americans felt at the threat of postwar Soviet expansionism and the worldwide spread of Communism. Two years before, Josef Stalin had closed all land approaches to Berlin. In response, the United States and its allies had launched the Berlin Airlift, or Air Bridge, continuous supply flights to keep the citizens of the old German capital in everything from food to fuel, clothes, medicine, and everything else necessary for their survival. Symington, as secretary of the air force, had played an important role in the airlift's ultimate success. Stalin lifted the land barricades in May of 1949.

Elsewhere, the Soviets had exploded their first atomic bomb, and just before Martha's return home from Israel that summer, the communist government of North Korea had launched an invasion of South Korea.

Martha flew to Washington to meet with Symington, who told her with "great gravity," as she recalled, about her responsibilities should she become associate director of the NSRB. The job sounded demanding but interesting. The money was right. The chairman wanted her to begin at once. Martha called Waitstill.

"In most families," he joked over the phone, "Johnny goes off to war. In ours, it is Martha." He advised her to take the position.

———— · ————

Martha's acceptance of a sensitive, high-level job with the federal government meant that the FBI would have another look at her—a long look. From the moment she was hired until she departed with the advent of the incoming Eisenhower administration in February 1953, the FBI would never stop investigating Martha. Its interest centered on Waitstill's signature of an anti-HUAC petition; the Sharps' possible 1945 membership in the National Committee of American Friends of Czechoslovakia, which had Communist ties; Martha's connections with the Joint Anti-Fascist Refugee Committee, which had funded some of her refugee work in Lisbon; and whether or not she had secretly been the US Communist Party's candidate in the 1946 congressional race.

Easily her severest critic was Ernie Adamson, the former HUAC counsel, who accused her of having run a "travel agency for communists" in Lisbon in 1945. The agent who interviewed Adamson noted, "He knows Martha Sharp to be an extremely intelligent, resourceful and politically active woman, he believes she is directly financed by Moscow."

No detail seemed to escape the FBI. An agent in Los Angeles reported that during World War II, Lion Feuchtwanger had written for a left-wing, German-language periodical based in Mexico. The Chicago field office found a 1949 article published in the *Chicago Maroon,* the student newspaper at the University of Chicago, reporting on an address Waitstill had made to a "crowded student audience" at the school. The article reported that Waitstill advised students to "keep out of tension areas," where the local housing battle sometimes turned violent. According to the agent, Sharp "had stated 'the discrimination problem is increasing in Chicago, with the rate of increase being only six percent for Caucasians, but 47 percent for non-Caucasians.'"

Given Waitstill's weakness for such statistics, the FBI file has the ring of authenticity. The agent continued quoting the article: "This factor, plus man's hatred of dissimilar persons, plus the frustration and boredom created by capitalism in urban life, foster Fascism in Chicago." That sounds like Waitstill too.

It is difficult to imagine more loyal Americans than the Sharps, and this was the message the FBI heard from the dozens of friends, acquaintances, and associates they interviewed. Yet the unfounded fear that Martha and Waitstill's sterling reputations for patriotism and civic-mindedness were simply a smoke screen to mask a communist agenda kept dozens of agents in cities all over the world busy for three years, a vast make-work project that would not cease until Martha at last left the NSRB in 1953.

— CHAPTER TWENTY-SEVEN —

Divergent Paths

After years of absentee marriage and fragmented home life, Martha's new job inspired hope in Martha and Waitstill that they could put their family life back together. The work of planning a civil defense program for women and children, then selling her ideas to various constituencies inside and outside the government, would challenge Martha, as India Edwards had said, on multiple levels. It was useful, important work.

The job paid well, and a generous travel allowance—one of her preconditions to accepting the position—meant that Martha could fly home to Chicago regularly. For the first year, she lived in an apartment in Washington but commuted home each weekend at NSRB expense. It seemed to be working. Even as late as 1953, after she left the White House at the beginning of the Eisenhower administration, Waitstill, in writing to a friend, referred to Martha as his "one in a million."

Then came the split.

Waitstill would recall Martha walking into the living room, sitting down on the couch opposite him, and removing one of her signature hats with a little flourish. Then Martha leaned forward on an elbow, looked him straight in the eye, and said, "Waitstill, I want a divorce."

They had seen so little of each other, and shared even less, that any sense they had of forward momentum was by now only inertia.

Waitstill and Martha's marriage had been a deep source of strength for each of them from the start of their lives together. When tempered by adversity during the war years, the bonds of that marriage grew even tighter, and the courage the husband and wife lent to each other helped them to persevere in the face of enormous challenges. But when the war was over and the relief mission they had taken on together came to a close, Waitstill and Martha's relationship was changed in fundamental ways. The intensity and ever-present dangers around them in Europe had pulled them together as a couple, but when they returned to the United States, their wartime experiences had the effect of pulling them apart. Despite what they courageously accomplished together in the war years, it had become easier for both to simply live in the present and let the past fade away.

Waitstill was shattered. Surprised, deeply upset, and ultimately angry over Martha's decision, he felt she had abandoned him. Martha believed that at least part of his hostility sprang from his fears of what a divorce might mean for his career in the ministry, to which he intended to return. It is true that he tried everything to protract the divorce proceedings, evidently hoping that Martha would have a change of heart.

She would not. They signed divorce papers in June of 1954.

Unsurprisingly, Waitstill's opposition to the divorce seems to have resonated in Unitarian circles. Reverend Leslie Pennington, one of the three references Martha had listed on her NSRB job application, wrote what he called a "Statement Concerning Rev. and Mrs. Waitstill H. Sharp" in support of Waitstill's efforts to return to the parish ministry.

"I have been very close to Mr. Sharp during these last two, difficult years," Pennington wrote.

He has been a faithful father to his daughter, Martha Content, who has been finishing her work at the Faulkner School in preparation for college. He has done everything he could to avoid the break in his marriage. He has been much more generous and tolerant of Mrs. Sharp's desertion of her family than many of us among his friends who have watched this situation develop.

Even after Mrs. Sharp had said that she would not discuss this matter with those of us who have known them both for many years, and we had given up hope of saving this marriage. Mr. Sharp maintained such love, trust and admiration for her that he had no thought of allowing the marriage to be broken. It was only after the realization of more than a full year of desertion, and her expressed word that the marriage could not be saved, that he acknowledged to himself and his friends the need for legal separation.

——— · ———

When asked which of her two parents she preferred to live with, Martha Content's emphatic answer was "neither." She graduated from Faulkner in the spring of 1954 and accepted a full scholarship to the University of Illinois at Champaign-Urbana. Martha objected to the choice and made what her daughter called "one of those entries into the picture." She decreed that Martha Content would attend either Radcliffe or Pembroke (the women's college at Brown University and Martha's alma mater), *not* a large public university in the Midwest. Martha Content replied that she had no money. She was working as a soda jerk at the time.

"It's all right," Martha said. "I will give you a bus ticket."

So Martha Content rode a Greyhound three days to Cambridge, where she arrived at the bus station in the early morning. A few hours later, when the Radcliffe interviewer asked, "What has *Beowulf* meant to you?" Martha Content couldn't take the question seriously and so took a pass on Radcliffe.

The visit to Pembroke College at Brown went more smoothly. Martha Content survived the interview, and her mother prevailed on Whitelaw Reid's wife, an alumna too, to arrange for everything else, including a scholarship for her daughter.

Martha Content's major would be classics. "Part of my reason for choosing classics was the romance of the past," she says. "And much of that came from my mother, who I remember describing all the fascinating places she'd been. Plus, the past was fixed, while the present was such a goddamn mess."

———— · ————

In 1953, Martha moved to New York City, where she joined Raymond Rich Associates, a public relations firm that specialized in representing nonprofit organizations. She also took care of Hastings, who, after dropping out of Harvard and entering the army, had suffered a severe head injury in a training accident on Mount Rainier in Washington State and received a medical discharge. They lived together in an apartment at 108 West Fifteenth Street.

Waitstill meanwhile was called to the pulpit of the Unitarian church in Davenport, Iowa, in 1954 and would lead that church for nine years. In the summer of 1955 he married Monica Clark, an attractive food stylist he'd met at the First Unitarian Church in Chicago.

At Brown, in 1955, Martha Content met and fell in love with Artemis Joukowsky II, then a senior majoring in sociology. They married in June of 1956 in dual ceremonies—Russian Orthodox and Unitarian—in New York City. Waitstill came from Iowa to officiate. Uncle Livingston Stebbins (Aunt Edna had since passed on) gave Martha Content away.

A few days later, Waitstill sent Martha a brief note. "I shall always hope," he wrote,

> that my coming really was Martha Content's chief wish as to my relationship to her wedding. I hope that she and Art will always know that I did my best. The service was the most difficult which I have ever conducted. I am sure that the tension was clear to all—because it must have been shared in by all—between affection and hope and faith on the one hand; and on the other the sense of the permanent tragedy of selfishness overarching every detail of the transient beauty and the historic conventions of the moment.
>
> We are left only with the hope that two can hear and guard the Word which two others once heard and failed to cherish.
>
> Sincerely yours, Waitstill.

As far as is known, this was the last personal communication between the Sharps.

———— · ————

In 1957, Martha married David H. Cogan, a wealthy inventor who'd helped develop key portions of early television and radio technology. Her second husband also prospered as a manufacturer of vacuum tubes and of complete radio and TV sets.

Over the coming years, Martha remained active in her support for Israel. In the mid-1970s, she took a special interest in "Beautiful Israel," an urban beautification and environmental education program founded by Aura Herzog, wife of Chaim Herzog, then the Israeli ambassador to the United Nations and later its two-term president.

———— · ————

In 1981, Waitstill departed Davenport for the Unitarian church of Flint, Michigan, site of Martha and Annabelle Markson's "Men of Flint" triumph of two decades before. From Flint he and Monica traveled on to Petersham, Massachusetts, where he retired from the ministry and then settled in Greenfield.

That same year, Waitstill attended Martha Content's twenty-fifth anniversary celebration. Martha came to the gathering as well. At some point in the evening she noticed a familiar-looking old man standing alone in the room. At first, she did not recognize Waitstill, who had aged much more than she had. They did not speak.

Waitstill died three years later of a stroke at the age of eighty-two. At that time, in 1982, Waitstill was an admired figure in the denomination. Jack Mendelsohn spoke for many when he said that Waitstill "was the kind of minister I wanted to be. That is, he wasn't just a minister of a parish church; he was a civic figure, he was interested in the community in which he worked. He was interested in world affairs. He was interested in the need for peace in the world."

Waitstill's eulogist portrayed a man who had grown less rigid and moralistic with age, one who had become slower to judge and who, when touched, was known to display a tear or two.

——— · ———

In December of 1990, to commemorate the fiftieth anniversary of Martha's 1940 children's emigration project, the Unitarians brought her together in New York with eleven of those she had rescued, including all six of the Theis sisters, for a two-day event. The meeting delighted her, although by now Martha was losing ground to old age and the early stages of dementia.

Mercedes Brown, the difficult child who had traveled most of the way from Marseille to Lisbon in Martha's lap, spoke eloquently for them all. "We were the first travelers," she said. "We salute you and thank you for our journey to freedom."

By that time, Martha was a widow, David Cogan having died in 1985. Martha Content, then living in Providence, had been urging Martha to come live with them. "But," as Martha Content has written, "she told us in no uncertain terms that she wanted to remain in New York where she could see her friends."

So it was settled at first that Martha would have a room in their house and visit whenever she could. She decorated the space with some of her favorite furniture pieces and her Rose Medallion china.

"She often spent the weekends with us when she could get away," Martha Content has written.

> With time, we knew that she had to move to Providence. Yet it also was evident that she wanted her independence. . . . So she purchased a lovely Cape Cod house a few doors down the street from us. We renovated it. She selected fabrics and colors, and we moved her furniture and favorite objects from New York so she would feel that she was in familiar surroundings."
>
> For years every Wednesday we would prepare lunch at our home and invite people she could relate to. She was in command, and we wanted her to feel that way. It was always a festive occasion and completely revolved around her. She was always made up, elegantly dressed with her hair coiffed, and chatter was always animated. She was the role model and always gracious. Any male

who happened to appear was always welcomed with her radiant smile and a sparkle in her eyes. With time, however, I could see a look in her eyes—the real world was slipping away.

The trips to the piano became more infrequent, her old files were rarely opened, and her old friend Winston, her dog, died. It came to a point when she couldn't manage the stairs, and we moved a hospital bed into the dining room. Her disposition was always pleasant and kind, and her charm continued to be directed to everyone, but it was but of a blush of her former brilliance.

She was diagnosed with "sundown syndrome," so we repainted the walls of the living room a soft peach color, and hung pastel flowered chintz drapes at the windows. Around the clock, bright lights were blazing, and we always had classical music playing. She loved Chopin and Smetana. With time she lost her balance; she frequently fell, and she was moved to a wheelchair from which she continued to orchestrate her life. Finally she was bedridden.

We talked about life and death, and she signed a living will. She wanted to be cremated and to have her ashes scattered wherever I thought she would want to be. After a while she didn't know where she was. Her thoughts were tangled, and whatever was said to her she didn't remember. Every now and then there was clarity in her eyes, and she would utter an intelligent definitive statement.

I think she knew who I was until she lapsed into a semi-comatose state. Did she suffer in death? I cannot know for sure, but I don't think she did.

Several years before Martha died, on December 6, 1999, her son, Hastings—Waitstill Hastings Sharp Jr.—came to live with her in Providence. We have no record of Hastings's feelings about his parents' frequent absences during his childhood or any sense of abandonment that he might have had. Childhood hurts are difficult to overcome completely, but it is possible that during the years that he spent with her a connection to the time when she took care of him after his army accident was made. Hastings died in 2012.

EPILOGUE

In 2006, the state of Israel formally proclaimed Martha and Waitstill Sharp "Righteous Among the Nations." This honor is bestowed upon non-Jews who risked their lives to save Jews during the Holocaust. The Sharps became two of only five Americans to be so honored by Israel—another being Varian Fry, with whom the Sharps collaborated on some rescues.

A ceremony celebrating the honor was held at Yad Vashem, the Holocaust memorial in Jerusalem, where Martha and Waitstill were described as "Heroes of the Spirit," and their names were added to an honor roll that included such well-known names as Oskar Schindler and Raoul Wallenberg. The Sharps were honored with tributes by a group that included family, dignitaries, international press, and eighty-year-old Rosemarie Feigl, one of Martha's rescued children. As part of the service, Martha Content and Rosemarie rekindled the Hall of Remembrance's eternal flame.

Speaking of her parents that day, Martha Content Joukowsky described them as "modest and thoughtful people who responded to the suffering and needs around them, as they would have expected everyone to do in a similar situation. They never viewed what they did as extraordinary. They would not have expected today to be singled out in this way."

But even among the honored at Yad Vashem, the Sharps were singled out—a point made clear by Mordecai Paldiel, head of the Department of the Righteous at the memorial. "The Sharps are an example of the minority among our righteous," Paldiel explained. "The rescue operation was not thrust upon them. This is not a case where a person knocks on the door and says, 'Help me! I just escaped from a ghetto, I need sanctuary. Can I stay in your home?' In such a case, the rescuer becomes a rescuer on the spot. With the Sharps, [it was] a different story. They were motivated from the beginning to go into the kingdom of hell and try to get some people out. For this, we honor them."[1]

Martha and Waitstill's names are engraved on vertical stone walls that partially enclose the Garden of the Righteous. There, on a gentle slope in the shade of some pine trees, Martha and Waitstill are honored and remembered. They are together once again, inspiring us to ask what we can do today to help others.

———— · ————

The Sharps never published their own memoirs and rarely spoke of their accomplishments in public. It is worth noting, however, that no matter how heartbreaking and disappointing the dissolution of their marriage may have been, in later years, when Martha and Waitstill began to speak to family members and researchers about their past, they remembered each other in a most respectful way, with words full of admiration and affection. In their later years, when they finally began to share their stories, they did in fact find a way to reconcile and to appreciate each other anew through memory.

Martha Content described her reckoning of her parents' choices:

We do not choose our parents but I do know that mine honestly followed their hearts and their ideals and threw themselves into their life courses. They were determined, tender, compassionate, and had a deep empathy to help others. They deeply cared and connected themselves to a larger life, showing kindness to, and saving, many people along the way.

As a child it was hard to know what they had witnessed, and they didn't want to talk with us children about their sustained work or the horrors and struggles they had seen or felt. And as an adult I was bewildered when I was told of their frightening life and death situations. Now I am less puzzled and realize that their passions were larger than life in spite of the dangerous worlds that they found themselves in. For the Sharps' moral compass was devoted to a fundamental battle for human rights—that was a war worth waging and winning. They were wise with gifts of courage and dedicated to reshaping the Nazi political landscape. We are better people and wiser for their personal experiences, and that is what they inspired us to be.

When the war raging around them unleashed the worst of human nature, Martha and Waitstill Sharp did all they could to protect the dignity and preciousness of human life. The Sharps saved lives and ministered to the immediate need for food and shelter of many trapped in the catastrophe of war.

There is always the tendency to want to quantify the extent of the work, to pin it down in terms of numbers actually saved, either through direct emigration assistance or through relief efforts that allowed people to survive hunger and cold. But to do so is impossible. The work was day-to-day in a chaotic environment with little chance for follow-up. Extant records regarding emigration, including a list of about fifty people who sailed from Lisbon in 1940 during the Sharps' tenure there and the rescues that can be directly attributed to them, suggest a number of about 125. But no one kept a tally, and valuable records, like those of the Committee for the Placement of Intellectual Refugees in Geneva, are lost. There are many intangibles that simply can't be forced into a statistic. Waitstill's feeding program at the Salvation Army in Prague, for instance, allowed 264 people to stay alive long enough to get out. Martha and Waitstill provided sustenance for eight hundred French children for a month. We have no idea how many of them survived the privations of the war. We don't know if the two women Martha helped in Agde, Anna Pollakova and Ella Adler, survived. To cover an emergency, Waitstill gave Joseph Schwartz of the American-Jewish Joint Distribution Committee a loan of nine hundred dollars. Did the money save lives? Probably, but if so, how many? We just don't know the answers to these questions. But we do know that Martha and Waitstill were there in the midst of unfathomable horror doing freedom's work with loving commitment. Perhaps what matters most is not the number they were able to help, but that they chose to help at all. With little more to guide them than innate decency, a keen sense of fairness, and a deep love for each other, the Sharps stood up to unspeakable evil and made a difference. By any measure, Martha and Waitstill Sharp were heroes.

RESCUE AND RELIEF ORGANIZATIONS

American Committee for Relief in Czechoslovakia (AmRelCzech)
American Friends Service Committee (AFSC)
American-Jewish Joint Distribution Committee (JDC)
American Unitarian Association (AUA)
British Committee for Refugees from Czechoslovakia (BCRC)
Carnegie Institute for Peace
Children to Palestine
Committee for the Placement of Intellectual Refugees
Displaced Persons Division of the Middle East Mission of the United Nations
    Relief and Rehabilitation (UNRRA)
Emergency Rescue Committee (ERC)
Hadassah
HICEM, Jewish emigration agency
International Labour Organization (ILO)
International Rescue Committee
Jewish Refugee Committee
Joint Anti-Fascist Committee
National Committee of American Friends of Czechoslovakia
National Security Resources Board (NSRB)
Red Cross of France
Red Cross of Portugal
Red Cross of Spain
Red Cross of the United States
Salvation Army
Society of Friends (Quakers)
Unitarian Case Work Committee
Unitarian Service Committee (USC)
US Committee for the Care of European Children (USCOM)
Women's International League for Peace and Freedom (WILPF)
YMCA
Youth Aliyah

──── ACKNOWLEDGMENTS ────

My purpose in telling Martha and Waitstill's story is to inspire a new generation of rescuers. It is a call for action. The Sharps' story shows that "ordinary people" can do extraordinary things, serving as an inspiration to all of us today.

After that first talk with my grandmother, I was impassioned to make a difference in the lives of others. I also knew I had to help her tell their story to the world. Since that time I have been working beyond being a family historian to become a kind of self-driven historian-at-large who could add a critical and consequential story to our understanding of the events around World War II. Thus began an adventure that entailed extensive research deep within library archives, travels to Europe for primary sources and interviews, and the tireless efforts of professional researchers, archivists, and historians across five countries who have all collaborated to bring this book—and the accompanying movie, archive, and curriculum—to life.

So, while the genesis of this book may trace back to my own ninth-grade humanities paper, getting the Sharps' story fully explored and expertly told has required the efforts and devotion of many to whom I am deeply indebted. There are many people to thank and acknowledge. Please see the Credits page on the website Defyingthenazis .org for a complete list of all the supporters, filmmakers, writers, and interns who devoted their passions and skills to bring this story to the world.

Between 1999 and 2005, Larry Benaquist, Bill Sullivan, and Tom Durnford, supported by the Cohen Center for Holocaust and Genocide Studies, helped break the case. They helped me uncover thirty boxes in my grandmother's basement and eight hundred primary documents of Unitarian Service Committee rescue. Among the files were four hundred case files of names of people that my grandparents had attempted to help. Who were these people and what happened to them? We hired a private detective to find some of the surviving children, and one who we discovered was Eva Rosemarie Feigl, who came to the United States with twenty-six other children. Rosemarie, as she is known, testified to the historians at Yad Vashem that "Martha Sharp saved my life." Because she was Jewish and over the age of fourteen, Rosemarie was a credible witness to verify that Martha Sharp risked her life to save her. As a result of that testimony, and others we made on behalf of Waitstill, the Sharps became just the second and third Americans to be honored as "Righteous Among the Nations" by the state of Israel.

Along with Ghanda DiFiglia and archivist Aleksandra Borecka of the US Holocaust Memorial Museum in Washington, DC, our team systematically worked our way through the voluminous files of the American Unitarian Association, visited several Holocaust centers in the United States and abroad, and scoured university libraries, historical society records, newspaper obituaries, and church and municipal archives across the United States, Europe, and Israel. The team undertook research where we retraced my grandparents' travels around Prague and elsewhere in Czechoslovakia and on to the south of France.

Each time we located someone on our list, whose family had been touched by the work of the Sharps, we would ask for copies of their personal documents, and soon our source material was growing exponentially. The private detectives we had engaged located those who had been directly saved by the Sharps, and we conducted interviews with other members of my family, as well as with Holocaust survivors and Holocaust experts, who might shed insight on the work of the Sharps. Those documents are a part of the film, book curriculum, and archives. Thanks to my scholarly advisory team for all your valuable feedback and insights, including Alan Adelson, Jeff Diefendorf,

Deborah Dwork, Henry F. Knight, C. Paul Vincent, James Wald, Yehuda Bacon, Yehuda Bauer, and David Wyman.

Thank you for those who we interviewed for the book and the film, including Peter Braunfeld, Clement Brown, Joanna Brown, Mercedes Brown, Margaret Carroll, Catherine Vakar Chvany, Mary Deutsch Edsall, Haim Genizi, Mary-Ella Holst, Amelie Holstrom, Alain Le Roux, Gerda Stein Mayer, Rev. Jack Mendelsohn, Paul Mirat, Hanna Papanek, Justus Rosenberg, Ruth Rogoff, Sylva Simsova, Evelyn Strange, Alex Strasser, Joe Strasser, Susan Subak, Laura Tracy, Henry Walsh, and Jeanne Whitaker. These landmark interviews will be housed at the Spielberg Collection at the United States Holocaust Memorial Museum (USHMM) in Washington, DC, for students and scholars to access and use in the future.

In addition to these film archives, the Sharps' archives are now digitally housed at the USHMM, as well as at the libraries of Brown University, the Divinity School at Harvard University, and the Cohen Center for Holocaust and Genocide Studies at Keene State College in Keene, New Hampshire. Special thanks to all the archivists (listed on our webpage), but special mention should be made to Brown librarian Harriette Hemmasi and archivist Holly Snyder, who have worked to showcase the collection, as well as to archivists Fran O'Donnell and Jessica Suarez at the Harvard Divinity School library. Beginning with the initial boxes of eight hundred documents in my grandmother's basement, the archive has grown to more than two hundred thousand digitized documents! Now there are thousands of related items at three institutions, which also includes links to libraries in the city of Pau, in Southern France, and to archives in London and the Czech Republic, where our teams continue to meticulously log, sort, and organize to give a more accurate depiction of the Sharps' achievements, historical contributions, and legacy.

This project would never have grown without the support of the Unitarian Universalist Service Committee (UUSC) and the leadership of the Dr. Charlie Clements, MD, a human rights activist, and the former president of UUSC, who was a critical supporter of this project from the moment we met, in 2005. He both guided my efforts and became my first co-executive producer. The current president of the UUSC, the Reverend William Schulz, and our partners at the UUA, including President Peter Morales, Carey McDonald, and Paul Twitchell, have played an instrumental role in telling this story and celebrating the founding of the UUSC in 1940.

Marina Goldman not only reads the voice of Martha Sharp in the film but started the Sharp Rescuer Prize, which has been awarded twice. The Sharp Rescuer Prize promotes humanitarian work in the example of Waitstill and Martha Sharp and seeks to empower rescuers today who are risking their lives for others. The first award was given to KaWDA—Katanya Women's Development Association—to prevent the spread of Ebola in West Africa, and the second went to Latifa, Alexandra, and Colin Woodhouse, who went to Lesvos to assist refugees on that small Greek island as a direct inspiration of the Sharps' story.

The big break was in 2013 when Ken Burns, America's leading documentary filmmaker, saw the film and said yes to re-editing it for PBS. Under Ken's tutelage and mentorship in filmmaking and his aesthetic vision of historical storytelling, we completely edited the film for airing on PBS. Together with producer Matthew Justus, editor Erik Angra, and an extensive team of storytellers, including my daughters Emma and Alexandra, we told the story through the actual journals and interviews that are the basis of both this book and film. Ken brought on renowned actor Tom Hanks to be the voice of Waitstill Sharp. It is safe to say that without Ken's support of the film and telling this unique American story, you would not be reading this book today. His support made this project happen, and for his mentorship, support, and friendship, I am deeply indebted.

Over the past ten years, I have worked with a number of filmmakers who helped craft this story, including Larry Benaquist, Bill Sullivan, Deborah Shaffer, Steven Wechsler, Coby Atlas, and Kyra Thompson. Together with Florentine Films, including David Blistein, Elle Carriere, Chris Darling, and Kim Klein of the Better Angels Society, we were able to finish the post-production of the film. Working closely with Outpost WGBH, Chris Fournelle, Brandon Kraemer,

Beth Golin Lillis and WETA, and PBS, including Dalton Delan, Jim Corbley, and Anne Harrington and advisors Joel Shames and Drew Patrick, we are proud to present the film and book as companions.

This project would not be possible without the support, love, and guidance of my dear family, starting with my inspirations, my mom, Martha Sharp Joukowsky, remarkable teacher and scholar of the prehistory of the Middle East, and my dad, Artemis Joukowsky Volynsky, the "first rescuers" I ever knew. My father and his family company, AIG, had the habit of rescuing employees during times of revolution and war, starting with the evacuation from China in 1938 from the impending Japanese invasion.

I thank my four beautiful daughters with all my heart—Emma Rose, Lydia Elena, Alexandra Sophia, and Natasha Sally. They have all made significant contributions to making this project happen, helping me organizing screenings and becoming my associate producers. They also tolerated work sessions in my home office and countless screenings enough for their entire lifetimes, and each in her own remarkable way has helped to tell this personal family story. Emma Rose worked two years on the making of the film and plays her great-grandmother Martha in the Mr. X scene. Alexandra Sophia helped to find the new Tom Hanks lines after Ken called and said, "We have good news. Tom Hanks has agreed to read the lines. The bad news is you have two weeks to double the size of the film, and remember, Tom Hanks is reading your grandfather, so find the best possible lines"—and Alexandra did! She and Emma both earned the credit of associate producers.

My sister Nina and my brother Misha, along with his wife, Jane, and their families, have also been there for me from the beginning, and I thank them with all my heart. Among the many, many efforts of support, it was Misha's leadership and initiative that solidified the worldwide importance of this story when we successfully testified together to Yad Vashem. Working closely with Stanlee Stahl of the Jewish Foundation for the Righteous, we were able to make a direct testimony to Dr. Mordecai Paldiel, who at the time was the director of the Righteous Among Nations Program at Yad Vashem. Without their guidance and support, this story would not be known today.

Acknowledgment to Stephen G. Michaud for his vital and much appreciated role in co-creating this book. He helped develop the narrative from thousands of pages of raw research and then helped me to craft both its pace and content.

I would also like to thank Richard Higgins, Chuck Crisafulli, and my original collaborator, Ghanda DiFiglia, for contributing their skills as well.

This book is a wonderful tribute to Livingston Stebbins, who with his wife, Edna (chapter 1), came and took care of my mom and uncle during the first tour in 1939. Livingston Stebbins was, at the time of supporting Martha and Waitstill, the publisher of Beacon Press! So we all think it is fitting that this book found its home where it all started. Words do not express my gratitude and appreciation for my editor, Rachael Marks, who helped me take the final stand to publish this book. Thanks to all the folks at Beacon, including managing editor Susan Lumenello, copy editor Chris Dodge, and, of course, Tom Hallock, marketing director, and Helene Atwan, the director of the press, who made this book possible.

Thanks to my mentors and teachers Dr. Fernando Flores, Russell Redenbaugh, Mickey Lemle, Arnold Slavet, Adele Simmons, Jonathan Lash, Greg Prince, and Vartan Gregorian. Thank you to my funders and supporters for over seventeen years, including Tom Tisch, Jan and Rick Cohen, Jonathan and Jeannie Lavine, the Righteous Persons Foundation, the Seastone Foundation, the Starr Foundation, and the entire Threshold Foundation community.

I could not have done this project without many of my institutional partners (see a complete list on our website). Facing History and Ourselves, our educational curriculum developer, is now being used in thousands of schools, and that is the result of the passion of Marc Skvirsky and Laura Tavares. They have collaborated as true partners in shaping the story as a teachable moment for students today. No Limits Media, our co-production company (with Florentine

Films, in association with WETA), also supported us. Larry Rothstein, executive director, and Steve Marx provided much-needed feedback and support throughout the past fifteen years. At Hampshire College, President Jonathan Lash, Clay Ballantine, and Professors Arron Berman and Myrna Breitbart mentored me through the process. The leadership of the US Holocaust Memorial Museum, in particular director Sara Bloomfield and her trusted team of Lorna Miles, Aimee Segel, Dana Marnie, and many others, has enabled this project to grow the research and education of this story. The Anti-Defamation League, J-Street, the Strassler Center at Clark University, Yad Vashem, and the Museum of Tolerance have also been partners.

I would like to give a shout-out to the "unlimited partners," the people who helped me day after day to bring this project to fruition, including Michelle Pinage, Anne Harrington, Elizabeth Bolger, Walter Strauss, Mark Ide, Lorenzo Gaines, Joseph Steig, Tom Stoner, Craig Sieben, Deanna Byck, Geralyn Dreyfous, Dewey Wigod, Jody Snider, the D'Arcy family, the Dumar family, Liz Sheehan, David and Catherine Hills, Jodie Evans, Annie Birdy, the Sennott family, Ibrahim AlHusseini, and Dan Cogan (the nephew through marriage to the late Martha Sharp Cogan), and the many other partners and friends who made this book—and related film, archives, and curricula—possible. On every level it has been life changing and affirming!

Finally, one of the most gratifying aspects of making this film and book was getting to know my uncle Hastings, whose imitations of Donald Duck provided comic relief at times when it was most needed.

It seems that after decades of effort, the world is going to learn of Martha and Waitstill Sharp. My deepest gratitude to all who have helped to make this possible.

——— NOTES ———

CHAPTER ONE: *The Eighteenth Choice*
1. Foote, "The Deadly Infection of Anti-Semitism," 708–9.
2. "Freiwilliger Schutzdienst," *Time,* May 23, 1938.
3. Robert Cloutman Dexter, unpublished manuscript, Elizabeth Dexter Papers, Box 37, John Hay Library, Brown University.
4. US Holocaust Memorial Museum, "Kristallnacht: A National Pogrom, November 9–10, 1938," *Holocaust Encyclopedia,* http://www.ushmm .org/wlc/en/article.php?ModuleId=10005201.

CHAPTER TWO: *Learning the Ropes*
1. Parker Marean, AUA treasurer, to Waitstill Sharp, December 4, 1939, Unitarian Universalist Service Committee (UUSC) Records.
2. "Reinhard Heydrich," Jewish Virtual Library, http://www.jewishvirtual library.org/jsource/Holocaust/Heydrich.html; Henry, *Norbert Fabian Capek,* 256–57, 262, 270–71.

CHAPTER THREE: *Witnesses to History*
1. Cogan, "Church Mouse."

CHAPTER FOUR: *The Dying Republic*
1. Wyman, *The Abandonment of the Jews,* 15.
2. London, *Whitehall and the Jews,* 146–47.
3. "The Story," *Nicholas Winton: The Power of Good* (Ann Arbor, MI: Gelman Education Foundation, 2006, 2009), http://www.powerofgood.net /story.php.
4. In her book *Prague Winter,* Gerda calls her sister "Anne." On the application that the Steins left with Martha, it's Johanna.
5. Mayer, *Prague Winter,* 33.

6. Emanuel and Gissing, *Nicholas Winton and the Rescued Generation,* 65.
7. Cogan, "Church Mouse." This may not be an accurate recollection of the opera. For the record, Martha notes in her datebook that the performance was "Dvorak." George Kennan, stationed at the American Legation at the time, notes that Dvorak's opera *Rusalka* was performed that night.

CHAPTER FIVE: *Einmarsch—The Invastion of Czechoslovakia*
1. Neville Chamberlain, speech, Birmingham, March 17, 1939, *The British War Bluebook,* Avalon Project, Yale Law School, http://avalon.law.yale.edu/wwii/blbk09.asp.
2. US Department of State, Publication 1983, *Peace and War: United States Foreign Policy, 1931–1941* (Washington, DC: US Government Printing Office, 1943), 453–54.
3. "The Holocaust in Bohemia and Moravia," *Holocaust Encyclopedia,* US Holocaust Memorial Museum, http://www.ushmm.org/wlc/en/article.php?ModuleId=10007323.
4. Chadwick, *The Rescue of the Prague Refugees,* 24.
5. Masaryk, *Alice Garrigue Masaryk,* 161–63, 179.

CHAPTER SIX: *Under the Swastika*
1. Kennan, *From Prague After Munich.*
2. "The Massacre at Lidice," Holocaust Education and Archive Research Team, 2008, http://www.holocaustresearchproject.org/nazioccupation/lidice.html.
3. De Haan, Daskalova, and Loutfi, *Biographical Dictionary of Women's Movements and Feminisms in Central Europe,* 439.

CHAPTER EIGHT: *Helping the Kulturträgers*
1. Because she and Waitstill had entered Czechoslovakia before the invasion, they possessed exit permits, *Ausreise,* good until April 30, that allowed them to leave the protectorate and return without having to get permission from Berlin. With no more than the show of a passport and the *Ausreise,* they were able to leave Prague periodically with the CVs of the professors, journalists, Social Democrats, and other professionals who were their primary clients.
2. Lydia Busch would reincarnate herself in the United States as Lydia St. Clair and appear in a number of dramatic productions on American

television. Her only movie credit came in Henry Hathaway's 1945 black-and-white drama *The House on 92nd Street*. Her character was Johanna Schmidt, a Nazi spy.

CHAPTER NINE: *Money Talks*
1. Waitstill Hastings Sharp interview, 1978.

CHAPTER TEN: *Last Days in the Protectorate*
1. Chadwick, *The Rescue of the Prague Refugees*.
2. De Haan, Daskalova, and Loutfi, *Biographical Dictionary of Women's Movements and Feminisms in Central Europe*, 439
3. Margaret Carroll interview, 2006.

CHAPTER ELEVEN: *The First Choice*
1. Correspondence concerning the formation of the USC, 1939, bMS 16003/2 (7), Unitarian Universalist Service Committee (UUSC) Records; "Unitarians Propose Further Refugee Work," *Christian Register*, November 30, 1939.
2. Elisabeth Dexter and Robert Dexter, report on trip to Europe (January 27–April 29, 1940), Elisabeth Dexter Papers, John Hay Library, Brown University.
3. Eliot letter to Waitstill, UUSC Records.
4. Shirer, *The Rise and Fall of the Third Reich*, 720–29.
5. "Dunkirk Evacuation, World War II," *Britannica Online Encyclopaedia*, http://www.britannica.com/print/topic/970448.

CHAPTER TWELVE: *In Lisbon*
1. Cogan, "Church Mouse."
2. Ibid.
3. Sharp and Sharp, *Journey to Freedom*, 13.

CHAPTER THIRTEEN: *Helping Hands*
1. Cogan, "Church Mouse."

CHAPTER FOURTEEN: *Reunion in Cerbère*
1. Waitstill Hastings Sharp interview, 1978.
2. Sharp and Sharp, *Journey to Freedom*, 8.

CHAPTER SIXTEEN: *The Emergency Rescue Committee*
1. Lowrie, *The Hunted Children*, 102–25.
2. Fry, "Surrender on Demand," 53–55.
3. Ibid.

CHAPTER SEVENTEEN: *The Milk Arrives*
1. *Report of the International Committee of the Red Cross on Its Activities During the Second World War* (September 1, 1939–June 30, 1947), vol. III, Relief Activities (Geneva, May 1948), 373; *Commission Mixte de Secours de la Croix-Rouge Internationale*, La Contribution de la Commission Mixte de Secours a L'Action D'Entraide en Faveur de L'Enfance des Hébergés Civils et des Civils Nécessiteux de France, 1941–1944 (Geneva, 2 July 1945), 191.

CHAPTER EIGHTEEN: *Refugees' Odyssey*
1. Mordecai Paldiel interview, 2006.
2. Deborah Dwork interview, 2006.
3. "Hitler Ridiculed as a Writing Man," *New York Times*, February 9, 1933.
4. "Nazis Raid Home of Lion Feuchtwanger," *New York Times*, March 18, 1933.

CHAPTER NINETEEN: *Escape from Marseille*
1. Sharp and Sharp, *Journey to Freedom*, 11.
2. Marino, *The Quiet American*, 166–71.
3. Marta Feuchtwanger, *An Emigre Life*.
4. Ball had worked with Varian's operation for a little less than two months when he mysteriously disappeared. His compatriots assumed that he was killed, but he seems to have quietly made it back to the United States and lived out a long life. "Leon Ivan 'Dick' Ball," *Find a Grave*, http://www.findagrave.com/.

CHAPTER TWENTY: *The Children's Journey*
1. Yehuda Bauer interview, 2006.

CHAPTER TWENTY-FOUR: *A Run for Congress*
1. FBI file on Martha Sharp.

CHAPTER TWENTY-FIVE: *Palestine*
1. Brita Stendahl, "Fellowship in Israel for Arab-Jewish Youth," unpublished paper, 1997.

CHAPTER TWENTY-SIX: *Civil Rights and Chicago*
1. *The Magnetic Tide*, Silverstone.

EPILOGUE
1. Mordecai Paldiel interview, 2006.

WORKS CONSULTED

Archives

Elisabeth Dexter Papers, John Hay Library, Brown University, Providence, Rhode Island

Hadassah, the Women's Zionist Organization, New York City

International Committee for the Red Cross and Federation of Red Cross and Red Crescent Societies, Geneva, Switzerland

Martha and Waitstill Sharp Collection, 1905–2005, John Hay Library, Brown University, Providence, Rhode Island

Martha and Waitstill Sharp Collection, ca. 1902–2006, US Holocaust Memorial Museum, Washington, DC

Unitarian Universalist Service Committee (UUSC) Records, ca. 1935–2006, Andover-Harvard Theological Library, Harvard Divinity School, Cambridge, Massachusetts

Books and Articles

Chadwick, William. *The Rescue of the Prague Refugees.* Leicester, UK: Matador, 2010.

De Haan, Francisca, Krassimira Daskalova, and Anna Loutfi, editors. *Biographical Dictionary of Women's Movements and Feminisms in Central Europe: Central, Eastern, and South Eastern Europe, 19th and 20th Centuries.* Budapest: Central European University Press, 2006.

DiFiglia, Ghanda. *Roots and Visions: The First Fifty Years of the Unitarian Universalist Service Committee.* Boston: Unitarian Universalist Service Committee, 1990.

Emanuel, Muriel, and Vera Gissing. *Nicholas Winton and the Rescued Generation: Save One Life, Save the World.* London: Vallentine Mitchell, 2002.

Feuchtwanger, Lion. *The Devil in France: My Encounter with Him in the Summer of 1940.* New ed. Los Angeles: University of Southern California Libraries, Figueroa Press, 2010.

Foote, Henry Wilder. "The Deadly Infection of Anti-Semitism." *Christian Register,* December 1, 1938.

Fry, Varian. *Surrender on Demand.* New York: Random House, 1945.

Gilbert, Martin. *The Holocaust: A History of the Jews of Europe During the Second World War.* New York: Henry Holt, 1985.

Greenberg, Marian G. *There Is Hope for Your Children: Youth Aliyah, Henrietta Szold and Hadassah.* New York: Hadassah, 1986.

Henry, Richard. *Norbert Fabian Capek: A Spiritual Journey.* Boston: Skinner House, 1999.

Kennan, George F. *From Prague After Munich: Diplomatic Papers 1938–1940.* Princeton, NJ: Princeton University Press, 1968.

London, Louise. *Whitehall and the Jews, 1933–1948: British Immigration Policy, Jewish Refugees, and the Holocaust.* New York: Cambridge University Press, 2000.

Lowrie, Donald. *The Hunted Children.* New York: W. W. Norton, 1963.

Marino, Andy. *The Quiet American: The Secret War of Varian Fry.* New York: St. Martin's Press, 1999.

Masaryk, Alice Garrigue. *Alice Garrigue Masaryk 1879–1966: Her Life as Recorded in Her Own Words and By Her Friends.* Compiled by Ruth Crawford Mitchell. Pittsburgh: University Center for International Studies, University of Pittsburgh, 1980.

Mayer, Gerda. *Prague Winter.* London: Hearing Eye, 2005.

Meyerhof, Walter. *In the Shadow of Love: Stories from My Life.* Santa Barbara: Fithian Press, 2002.

Schofield, Victoria. *Witness to History: The Life of John Wheeler-Bennett.* New Haven, CT: Yale University Press, 2012.

Sharp, Martha. "Emigration Held Key to Ease French Prison Plight," *Christian Science Monitor,* April 14, 1941.

———. "Refugee Army Languishes in French Camps," *Christian Science Monitor,* April 12, 1941.

Shirer, William L. *The Rise and Fall of the Third Reich.* New York: Simon and Schuster, 1960.

Subak, Susan Elisabeth. *Rescue and Flight: American Relief Workers Who Defied the Nazis.* Lincoln: University of Nebraska Press, 2010.

"Unitarian Service Committee in World War II." *Christian Register,* January 1946.

"Unitarians Propose Further Refugee Relief Work." *Christian Register,* November 30, 1939.

Warriner, Doreen. "Winter in Prague." *Slavonic and East European Review* 62, no. 2 (April 1984): 209–40.

Wyman, David S. *The Abandonment of the Jews: America and the Holocaust, 1941–1945.* New York: Pantheon, 1984.

———. *Paper Walls: Americans and the Refugee Crisis, 1938–1941.* Amherst: University of Massachusetts Press, 1968.

Film and Microfilm

Erica Mann and Klaus Mann, Escape to Life, Boston, Houghton Mifflin, 1939 (microfilm).

The Magnetic Tide. Produced and directed by Dorothy Silverstone, 1950. Spielberg Jewish Film Archive. Available on YouTube, https://www.youtube.com/watch?v=2VEW8KVB_14.

Interviews

Yehuda Bauer, interview by Deborah Shaffer, Israel, 2006.

Margaret Carroll, interview by Stephen G. Michaud, 2006.

Martha Sharp Cogan, interview by Ghanda DiFiglia, New York City, April 1979.

Martha Sharp Cogan, interview by Artemis Joukowsky, April 1977.

Deborah Dwork, interview by Deborah Shaffer, Israel, 2006.

Martha Sharp Joukowsky, interview by Stephen G. Michaud, Providence, Rhode Island, 2009.

Martha Sharp Joukowsky, interview by Ghanda DiFiglia, Providence, Rhode Island, 2015.

Gerda Stein Mayer, interview by Deborah Shaffer, New York City, 2006.

Marne Mette, interview by Deborah Shaffer, Wellesley Hills, Massachusetts.

Mordecai Paldiel, interview by Deborah Shaffer, New York City, 2006.

Hastings Sharp, interview by Artemis Joukowsky and Matthew Justus, April 2012.

Hastings Sharp, interview by Stephen G. Michaud, Providence, Rhode Island.

Waitstill Hastings Sharp, interview by Ghanda DiFiglia, Greenfield, Massachusetts, October 1978.

Waitstill Hastings Sharp, interview by Artemis Joukowsky, August 1981.

Alexander and Joseph Strasser, interview by Artemis Joukowsky, April 2013.
Priscilla Sweet, interview by Deborah Shaffer, Wellesley Hills, Massachusetts.

Manuscripts
Cogan, Martha Sharp. "Church Mouse in the White House." Unpublished
    memoir written between the 1940s and 1980s.
DiFiglia, Ghanda. "To Try the Soul's Strength: A Woman's Participation
    in the History of Her Time." Unpublished biography of Martha Sharp
    Cogan, 1998. Martha and Waitstill Sharp Collection, box 43, folder 104,
    John Hay Library, Brown University, Providence, Rhode Island.
Feuchtwanger, Marta. *An Emigre Life: Munich, Berlin, Sanary, Pacific
    Palisades,* vol. 3. Interviewed by Lawrence M. Weschler. Oral History
    Program, University of California, Los Angeles, 1976. https://archive
    .org/details/emigrelifeoralhi03feuc.
Fry, Varian. "Surrender on Demand," manuscript 2, 53. Varian Fry Papers,
    Columbia University, New York.
Sharp, Waitstill Hastings. "Freedom of the Human Spirit." Unpublished
    memoir.
White, Arthur Henry. "Campaign: Martha Sharp for Congress 1946: A
    Case Study." Senior honors thesis, Harvard University, 1947. Harvard
    University Archives.

Online Sources
Holocaust Education and Archive Research Team, http://www
    .holocaustresearchproject.org.
Holocaust Encyclopedia, United States Holocaust Memorial Museum,
    http://www.ushmm.org/learn/holocaust-encyclopedia.
Jewish Virtual Library, http://www.jewishvirtuallibrary.org.
Warnes, Kathy. "Wilbur Carr, the Imperial State Department and Immigra-
    tion: 1920–1945." *Discover Fun History in Clio's Cave.* http://discover
    funhistory.webs.com/.

Reports and Documents
Commission Mixte de Secours de la Croix Rouge Internationale, record
    of condensed and powdered milk sent to France 1941–44, Red Cross
    Archives, Geneva.
Dexter, Elisabeth, and Robert Dexter, report on trip to Europe (January
    27–April 29, 1940), Elisabeth Dexter Papers, John Hay Library, Brown
    University.

Dexter, Robert. *Preliminary and Confidential Report from Robert C. Dexter to the American Unitarian Association,* November 16, 1938, Unitarian Universalist Service Committee Records, ca. 1935–2006, Andover-Harvard Theological Library, Harvard University.

FBI file on Martha Sharp, received through the Freedom of Information Act.

Hadassah National Board, meeting minutes, March–April 1948, Hadassah archives, New York City.

Hadassah National Board, meeting minutes, December 1958, Hadassah archives, New York City.

In Memoriam, Samuel Atkins Eliot, Hadassah Executive Committee, Children to Palestine, 1950.

Sharp, Waitstill, and Martha Sharp. *Journey to Freedom.* Unitarian Service Committee, 1941.

Sharp, Waitstill Hastings, Martha Sharp, and Robert C. Dexter. *How Americans Helped a Nation in Crisis.* Report of the Commission for Service in Czechoslovakia, 1939.

INDEX